Principles of small business

Principles of small business is designed to help small business practitioners to understand the complex issues involved in creating a professional and successful firm. It addresses the issues in three sections: The difficulties of getting into business; the difficulties of staying in business; the difficulties of deciding whether to invest or to sell the business. Using case examples drawn from the MBA and Business Growth Programmes at Cranfield, this book illustrates the key problems entrepreneurs will face and explains solutions to those problems so that they can map out a route to success.

Colin Barrow and **Robert Brown** are lecturers in the Enterprise department at the Cranfield School of Management. Their other books include *The Business Growth Handbook* and *The Business Plan Workbook*.

Principles of management
Edited by Joseph G. Nellis

This International Thomson Business Press series in the principles of management offers stimulating approaches to the core topics of management. The books relate the key areas to strategic issues in order to help managers solve problems and take control. By encouraging readers to apply their own experiences, the books are designed to develop the skills of the all-round manager.

Principles of marketing
G. Randall

Principles of information systems management
John Ward

Principles of law
A. Ruff

Principles of applied statistics
M. Fleming and J. Nellis

Principles of accounting and finance
P. Sneyd

Principles of operations management
R. L. Galloway

Principles of human resource management
D. Goss

Principles of international strategy
S. Segal-Horn and D. Faulkner

Principles of small business

Colin Barrow
and
Robert Brown

INTERNATIONAL THOMSON BUSINESS PRESS
I(T)P® An International Thomson Publishing Company

London • Bonn • Boston • Johannesburg • Madrid • Melbourne • Mexico City • New York • Paris
Singapore • Tokyo • Toronto • Albany, NY • Belmont, CA • Cincinnati, OH • Detroit, MI

Principles of small business

First published by International Thomson Business Press

I(T)P® A division of International Thomson Publishing Inc.
The ITP logo is a trademark under licence

British Library Cataloguing-in-Publication Data
A catalogue record for this book is available from the British Library

Library of Congress Cataloging-in-Publication Data
A catalog record for this book is available from the Library of Congress

---

First edition 1997

Typeset by Acorn Bookwork, Salisbury, Wilts
Printed in the UK by the University Press, Cambridge

ISBN 1-86152-188-X

International Thomson Business Press
Berkshire House
168–173 High Holborn
London WC1V 7AA
UK

International Thomson Business Press
20 Park Plaza
13th Floor
Boston MA 02116
USA

http://www.itbp.com

Contents

List of Figures

List of Tables

Series editor's preface

In recent years there has been a dramatic increase in management development activity in most western countries, especially in Europe. This activity has extended across a wide spectrum of training initiatives, from continuing studies programmes of varying durations for practising managers to the provision of courses leading to the award of professional and academic qualifications. With regard to the latter the most prominent developments have been in terms of the Master of Business Administration (MBA) and Diploma in Management (DMS) programmes, particularly in the UK where virtually every university now offers some form of post-graduate and/or post-experience management qualification.

However, the explosion of formal management training programmes such as the MBA and DMS has tended to be in advance of suitably tailored management textbooks. Many of the core functional areas of these programmes have had to rely on some of the more specialized and thus more narrowly focused textbooks, which are more appropriate for undergraduate requirements. They have generally not provided a suitable balance between academic rigour and practical, business-related relevance. This series covering the principles of management has been specifically developed to service the needs of an expanding management audience. The series deals with the full range of core subjects as well as many of the more popular elective courses that one would expect to find in most MBA and DMS programmes. Many of the books will also be attractive to those students taking professional exams, for example in accountancy, banking, etc., as well as managers attending a wide range of development courses. Each book in the series is written in a concise format covering the key principles of each topic in a pragmatic style which emphasizes the balance between theory and application. Case studies, exercises, and references for further reading are provided where appropriate.

Joseph G. Nellis
Cranfield School of Management

Acknowledgements

We have been greatly assisted by Cranfield Graduate Enterprise Programme participants, MBA and Firmstart students, as well as by Business Growth Programme participants and visiting lecturers at Cranfield School of Management. We would like to thank them all for their contributions and for permission to quote them in this book. Our most particular thanks are due to Robert Wright, whose entrepreneurial career has provided a format for the book.

Introduction

We have written this book in three main sections, suggested to us by Robert Wright, founder of Connectair, now City Flyer Express. While flying to America in the late 1980s, to negotiate the sale of his fledgling yet valuable company, Robert's business class companion, on discovering the purpose of his visit, congratulated him on having covered in five short years the 'three basic difficulties of small business'. These were:

1 the difficulties of getting into business;
2 the difficulties of staying in business;
3 the difficulties of deciding whether to invest further, or to sell the business.

Each stage, we felt, corresponded with a distinctive business planning requirement, to cope with quite different and distinct problems, i.e.:

1 A business plan, to minimize start-up risks.
2 Operating and budget plans, to control the growing business.
3 A strategic 'overview' plan, to give basic direction to a maturing business.

As Professor Storey[1] (1994) has noted, 'formal planning procedures and their monitoring appears to be more characteristic of larger businesses ... business planning is almost wholly absent from the UK micro-business sector'. Our own research at Cranfield (the Cranfield/Kellock research project) found that 50% of companies with a turnover under £5 million did not have a written marketing plan. Even more alarming was that a quarter of firms with a turnover of more than £10 million were similarly ill-equipped. Yet we are not making the 'leap of faith' that 'planning' per se is thus the 'missing link' for assured business growth.

We fully recognise that no plan or management system, however capable, can compensate forever for human error or prolonged management absence.

EXAMPLE: Young graduate entrepreneur Farshad Rouhani, after five hard years of building The Pasta Factory's manufacturing sales to near a million pounds, while operating fresh pasta retail outlets in Harrods, the Hilton (Wembley) and Selfridges, decided to take a year out travelling the world. He felt that the reporting procedures and controls he had established would provide a sufficient framework for his trusted staff and enable him to manage the business via regular fax reports to five-star hotels across the world! Eighteen months later, having sated his travel appetite, Farshad was back putting his retail outlets into receivership in order to save his manufacturing capacity, as the economic recession of the early 1990s took its toll!

Although this is a somewhat extreme (and youthful) example, it simply confirms that planning and control systems can only support an active and involved management. Such systems are also as old as the study of management itself, beginning in the Springfield Armoury, USA, in the early nineteenth century.[2] Yet in the present-day newly competitive world, where Professor David Birch, following his landmark work in emphasizing the importance of small firms,[3] has estimated that about 7–8% of the roughly 8 million enterprises operating in America close every year (and the percentage is comparable in the UK), meaning that 'every five to six years, we have to replace half of the entire US economy',[4] re-instatement of some of the essential building blocks of the company may not be amiss.

In particular we have been influenced by two major teaching experiences at Cranfield in the last 10 years:

1 In helping to launch some 150 new businesses on the Graduate Enterprise Programme (GEP) at Cranfield, the majority of which could never have started in the current business climate without the benefit of a written business plan.
2 In working since 1989 with nearly 300 companies, with turnover between £1 million and £20 million, enrolled on the Business Growth Programme at Cranfield, we have been impressed by the variety of reporting methods and business controls utilized, without which owner-managers would not have been able to realize the ultimate wealth of their companies.

Using case examples sometimes drawn from the Business Growth Programme, as well as from enterprising Cranfield graduates such as Robert Wright, we have tried to illustrate the key questions entrepreneurs and their teams must address at each of the three key 'stages of difficulty' in guiding their companies' development The detailed format we have used is shown in Figure I.1, where the main issues to be explored are detailed in terms of environment, people and operations, marketing and finance.

The aim of our book is to help small business practitioners, actual and potential, to better understand what Professor Elizabeth Chell has described as 'the many complex issues involved in the process of moving from an

GROWTH PHASES IN A NEW BUSINESS

QUESTIONS TO ADDRESS	PART A The difficulties of getting into business *NEED* – BUSINESS PLAN	PART B The difficulties of staying in business *NEED* – OPERATING PLANS AND BUDGETS	PART C The difficulties in deciding whether to re-invest/get out of business *NEED* – STRATEGIC OVERVIEW PLAN
Environment:	**1. Is there a market opportunity in your business sector?** – define vision statement and quantify market sector – market research to show your product or service needed – desk research – field research	**5. What are key factors for success in your business sector?** – service levels & company competencies – customer continuous research & competitor analysis	**9. What is changing in your business environment?** – PEST analysis: political, economic, social & technology – SWOT analysis: strengths & weaknesses opportunities & threats
People:	**2. Do you have the right personal qualities for success?** – entrepreneurial types – team – legal form of company	**6. Can you develop a balanced management team?** – leadership & team roles – recruitment & selection – training employees	**10. Can you change from owner to manager?** – management needs of business – motivation & appraisal – human resource management
Marketing:	**3. What is your marketing entry strategy?** – market segment & competitive analysis – strategy to emphasize focus & differentiation	**7. Can yu further develop your market differentiation?** – developing quality image – optimizing margins & promotion activities – performance	**11. Can you optimize marketing strategy?** – product portfolio analysis – improving productivity – increasing volume sales
Finance:	**4. Can you make a profit?** – first break even/s – cash flow needs – balancing financial risk & business risk – sources of start up finance	**8. How do you fund growth?** – internal sources of funds – ploughing back profits – external sources of funds – gearing limits – hire purchase & factoring	**12. Can you stand the financial pressures?** – to sell or not to sell – exit routes & valuation – floatation vs. trade sale

Figure I.1 Growth phases in a new business

entrepreneurial to a professionally managed firm, the resolution of which is critical to ensure the continued survival and future success of business organisations'.[5] We are not trying to develop a new 'life-cycle model' of business development, of which many useful models exist,[6] but more to look at some of the decision-making processes taken by owner managers.[7] Our concern is less with what an economist once famously described as 'the effort to construct a "science" of management that embodies enduring truths similar to those of medicine, [which] is doomed to fail', but more with that which the economist recommended: 'what businessmen require, is a tool kit to rummage through when facing a challenge'.[8]

We agree with Professor Arthur Francis that 'it is the competitiveness of UK firms that needs improving, not the competitive energy of the UK'.[9] If in our courses and writing we can help the number of successful new business start-ups, and see more than the average of 100 new business-seeking public listings each year, we will have achieved our primary concern. We share Professor David Storey's view that 'it is the failure of UK small enterprises to grow into large enterprises that may be at the heart of the country's long-term poor economic performance'.[10] We wish to contribute to this process and to show, where possible, examples of good practice from growth companies which have coped well with each of 'the three difficulties of small business'.

Notes

1 Storey, D.J. (1994) *Understanding the Small Business Sector*, Routledge, London.
2 Best, M.H. (1990) *The new Competition: Institutions of Industrial Restructuring*, Polity Press, Cambridge, cited in A. Francis (1995) Improving the UK's industrial competitiveness, *RSA Journal*, **CXLIII**, 5436, (October).
3 Birch, D. (1979) *The Job Generation Process*, MIT Program in Neighborhood and Regional Changes, Cambridge, Mass.
4 Birch, D. cited in Best, M.H. (1990) *op. cit.* p. 256.
5 Chell, Elizabeth and Adam, Elaine (1993) Translittoral issues in moving from an entrepreneurial to professionally managed firm, Nottingham Small Business Conference, Institute of Small Business Administration, Nottingham.
6 Churchill, N. and Lewis, V.L. (1983) The five stages of small business growth, *Harvard Business Review*, **6**, (3): 43–54, Scott, M. and Bruce, R. (1987) Five stages of growth in small business, *Long Range Planning*, **20**, (3): 45–51.
7 Storey, D.J. (1994) *op. cit.*
8 Economic focus, *The Economist*, 17th April, 1993.
9 Francis, Arthur (1995) Improving the UK's industrial competitiveness, *RSA Journal*, **CXLIII**, 5436, (October): 35
10 Storey, D.J. (1994) *op. cit.* p. 159.

Part 1

The difficulties of getting into business

The period since the Bolton Committee Report (1971),[1] which was the committee appointed by the government to investigate the state of the small business sector, has seen a resurgence of small firms in the UK. While for the most part this has been fuelled by the growth in self-employment, rising from 6.5% of the UK labour force in 1965 to nearly 12% by 1990, by this latter date there were approximately 1.7 million businesses registered for VAT in the UK. The annual births and deaths of firms, indeed, occur on a large scale, e.g. in 1990 new firms registering for VAT numbered 235,000, while some 185,000 were de-registering, giving a net new addition to stock of 50,000 in the year.

While the growth in self-employment and new firm creation has been stronger in the UK in the last 15 years than in Europe, it has to be seen as being part of practically a worldwide interest in stimulating new enterprise. Ever since the work of David Birch at MIT in 1979, in demonstrating that two-thirds of the increase in employment in the United States between 1969 and 1976 had been in firms with fewer than 20 workers, many 'free-world' governments have been attempting to develop programmes to stimulate entrepreneurship (e.g. among indigenous Malays in Malaysia) or to provide support to the growing small business sector (e.g. the work of the Small Business Administration in the USA).

Coinciding with all this has been the development of what the *Harvard Business Review*[2] has described as a 'new growth industry' of business plan writing. Yet the US entrepreneurial magazine *Inc* has shown that nearly two-thirds of new businesses started without a formally produced business plan. (Of *Inc*'s top 100 fastest growing companies in 1989, 41% had started with no business plan at all, and 26% 'back of envelope' only.) Writing a business plan is no guarantee of future business success: the survival rate of Graduate Enterprise Programme (GEP) businesses at Cranfield at just over 50% after three years was neither better nor worse than national figures for VAT company de-registrations over a similar period – although given the average age of participants, 22, and their lack of work experience, such an achievement might be regarded as exceptional. There are, nevertheless, several compelling arguments for undertaking such an exercise of business plan writing prior to launching the business on an unsuspecting public. These include the following:

(a) It is usually less costly to make your first mistakes on paper rather than in the marketplace (i.e. failing in the market research phase of plan preparation to locate sufficient 'real' customers to justify the venture, rather than without research, taking premises and lease obligations, and coming to the same negative conclusions!).
(b) The business 'idea' and concept will undergo modifications and perhaps improvement in the rigorous process of researching markets and presenting findings to potential investors.

EXAMPLE: GEP student Mark Sanders originally planned to design and manufacture himself his innovative Strida bicycle, but market size and product costings quickly convinced him of the need to sub-contract manufacture, thereby reducing risk to himself and ensuring quicker access to the market.

(c) Those entrepreneurs needing financial assistance either from the outset or at a later stage, whether from banks, venture capitalists or business angels, will all find preparation and presentation of a business plan to be an essential and learning part of the financial negotiation.

EXAMPLE: It was Robert Wright's fourth business plan, written and re-presented over a period of 18 months, which finally secured venture capital support from 3i for Connectair. The fourth plan had identified a viable customer, British Caledonian, and a totally different airport connection from his original idea, in part suggested by the venture capitalist organization.

New business ideas that derive from what might be termed the 'supply side', i.e. originate from their owners' hobbies or particular skills (e.g. cooking, software, writing skills, etc.) need to prove that there is a market for such activities. While ideas which derive from the 'demand side', e.g. products or services known to be available in one market town but not another, need to demonstrate less that there is a market need for such activities, but more that they can be provided at an acceptable price and quality.

EXAMPLE: Mark Ranson spent time in hospital and quickly grew tired of the 10-year old copies of *Punch* magazines for patients to read. Upon discharge, he approached top magazine producers to see if he could buy magazines that were just one month old but had been withdrawn from newsagents' shelves to make way for the next edition. The publishers had to pay to have them pulped and Mark offered to pay a nominal fee for them. Winning many major publishers over enabled him to supply quality magazines (*House & Garden*, *Vogue* and *Tatler*) at about half price or less to doctors and dentists for their waiting rooms. Magpak was soon established in hospitals as well, offering good value for money to the NHS.

Whether the idea is 'supply' or 'demand' side it is the function of the business plan to provide the supporting evidence for the venture. Would-be entrepreneurs, whether with or without adequate funding, would be well advised to complete the essential steps of the business planning process, for in essence the business plan is designed to reduce risk for the entrepreneur and investors alike by attempting to determine that:

1 there is a definite market opportunity for the product/service proposed
2 the entrepreneur and potential team are credible managers for the tasks in hand
3 the marketing entry strategy proposed is suitable
4 the venture holds out the prospect of being eventually profitable!

Each of these elements will be examined in the following chapters, designed to help new and potential owner-managers approach the market in a vigorous and credible way. We may lament, as Ms Prue Leith did at an RSA lecture (October 1995) that in starting her own catering business she 'had never had a business plan, neither had Richard Branson'. At the same time Ms Leith noted the passing of 'relationship banking', wherein local bank managers who might have known the entrepreneurial family or local business area well, no longer existed! Because the financial world has changed so dramatically, so the need for properly researched plans has become imperative.

NOTES

1 Bolton, J.E. (1971) *Report of the Committee of Enquiry on Small Firms,* 411, HMSO, London.
2 Bhide, Amar (1992) Bootstrap finance: the art of start-ups, *Harvard Business Review,* Nov–Dec, pp. 109–17 and (1994) How entrepreneurs craft strategies that work, *Harvard Business Review,* Mar–Apr, pp. 150–61.

Chapter 1

Is there a market opportunity in your business sector?

At the outset it is important for the owner manager to define the business sector within which the new enterprise will function. One effective way to do this is to write a vision statement for the enterprise.

VISION STATEMENTS AND OBJECTIVES

A common characteristic of successful entrepreneurs, according to research by Mathew Manimala, of the Administrative Staff College of India,[1] is that they have a clear goal vision, even if they are not sure how to achieve it!

Vision statements and objectives are important in two main ways:

- To concentrate your own and your future employees' efforts in a specific market.
- To concentrate attention on problems to be solved.

Large companies may spend long weekends at country mansions wrestling with the fine print of their vision statements; in principle, given the narrower scope of the new business, the task facing the new business owner should be less daunting.

To take vision statements and objectives first, as they are inevitably intertwined, these are direction statements, intended to focus your attention on essentials, to encapsulate your specific competence(s) in relation to the markets/customers you plan to serve.

First, the vision should be narrow enough to give direction and guidance to everyone in the business. This concentration is the key to business success because it is only by focusing on specific needs that a small business can differentiate itself from its larger competitors. Nothing kills off a new business faster than trying to do too many different things at the outset.

Second, the vision should open up a large enough market to allow the business to grow and realize its potential.

In summary, the vision statement should explain:

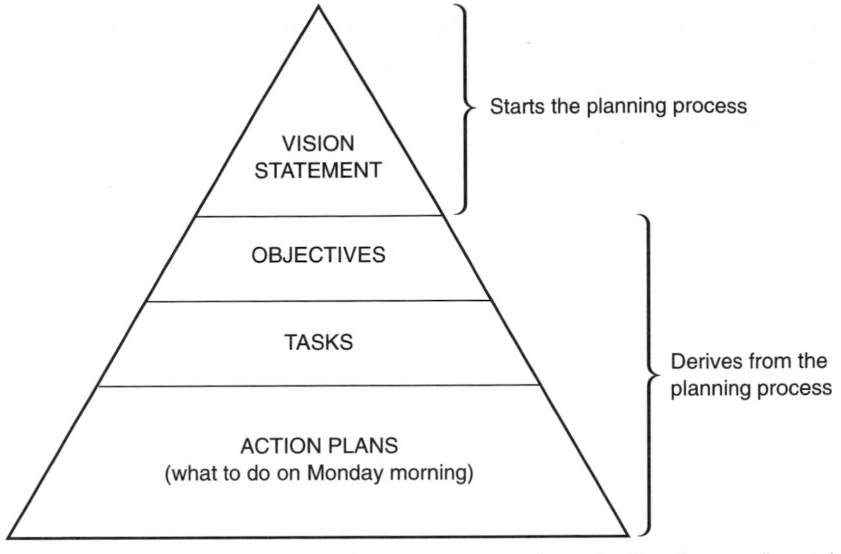

Note: Mission and objectives are 'what' statements, tasks and action plans are 'how to' statements.

Figure 1.1 The pyramid of goals

- What business you are in and your purpose (e.g. Quantum Cars 'we are in the kit-car business and the plan is to develop, build and market a four-seater sports car for the family man').
- What you want to achieve over the next one to three years, i.e. your strategic goal (e.g. Bagel Express 'we want to do for bagels in London what McDonalds have done for hamburgers in America, while being profitable within 18 months of start-up').
- How, i.e. your values and standards (e.g. Quantum Cars 'we will build a car using a lightweight, glass fibre construction, but with sporting performance and appearance').

Above all, mission statements must be realistic, achievable – and brief.

Many companies separate out their specific objectives, which they wish to keep confidential, from the vision statement, which they realize they must communicate widely, via meetings and company literature, to promote greater company cohesion and concentration. Specific objectives, such as breaking even within 18 months, achieving a suitable return on capital, etc., and the tasks to achieve them, will be discussed in later chapters.

Having narrowed your market focus by completion of your vision statement (kit-cars segment of automobile market for Quantum, commuter/ feeder airlines for Connectair), effort should now be concentrated on researching the specific market segment, to determine the need for your own product or service.

MARKET RESEARCH

You do not have to open a shop to prove there are *no* customers for your goods and services; frequently some modest do-it-yourself (DIY) market research beforehand can give clear guidance as to whether your venture will succeed or not.

The purpose of practical DIY market research for entrepreneurs seeking to prove, as far as possible, that there is a real market opportunity for their business idea is, therefore, twofold:

1 To build *credibility* for the business idea; the entrepreneur must prove first to his or her own satisfaction, and later to outside financiers, a thorough understanding of the marketplace for the new product or service. This will be vital if resources are to be attracted to build the new venture.
2 To develop a *realistic* market entry strategy for the new business, based on a clear understanding of genuine customer needs and ensuring that product quality, price, promotional methods and distributions chain are mutually supportive and clearly focused on target customers.

Otherwise there is a danger of fools rushing in, where angels fear to tread; while as they say in the Army, 'time spent in reconnaissance is rarely time wasted'. The same is certainly true in starting a business, where you will need to research in particular:

1 *Your customers* – who will buy your goods and services? What particular customer needs will your business meet? How many of them are there?
2 *Your competitors* – which established companies are already meeting the needs of your potential customers? What are their strengths and weaknesses?
3 *Your product or service* – how should it be tailored to meet customer needs?
4 *What price should you charge* to be perceived as giving value for money?
5 *Which promotional material is needed* to reach customers; what newspapers, journals do they read?
6 *Where should you locate* to reach your customers most easily, at minimum cost?

Research, above all else, is not just essential in starting a business, but once launched, must become an integral part in the on-going life of the company. Customers and competitors change; products have life-cycles.

Once started, however, on-going market research becomes easier, as you will have existing customers (and staff) to question.

First steps

There are two main types of research in starting a business:

1 Desk research, or the study of published information.
2 Field research, involving fieldwork in collecting specific information for the market.

Both activities are vital for the starter business.

Desk research

There is increasingly a great deal of secondary data, available in published form, and accessible via business sections of public libraries throughout the UK, to enable new starters to both quantify the size of market sectors they are entering and to determine trends in those markets. In addition to populations of cities and towns (helping to start quantification of markets), libraries frequently purchase Mintel Reports, involving studies of growth in different business sectors, and have access via CD-Roms and computer screens to a wide range of business data and individual company results. Government statistics, showing trends in the economy, are also held (*Annual Abstracts* for the country as a whole, *Business Monitor* for individual sectors). It is important to demonstrate that your sector is growing (you have the wind behind you, like Anita Roddick with the 'green' movement behind her Body Shop's 'natural' beauty products), or if the sector is declining, you can demonstrate why your product/service will be different and will not be affected by this trend (e.g. although UK car manufacturing has declined, the makers of 'kit cars' have focused on a growing profitable niche of enthusiasts). It is not always necessary to be in a high growth sector (e.g. computer peripherals, +20% pa growth in the 1980s), as such sectors frequently attract many competitors. Lower growth sectors (e.g. vehicle population in UK increasing at real 3% pa) can also produce attractive opportunities, for example in vehicle spare parts, without attracting as many new entrants.

If you plan to sell to companies or shops, Kompass and Kelly's directories list all company names and addresses (including buyers' telephone numbers). The Registrar of Companies, in Cardiff, contains Extel card information on the 3,000 major quoted UK companies (£10 per card). Many industrial sectors are represented by trade associations, which can provide information (see *Directory of British Associations, CBD Research*), while Chambers of Commerce are good sources of reference for import/export markets.

Mark and Harvey Wooldridge were able in the mid-1980s, via library and magazine research, to come up with precise definitions of their industry size and direction, as well as information on customers and competitors, useful in determining the quality and likely price of their first model car for production.

EXAMPLE: Quantum Cars

Kit Cars – Introduction
The origins of the British kit car industry date back to the early 1970s. Since this time the industry has grown into a multi-million pound business. Growth is continuing at a healthy pace. In the last three years, capacity has doubled and there is no sign of any moderation in this growth.

Industry Definition – Kit
Information relating to the kit car industry is difficult to isolate. There is no clearly recognized definition. A kit can vary from a body shell in fully built or disassembled form for the mechanically minded enthusiast through to a completed car, built by the kit car company to the customer's specification.

The companies involved in this market have created a niche among the current production car companies, getting around the current legislation for type approval by selling a vehicle that supposedly requires minor work for completion prior to vehicle registration (type approval costs £20,000 minimum).

The Market
The market contains many players. One major player, Dutton, with 70 employees, controls around 30% of the market. There are many successes and failures in an industry of this type. The successes are those who are able to exploit a particular segment with their product offering and do not try to grow too fast, diverting resources to unnecessary and unrelated work.

The market consists of around 100 companies, but the top 10 cover up to 75% of the market. The majority of companies are small businesses many of whom are relatively new and will unfortunately never succeed in making a viable business. (See Current industry problems below.)

The range of model varies from cheap fun cars to machines with the performance of a Porsche or Jaguar. The majority are of the two-seater sports car/replica type but the other sectors are growing as the kit car image improves and customer tastes become more sophisticated. The larger production car companies are by their size slow to respond to consumer tastes and this represents an opportunity for this industry.

In the UK the kit car market is estimated at 3,000 cars per annum, the speciality car market (e.g. Morgans, Reliant) at around 15,000 per annum, total new car market around 2 million cars per annum, and total used car market at over 4 million cars per annum!

Customers

Contact with the kit car magazine companies, manufacturers and research libraries has shown that no major research has been undertaken for the industry regarding customer type and numbers. Individual manufacturers have, however, released details of the type of customer to whom they specifically sell cars and there are common traits. These can be summarized as follows:

- aged under 30, often unmarried
- average salary, less than £10,000 pa
- consider the car to express their personality
- mechanically minded individuals
- often have built a car before.

The kit must be seen as good value for money, providing good performance using readily available car components.

More recently the age profile of the average customer is rising and there is an increasing need for cars to be provided ready-built. There is currently no pressure for the industry to provide special warranties and guarantees.

Products and prices

The market can be viewed as consisting of a number of separate, distinct product sectors:

- saloon cars
- sports/saloon cars
- off road/four wheel drive
- production replicas
- fibreglass bolt-ons to metal bodies

Kits can be built using new or second-hand parts dependant on the customer's budget. Fibreglass is the most common material for body construction but for some of the luxury, expensive kits, aluminium is often used.

Prices are highly variable (£1,000 for a basic kit at the lower end of the market, to £30,000 for a fully built classic replica). The majority of customers are in the market for a car, on the road, for less than £10,000, which usually will not include any parts and labour warranty.

The kit car market is therefore getting close to production car pricing and competition will become very interesting as kit quality improves and these vehicles become a more acceptable alternative.

Support industries

As the kit car industry has grown, a number of related companies and groups have grown up to support the various activities involved in producing and marketing a kit. These include:

- component reconditioning
- fibreglass body builders
- specialist insurance companies
- kit car magazines
- specialist kit car clubs.

This kit car industry will increasingly turn to many of the companies who support the production car industry as they attempt to improve their image.

Current industry problems

Finally, these are the key problems facing the kit car industry today:

- companies are seen as a poor relation of the car industry
- high growth needs to be well managed to prevent companies going out of business
- too many failures
- no research and development
- obtaining finance for expansion is difficult
- poor quality products
- vehicles often not type approved.

These problems all hinge around the image of the industry and the product on offer.

Most of the kit car manufacturers could take a lesson from Morgan cars, who have successfully positioned themselves in the market between the major production car manufacturers and those companies offering a fully built kit. The difference is the customer perceived image.

Following the desk research, the Wooldridge brothers were encouraged to conduct field research at kit car exhibitions to confirm their understanding of customer needs and competitive offerings. Unlike the Wooldridge family, graduate farmer William

> Alexander, attempting to desk research the market for UK dried flower production in the mid-1980s, was unable to find any supporting material at all! Rather than be disheartened by this, he realized that this confirmed his opinion that here really was an exciting opportunity for him to be the pioneering dried flower producer in England!

Field Research

Some entrepreneurs considered opening a classical musical shop in Exeter focused on the young. Desk research revealed that out of a total population of 250,000 there were 25% under 30 years olds, but this did not tell them what percentage were interested in classical music or how much they might spend on classical records. Field research (questionnaire in the street) provided the answer of 1% and £2 a week spent, suggesting a potential market of only £65,000 a year (250,000 x 25% x 1% x £2 x 52!). The entrepreneurs in question decided to investigate Birmingham and London instead! But at least the cost had only been two damp afternoons spent in Exeter, rather than the horrors of having to dispose of a lease of an unsuccessful shop.

Fieldwork is now becoming big business in the UK, for example expert market research companies turned over more than £500 million in the early 1990s. Most fieldwork consists of interviews, with the interviewer putting questions to a respondent. We are all becoming accustomed to it, whether being interviewed while travelling on British Rail, or resisting the attempts of enthusiastic salesmen posing as market researchers on doorsteps ('sugging', as this is known, has been illegal since 1986). The more popular forms of interview are:

- personal (face-to-face) interview: 55% (especially for consumer markets)
- telephone: 32% (especially for business and companies market)
- post: 6% (especially for industrial markets)
- test and discussion group: 7%.

Personal interviews and postal surveys are clearly less expensive than getting together panels of interested parties or using expensive telephone time. Telephone interviewing requires a very positive attitude, courtesy, an ability not to talk too quickly and listening while sticking to a rigid questionnaire. Low response rates on postal services (less than 10% is normal) can be improved by accompanying letters, explaining its purpose and why respondents should reply by offering rewards for completed questionnaires (small gift), by sending reminder letters and, of course, by providing pre-paid reply envelopes.

All methods of approach require considered questions. In drawing up the questionnaire attention must be made first to:

- Defining your research objectives; what exactly is it that you need vitally to know? (e.g. how often do people buy, how much?)
- Who are the customers to sample for this information? (e.g. for DIY products, the Ideal Home Exhibition audience might be best).
- How are you going to undertake the research? (e.g. face to face in the street).

When you are sure of the above, and only then, you are ready to design the questionnaire. There are six simple rules to guide this process:

1 Keep the number of questions to a minimum.
2 Keep the questions simple! Answers should be either 'Yes/No/Don't Know' or offer at least four alternatives, which could be ranked in order of importance (1–4).
3 Avoid ambiguity – make sure the respondent really understands the questions (avoid 'generally', 'usually', 'regularly').
4 Seek factual answers, avoid opinions.
5 Make sure at the beginning you have a cut-out question to eliminate unsuitable respondents (e.g. those who never use the product/service).
6 At the end make sure you have an identifying question to show the cross-section of respondents.

The introduction to a face to face interview is important. Make sure you are prepared, either carrying an identifying card (e.g. student card, Association of Market Researchers watch-dog card), or with a rehearsed introduction (e.g. 'Good morning, I'm from Westminster University [show card]. We are conducting a survey and we would be grateful for your help.') You may also need visuals of the product you are investigating (samples, photographs), to ensure the respondent understands. Make sure these are neat and accessible. Finally, try out the questionnaire and your technique on your friends, prior to using it in the street. You will be surprised at how questions which seem simple to you are incomprehensible at first to respondents!

The size of the survey undertaken is also important. You frequently hear of political opinion polls taken on samples of 1,500–2,000 voters. This is because the accuracy of your survey clearly increases with the size of sample as the following table shows:

With random sample of:	*95% of surveys are right within ... points*
250	6.2
500	4.4
750	3.6
1,000	3.1
2,000	2.2
6,000	1.2

If, on a sample size of 600, your survey showed that 40% of women in the town drove cars, the true proportion probably lies between 36% and 44%. For small businesses, we usually recommend a minimum sample of 250 completed replies. An example of a questionnaire, with results, administered to participants at Rye House Greyhound Stadium is included in the Appendix to this chapter, showing also interesting publicity results for the stadium as an incidental outcome of the research.

Remember, though, that questioning is by no means the only or most important form of fieldwork. Sir Terence Conran, when questioned on a radio programme, implied that he undertook no market research fieldwork at all (i.e. formal interviews). Later in the programme he confessed to spending nearly 'half of his time, visiting competitors, inspecting new and rival products, etc.'. Visiting exhibitions, buying and examining competitors' products (as the Japanese have done so methodically) are clearly important fieldwork processes. David Sinclair, founder of Bagel Express, used his competitive survey to justify his first year sales forecast.

EXAMPLE: Bagel Express – Competition Field Study

A survey of competitors has been completed to confirm Bagel Express' forecast of £216,000 worth of sales in the first year of trading, equivalent to £18,000 a month, or £600 a day, or £37.50 an hour. Assuming an average spend of £1.00, that is roughly one purchase every 2 minutes – 60 customers in a 16-hour day. Market research on competitors conducted by Bagel Express suggests this figure is easily obtainable (see Table 1.1).

Sales of £600 a day are significantly above the sales required for Bagel Express to break even (on the assumed cost structure).

$$\text{Break-even sales} = \frac{\text{Fixed costs}}{\text{Gross profit margin}} \times 100$$

$$= \frac{£99{,}550 + £12{,}000}{70\%}$$

$$= £159{,}357$$

In order to break even, Bagel Express must achieve sales of £159,357 a year, or £422 a day or only £27 an hour. This is one sale every 133 seconds, compared with the one every 7 seconds sold by Ben's Bagels.

Just as important, test marketing by selling from stalls on a Saturday, or taking part in an exhibition, gives an opportunity to question interested customers and can be the most valuable fieldwork of all.

Table 1.1 Customer counts at various stores

Date	*Store*	*Location*	*Time*	*Customers per Period*	*Customers per hour*
20.8.88	Ben's Bagel	Hendon	10.00pm–2.00am	2,000	500
23.8.88	Cafe Croissant	King's Road	11.30am–12.00pm	27	54
			1.20pm–1.30pm	31	
			2.00pm–3.00pm	125	
23.8.88	The Coffee House	King's Road	3.00pm–3.30pm	44	88
23.8.88	Sharaton's	Victoria Street	12.00pm–1.00pm	300	300

EXAMPLE: William Alexander began to suspect that there was a market for dried hop bines when he detected that numbers of bines were being stolen from his hop fields! But marketing bines which he dried over his domestic Aga that winter to local public houses proved fruitless. Acting on a recommendation, however, he drove up to Covent Garden market at Nine Elms, Battersea, early one morning, and while standing in a queue at a major flower wholesaler, he was approached and offered cash for the hop bines he and his wife Caroline were carrying!

Looking back on his later success with his 'Hop Shop' dried flower business, William concluded, 'I would recommend to any young farmer, thinking about diversifying, to go early morning to Covent Garden, look around and you will see many opportunities, just as we did, to change your business.'

All 'research' methods are equally valid, and the results of each should be carefully recorded for subsequent use in presentations and business plans. Once the primary market research (desk and field research) and market testing (stalls and exhibitions) are complete, pilot testing of the business should be undertaken in one location or customer segment, prior to setting targets and subsequently measuring the impact of a full regional launch.

SUMMARY

By closely defining your market sector in your vision statement and by conducting detailed desk and field research, the basis should be set for tailoring your product/source ideas to the needs of the market. You should be able to draw confidence for yourself and potential backers that your project is both timely and appropriate for identified customers. The activities you need to undertake to bring your business idea to market should be identified and planned, as shown in Quantum Cars' original market research plan (see Figure 1.2).

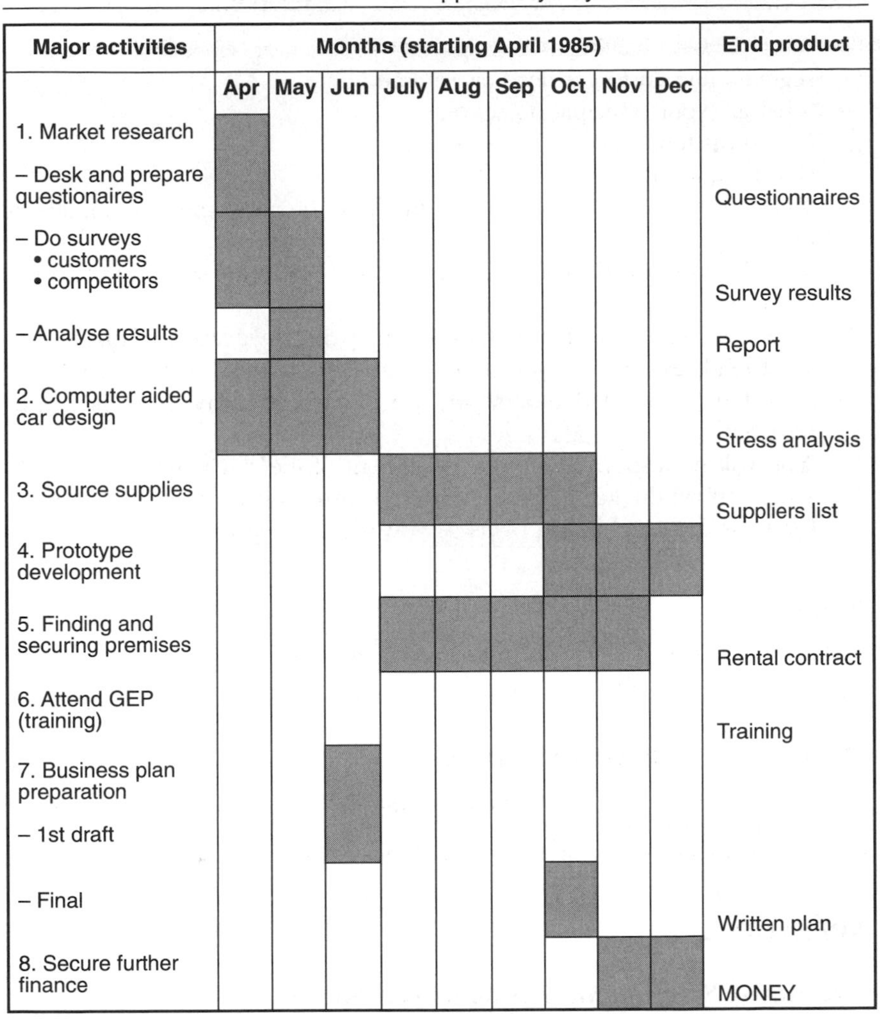

Figure 1.2 Quantum Cars action plan

Although development of a successful prototype took a further 12 months, Quantum's carefully planned approach to the market produced a successful kit-car manufacturing business, now producing two cars a week to order, despite the dearth of British owned car manufacturers.

EXERCISES

1 Explain how you arrived at your business idea.
2 What makes you believe it will succeed?

3 Write a vision statement linking your product or service to the market segment and customer needs it is aimed at.
4 What are your principal objectives?
   (a) short term
   (b) long term
5 What information do you currently have on customers, competitors, markets, etc.?
6 What information do you still need to find, and why specifically do you need it?
7 What desk research will you have to carry out to answer this question?
8 What field research will you have to carry out to answer this question?
9 How much time and money will be needed to carry out this market research?
10 Who will be responsible for each element of the research?
11 When will all the key market research information be available?
12 List your tasks and action plans as you see them at present.

NOTES

1 Manimala, Mathew (1992) 'The entrepreneurial personality', *Journal of Business Venturing*, **7**, 477–504.

SUGGESTED FURTHER READING

Barrow, Colin (1995) *The Small Business Guide*, 4th edn, BBC Publications, London (for desk research guidance).
Crimp, Margaret (1995) *The Market Research Process*, 3rd edn, Prentice-Hall, London.

APPENDIX 1

Rye House Stadium Market Research Survey

Questionnaire

Greyhound racing is going through a period of change. Increased competition from other forms of entertainment and particularly the potential evening opening of betting shops make it essential that we assess the views of our customers.

We would therefore be very grateful if you would take a few minutes to complete the following questionnaire to allow us to understand your opinions more clearly.

We ask for your co-operation in this survey. To make it more attractive, every form received will go into a lucky draw. The first three picked out will permit the winners free entry and racecard until 1st January 1993.

1. How far have you travelled to get to the Stadium tonight?

   Less than 1 mile______ Between 1 and 5 miles _____

   Between 5 and 10 miles _____ Over 10 miles _____

2. How did you get here?

   Bus _____ Car _____ Walk _____ Train _____

3. How often do you attend meetings?

   1 per week _____ 2 per week _____ 3 per week _____ occasionally _____

4. Do you come to the meeting?

   On your own _____ With wife/husband _____

   With friends _____ With children _____

5. Do you bet on the races? Yes/No

   If so do you use Tote _____ Bookmakers _____ Both _____

6. What would you most like to see changed at the stadium?

   Tote facilities _____ Restaurant facilities _____

   Race night _____ Viewing facilities _____

   Bar facilities _____ Level of open races _____

7. Would you like to see any changes made to the tote?

   Introduction of a trio pool _____

   Introduction of a forecast jackpot pool _____

   Introduction of a win jackpot pool _____

   Deletion of a place pool _____

   No changes to current tote pools _____

8. Which days would you prefer to see racing on? (Please tick three or less only)

   Mon _____ Tues _____ Wed _____ Thurs _____ Fri _____ Sat _____

9. Would you use any of the following facilities at the stadium if they were provided?

   Snooker ____ Squash ____ Badminton ____ Sunbeds ____ Gym ____

5-a-side _____ Swimming pool _____

Other suggestions:..

....

10. What aspect of the racing would you like to see changed?

    More/Less/Same open races __________

    More/Less/Same inter track races__________

    More/Less/Same sprint races __________

    More/Less/Same stayers races _______

    More/Less/Same competitions _______

11. Do you attend the Speedway meeting?

    Yes/No/Sometimes

12. Do you or your family use the Go-Kart track?

    Yes/No

13. Would you use a 'Sit down and View' Restaurant if provided?

    Frequently (once a week) ______
    Occasionally (once a month) _____
    Rarely __________
    Never __________

14. Do you have any other comments about Greyhound Racing at Rye House?

Thank you for your time. In order to enter the prize draw please give your name and address

Name: Mr/Mrs/Miss ____________________________

Address: ____________________________
____

Rye House Stadium Market Research Survey

Summary of results

First of all we would like to thank all the 310 people who took the time and trouble to complete our questionnaire. It was an excellent response and we have found the results both interesting and useful. Here is a summary of the results:

The responses were split as follows:

Male: 216 Female: 73 Did not indicate: 16

An overwhelming majority of our customers travel to Rye House by car (285), 169 of whom travel over 10 miles. Only 80 people travel less than five miles, only 14 come by train and no-one uses the bus.

Most people attend meetings regularly each week (235) with twice a week being the most popular (89).

The survey also showed that greyhound racing is enjoyed by all the family; 127 attended with their wife/husband and 48 attend with children.

Only 13 respondents said they did not bet and of the rest that did bet they tended to use both the Tote and Bookmakers for their investments. 62 people said they would like to see some change made to the Tote, but significantly more people (150) would like to see the introduction of a trio pool. The introduction of a win jackpot and forecast jackpot were also very popular.

The other facility most people wanted to see changed was the viewing facility with the lack of seating, view of the first bend and winning line coming in for special mention from many of you.

In terms of race nights we seem to have got it about right, with Monday and Saturday coming out as the most popular and it was very close between Wednesday and Thursday as the third night.

The racing content question brought a large and varied response. The overall conclusions being that you would like to see more stayers races and fewer sprint races. You would also like to see more inter track races and competitions, although these responses were significantly less than the request for more stayers races. There was also a marginal preference for more opens.

Few people attend the Speedway meetings (9) or use the Go-kart track (20). However, we had many additional facilities being suggested. The most popular being snooker, a swimming pool, sunbed and a gym. One or two of the suggestions were interesting but perhaps not suitable for publication!

All comments and suggestions have been noted. A few of the recurring comments included a request for children's play area (21), improvements to the toilets (24), general housekeeping/safety improvements (19), automatic starting traps (14) and increased prize money (13).

During the following weeks more detailed responses will be published.

Once again thank you for completing the questionnaire, possibly the most encouraging fact we discovered is that Rye House attracts people from no less than 5 counties – so it can't be all bad!!

GREYHOUNDS RACING POST

Rye survey novel but no surprises.

The results of a survey amongst Rye House racegoers was revealed yesterday and makes particularly interesting reading for anyone familiar with the track.

Indeed, bigger circuits could do worse than follow the example of a 'minnow' like the Rye and undertake such a detailed survey to find out what their patrons think.

As Rye regulars would probably expect, improvement of viewing and dining facilities came out top amongst the 310 people who replied to the questionnaire, 235 of whom were regulars.

As far as viewing was concerned, 35 per cent wished to see an improvement with lack of seating and vantage points at the first bend and winning line singled out.

And there was a huge nudge for promoter Eddie Lesley to better the dining facilities with 80 per cent of the respondents claiming they would use a restaurant, 43 per cent 'frequently'.

There is a dining area but it is small and tucked underneath the main stands well out of the way. What is obvious though, is that the policy of providing creature comforts as at the likes of Peterborough and Yarmouth, is what racegoers require.

At first sight, it was somewhat surprising that 84 per cent thought there should be more inter-track races, compared to 66 per cent for extra opens. However, the local runners are very hard to beat on their home patch and there was probably a touch of feathering their own nests from the track regulars.

An overwhelming majority (87 per cent) thought there should be more stayers racers with 66 per cent calling for more competitions. However, the sprint events came in for the thumbs down, over half feeling there should be less. This probably ties in with the feelings of main trainers at the track, that the long run to the bend for the 255 metre trip, allied to a tight turn, makes for plenty of trouble.

On thing that should perk up the management is the fact that people seem prepared to travel from miles away to get to the track – 55 per cent came from more than ten miles away. But the downside of this is just 26 per cent are 'local' ie under five miles away – room for improvement there.

And the fact that 93 per cent of those questioned arrive at the track by car highlights the problem of parking spaces – there are often none to be found.

The weakness of the tote at the Rye is legendary so it was somewhat surprising that 34 per cent bet on the 'nanny' only, with 57 per cent using both tote and bookmakers. But once again the lure of the big win was at the top of the agenda for most, with an introduction of trio and jackpot pools getting the thumbs up.

The management should be congratulated for bothering to find out what their patrons think. But with the long term future of the venue yet to be publicly announced, and in the middle of a recession, as well, whether they act on the findings is another matter.

Chapter 2

Do you have the right personal qualities for success?

If your business idea stands up to the rigours of market research the next question you need to ask yourself is – can I do it? In answering this question you will need to address three issues:

1. *Am I really the entrepreneurial type?* The high failure rate for new business would suggest that some people are seduced by the glamour of starting up on their own, when they might be more successful and more contented in some other line of endeavour.
2. *Are my motivations and aims realistic?* Running a business is never easy and on an hourly wage basis is often less well paid than working for someone else. So why do people set up their own business, and do your aims seem realistic in that context?
3. Is this business right for me? Even if your answers to 1 and 2 above are sound, this particular proposition might not be right for you.

AM I THE ENTREPRENEURIAL TYPE?

To launch a new business successfully calls for a particular type of person. The business idea must also be right for the market and the timing must be spot on. The world of business failures is full of products that are ahead of their time.

The stereotyped idea of the entrepreneur is of someone who is always bursting with new ideas, highly enthusiastic, hyperactive and insatiably curious. But this is not always the case: people who start businesses have many different personality types.

Peter Drucker, the international business guru, describes what his research has revealed:

EXAMPLE: Some are eccentrics, others painfully correct conformists; some are fat and some are lean; some are worriers, some relaxed; some drink quite heavily, others are total abstainers;

> some are people of great charm and warmth, some have no more personality than a frozen mackerel.
>
> *Source*: Drucker, P. (1985) Innovation and Entrepreneurship, Heineman, London.

There is little point, therefore, in trying to match yourself up to this or that personality type. However, there are some fairly broad characteristics that are generally accepted as being essential, if you are going to make a success of your own business.

A lot of commitment and hard work

Small business founders have complete faith in their business idea. This self-belief is necessary if they are to convince the sceptics (such as the bank manager), whose help they need. They are usually single-minded and more than capable of putting in an 18-hour working day. This can put a strain on other relationships, so successful small business founders usually involve their families and get them on their side too.

Small business proprietors are also likely to put in many more hours at work than their employees. This is true for both male and female small business people, although generally male proprietors do seem to work longer hours than females.

In the UK, at any rate, over the decade of the 1980s the proportion of small business people working more than 41 hours per week increased. For male business founders this increase was more noticeable. (This is probably because many female business founders have part-time ventures.)

In the 1980s it was the workaholic that epitomized the spirit of enterprise. However, much research has been carried out showing this behaviour is probably counter productive. People can be productive for up to 50 hours a week, but after that performance drops sharply. After about 70 hours people are very often contributing nothing of value – and perhaps causing even more problems. They are certainly doing little to improve the lives of their families and colleagues.

While most British firms remain unaware of the damage that prolonged stress can do, some are now addressing the problem. High technology companies such as Rank Xerox and IBM operate counselling schemes to help employees spot the danger signs, while some divisions of ICI give their entire workforce stress management training. This is not altruistic. The company wants to encourage balanced employees because they are more productive, so the reasons are completely mercenary.

Table 2.1 Self-employed and employees by hours worked

No. of hours worked	1981 Employee %	1981 Self-employed %	1989 Employee %	1989 Self-employed %
All				
0–12	6	5	7	7
13–32	16	9	16	12
33–40	62	29	36	20
41–56	13	29	34	34
57+	3	29	6	27
All	100	100	100	100
Male				
0–12	1	2	2	3
13–32	4	4	3	6
33–40	71	31	35	21
41–56	20	32	50	39
57+	4	31	10	31
All	100	100	100	100
Female				
0–12	12	17	14	21
13–32	34	26	31	29
33–40	50	22	38	17
41–56	3	16	15	18
57+	1	20	2	15
All	100	100	100	100

Source: *Employment Gazette*, March 1991.

But where does the balance lie? There is probably nothing wrong with working hard as long as you are having fun. The thing to remember is that running a business is more like running a marathon than running a sprint. Workaholics rarely seem to enjoy their work and behave more like addicts than enthusiasts. Jim Henson, creator of the Muppets, who died suddenly at 50, is being held up as a warning to stoics and workaholics who persist in carrying on as usual during or after bouts of illness. A vigorous man in excellent health and with £90 million in the bank, Henson kept to his usual punishing work schedule while complaining of flu. He consulted a doctor on the Saturday who prescribed aspirin, and on Tuesday, after continuing to work, was admitted to hospital where he died of gallopping pneumonia 16 hours later.

Acceptance of uncertainty

Managers in big business tend to seek to minimize risk by either calling up more information or delaying decisions until every possible fact is known.

This response to uncertainty is one that challenges the need to operate in the unknown. There is a feeling that to work without all the facts is not prudent or desirable.

Entrepreneurs, on the other hand, know that by the time the fog of uncertainty has been completely lifted too many people will be able to spot the opportunity clearly. In point of fact an entrepreneur would usually only be interested in a decision that involved accepting a degree of uncertainty and would welcome and on occasions even relish that position.

Good health

Apart from being able to put in long days, the successful small business owner needs to be on the spot to manage the firm every day. Such owners are the essential lubricant that keeps the wheels of the business turning. They have to turn their hands to anything that needs to be done to make the venture work and they have to plug any gaps caused either by other people's sickness or because they just cannot afford to employ anyone for that particular job. They themselves cannot afford the luxury of sick leave. A week or two for a holiday is viewed as something of a luxury in the early years of a business life.

Self-discipline

One of the most common pitfalls for the novice businessman is failure to recognize the difference between cash and profit. Cash can make people feel wealthy and if it results in a relaxed attitude to corporate status symbols such as cars and luxury office fittings, then failure is just around the corner.

Owner managers needs strong personal discipline to keep themselves and their business on the schedule set out in the business plan. They must set the example for everything in their firm. Get that wrong and wrong signals are sent to every part of the business – both inside and out.

Self-confident all rounders

Entrepreneurs are rarely geniuses. There are nearly always people in their business who have more competence, in one field, than they could ever aspire to. But they have a wide range of ability and a willingness to turn their hand to anything that has to be done to make the venture succeed. They can usually make the product, market it and count the money, but above all they have self-confidence that lets them move comfortably through uncharted waters.

EXAMPLE: Paul Smith, who left school at 15, launched his clothing business in 1974 and within a decade had opened three shops in London, one of which is in Covent Garden, and a further one in Tokyo. Turnover is now above £2 million pa.

Explaining his success he states: 'It's not that I'm a particularly brilliant designer or businessman, but I can run a business and I can design. There are so many excellent designers or excellent business people but so often the designers can't run the business and businessmen do not have the right product.'

Bob Payton, founder of Chicago Pizza Pie Factory, explained how his first venture got started. 'I had no catering experience, but I've got a nose for what's going on. I flew to Chicago, located the best pizza chef and spent two weeks learning the business. I made dough, waited at tables and washed dishes – and then I set out to raise £25,000 to start up.'

Innovative skills

Almost by definition, entrepreneurs are innovators who either tackle the unknown, or do old things in new ways. It is this inventive streak that allows them to carve out a new niche, often invisible to others.

EXAMPLE: The entrepreneurial Elizabeth Taylor (no relation) read an article about organic markets in France, les Marches Biologiques, and wondered why there was none in the UK. She asked organic producers if they would be interested in a market and received enough positive responses to go ahead.

In May 1992 she had 40 different organic producers and suppliers under one roof. Spitalfields, once a wholesale fruit and vegetable market, has been taken over as a leisure venture with around 200 stalls selling crafts and bric-a-brac plus sporting attractions in a covered area larger than Covent Garden.

The organic food stalls will be there on Sundays and eventually, if there is enough interest from customers and caterers, may become a daily fixture. 'Farmers like to see things going from the farm straight to the table,' said Elizabeth Taylor. 'But they've never had a market designed especially for them.' In creating one she has inadvertently made a move towards alternative methods of selling that could have great significance for organic farming.

The Soil Association sees this development in more political terms, as possibly changing the relationship between consumer and producer. 'Part of the organic ethic is to shorten the chain and look at ways of bringing consumers and producers back together,' said its spokesman Patrick Holden. 'The market concept is a very exciting example of that.'

Brian Tustian, who has farmed organically for five years, is looking forward to the opportunity of dealing with his customers personally; it gives him a chance to put the case for organic produce himself, and he can cope better with the variable quantity if he sells at a market. His hens, although merrily producing eggs now, do not lay to order as battery hens can. He'll be selling his Grade 1 eggs for about £2 a dozen – £1 less than eggs from organically reared hens usually cost. He also sells organic chicken at about the same price supermarkets charge for non-organic (£1.25 per lb), and organic pork for £1.20 per lb.

Successful people set themselves goals and get pleasure out of trying to achieve them. Once a goal has been reached, they have to get the next target in view as quickly as possible. This restlessness is very characteristic. Sir James Goldsmith is a classic example, moving the base of his business empire from the UK to France, then the USA – and finally into pure cash, ahead of the 1987 stock market crash.

James Gulliver, who built the Argyll group up to the fourth largest food retailer in the UK in around a decade, also exhibited this restless streak when he resigned in November 1987, still only in his fifties, to make a third 'fresh' start in his career, sadly without great success when his Queensway business failed.

SELF-EVALUATION FOR PROSPECTIVE BUSINESS STARTERS

The following self-evaluation questions probe only those areas which are important to successfully starting up a business and can be controlled or affected by the individual. If the statement is rarely true, score 1; if usually true, score 2; and if nearly always true, score 3.

1 I know my personal and business objectives.
2 I get tasks accomplished quickly.
3 I can change direction quickly if market conditions alter.
4 I enjoy being responsible for getting things done.
5 I like working alone and making my own decisions.
6 Risky situations don't alarm me.

7 I can face uncertainty easily.
8 I can sell myself and my business ideas.
9 I haven't had a day off sick.
10 I can set my own goals and targets and then get on with achieving them.
11 My family are right behind me in this venture – and they know it will mean long hours and hard work.
12 I welcome criticism – there is always something useful to learn from other people.
13 I can pick the right people to work for me.
14 I am energetic and enthusiastic.
15 I don't waste time.

A score of 30 plus is good; 20–30 is fair; below 20 is poor. A high score will not guarantee success but a low one should cause a major re-think.

Are my motivations and aims realistic?

Few people get rich working for someone else. Running a business at least provides the opportunity to make more money, but whether you become wealthy depends very much on the success you make of it. If the business does well, you – as the founder – can determine the amount of money you take out as salary and can claim extra benefits on the firm (e.g. cars, pensions). Big businesses are only small businesses that succeed. If a business makes it to the big time the founder might consider going public, which will dramatically increase the value of the business, or they may decide to sell out for a large profit and retire in luxury.

More important than riches to many an entrepreneur, though, is the freedom which comes from being your own boss. Proprietors are totally independent and can plan the business and run it on a day-to-day basis the way they want. It is also an opportunity to work in a field they really enjoy.

There are tax advantages too. Self-employed people have more allowances against income than employees. Directors of their own limited liability companies, though, are not classified as self-employed for tax purposes, but the benefits they can take from the company frequently mitigate their tax bills.

Disadvantages

Running a business is much more risky than working for someone else. If the business fails you stand to lose far more than just your job. Not only will all your hard work have been to no avail, but you might suffer severe financial hardship if your business owes money since, as a self-employed person, you are personally liable to your creditors. This might mean selling your assets, including your home, and, at the worst, may result in bankruptcy. If you form a limited company your personal liability to creditors is limited to the value of the shares you hold – in theory. But, in practice, banks usually require a personal guarantee from the director(s) to secure an overdraft or loan for the business, which to some extent negates the benefits of limited liability status.

You are totally responsible for the success or failure of your business. This can be very exhilarating, but it is, inevitably, very stressful: constant pressure and long hours are par for the course for most entrepreneurs. This can drastically affect your social and family life, also your health.

To give a flavour of what it is like being your own boss, here in their own words are selected comments from some small business founders.

EXAMPLE: It gives you a feeling of being totally in control of your own destiny which is very exciting.

You feel totally productive. You use your own time as you wish to spend it. Often this means working all hours of the day, six days a week – permanently. But it isn't a grind if you're doing it for yourself.

I have earned far more in personal reward than I have financial benefits. It has given me self-confidence which has made me calmer, less neurotic and more prepared to take risks than hitherto.

No longer being involved in office politics has given me an enormous feeling of freedom.

You get pleasure from the simplest things – just the fact that the office copier is working!

The ability to buy more and better material possessions is irrelevant compared to the sense of achievement you feel.

To begin with it's a very exciting feeling, you've struck your flag in the sand. Then ... there is a deadly pause while you sit and wait for the business to pour in. The bank manager or your spouse are going berserk and you wonder why you've done it. If you're sensible, you ride out this period by concentrating on planning the business properly and making sure you've got your costings right.

It's food for the soul.

It's good fun.

But...

It's very lonely knowing you are totally responsible for the success or failure of the business.

You have to be totally single-minded which can make you appear selfish to family and friends. It bust up my marriage.

You have to be prepared to turn your hand to anything that needs doing. A small firm can't afford all the back-up services – typing help, tea lady, mail boy – you might have become accustomed to as an employee.

Some aspects of the work are unpleasant – e.g. cold canvassing for clients, chasing up slow payers, and doing VAT returns.

You must develop a strong sense of responsibility to your staff. You can't be cavalier with them, after all, their careers and jobs are in your hands.

You must be prepared to be ruthless however friendly you are with staff or suppliers. If staff are no good you must fire them. If suppliers let you down get rid of them.

It was a great relief going back to being an employee since I no longer had the burden of finding staff salaries each week.

These days everyone is trying to live on credit so the biggest problem is cashflow.

It's very terrifying at the beginning. You sit there waiting for the phone to ring and when it does you hope like hell it's a potential customer rather than someone you owe money to.

The paperwork and form filling is time-consuming and irritating. The Department of Employment returned a form to us because we omitted to indicate the type of business of a client even though the client was called the Bank of America!

I find the responsibility a constant worry – it brings me out in cold sweats every night.

Despite the complaints, most business owners are pleased to have gone on their own and would have no hesitation in starting up another business rather than work for someone else. In 1991 some 800 independent profitable companies with turnover of less than £25 million were asked what motivated them to start up and run their own businesses. The majority of the responses, 73.5%, had turnover between £1 million and £10 million.[1]

A massive 98% of respondents rated personal satisfaction from success as an important motivator, with 70% of these rating it very important; 88% rated 'ability to do things my own way' and 87% rated 'freedom to take a longer term view' as important or very important, indicating that independence is a key motivator. Evidently, financial rewards register as an important motivator, but it is interesting to note that they are rated less highly than personal satisfaction, and only marginally more highly than independence. To assume, as some do, that business founders are motivated purely by pecuniary gain is

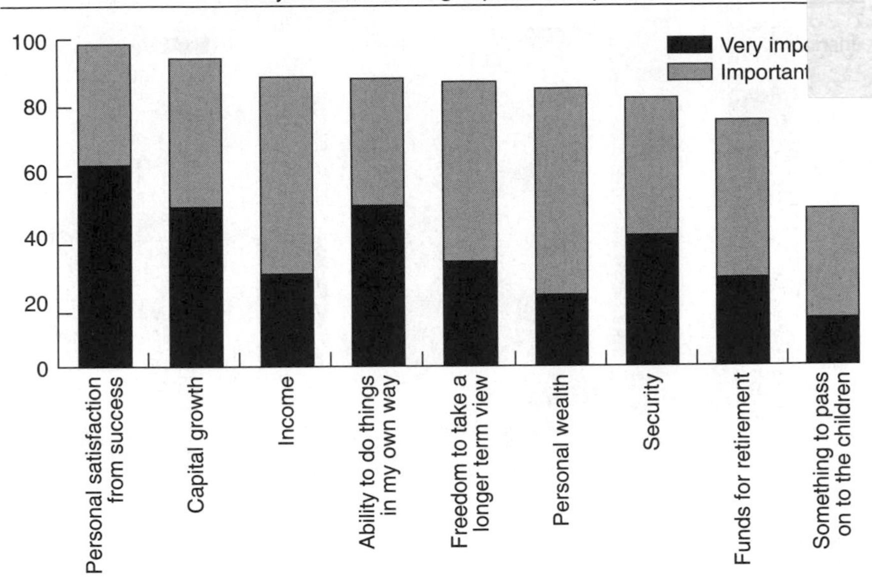

Figure 2.1 Ranking of small business motivators[1]

Source: Cooper and Lybrand, 1991

not only naive but also demonstrates a lack of understanding of entrepreneurs' personal goals.

Few were highly motivated by 'something to pass on to the children' – only 15% rated this as very important. Does the idea of a family company belong to the past?

Study Figure 2.1. What do you think are your principal motivations in running your business?

HOW SMALL BUSINESS FOUNDERS MEASURE SUCCESS

The same study echoes other studies that have revealed how small business proprietors measure success in their business: 82% of responding companies see the quality of their product or service as a very important measure of business success – compared with 67% for pure financial performance. The message is clear, and is, in reality, common sense. Quality and customer service are the keys to long-term prosperity. It is the combination of quality and financial performance that provides the most acute measure of success.

Quality, of course, also reflects entrepreneurs' feelings of a job well done, matching the importance placed on personal satisfaction as a motivator. Ego evidently plays little part in entrepreneurs' minds as only 8% rated 'standing in the business community' as a very important measure of success. A developing business is only as good as the people involved in its development, so

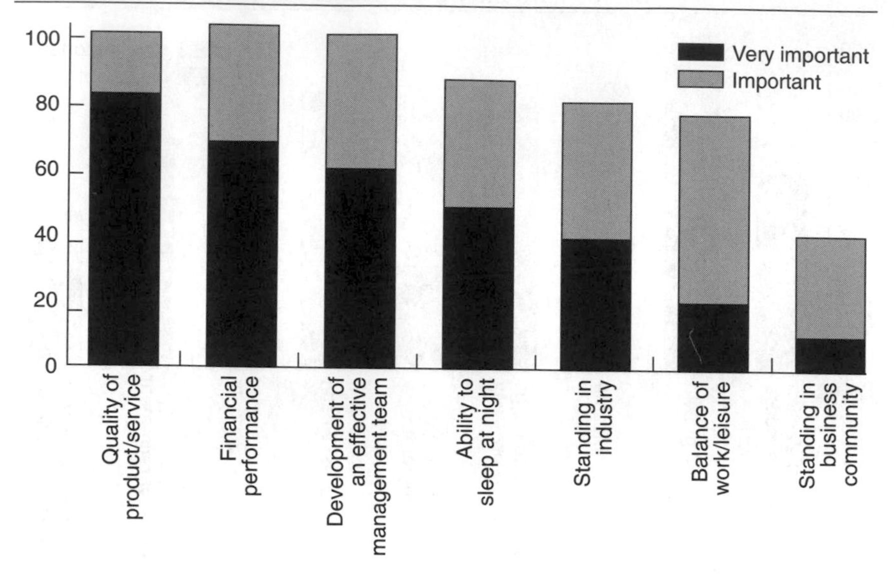

Figure 2.2 Ranking of how small business proprietors measure success
Source: Cooper and Lybrand, 1991

it is good to see that 98% of respondents rated the development of an effective management team as an important or very important measure of success (see Figure 2.2).

IS THE BUSINESS RIGHT FOR ME?

So much for general self-analysis. Now to the particular. Here is an exercise which might help your decision process. Take a sheet of paper and draw up two columns. In the left-hand column, list all your hobbies, interests and skills. In the right-hand column, translate them into possible business ideas.

For example:

Interest/skills	*Business ideas*
Motor cars	motor car dealer/repair garage/home tuning service
Cooking	restaurant/home catering service/bakery shop providing produce for freezer outlets
Gardening	supplier of produce to flower or vegetable shop/running a nursery/running a garden centre/landscape design

Typing	typing authors' manuscripts from home/typing back-up service for busy local companies/running a secretarial agency

. . . and so on

Having done this exercise, you need to balance the possibilities against the criteria; which are most important to you? These might be: small amount of capital required; good anticipated profit; secure income; work satisfaction; no need to learn new skills; variety of work; the possibility of working hours that suit your lifestyle; opportunity to meet new people; minimal paperwork; opportunity to travel.

Select your criteria

You may have other criteria not on this list. Decide the most important criteria and place them in order of importance. Allocate each chosen criterion a weighting factor of between 1 and 5. Now list the possible business opportunities you have identified from the first exercise and measure them against the graded criteria.

A simple example: Jane Clark, an ex-secretary with school-aged children, needed work because her husband had been made redundant and was busy looking for another job. She was not in a position to raise much capital, and she wanted her hours to coincide with those of her children. She wanted to run her own show and she wanted to enjoy what she did. The criteria she selected were:

Criteria	*Weighting factor (out of five)*
Minimal capital required	5
Possibility to work hours that suit lifestyle	5
No need to learn new skills	4
Minimal paperwork	3
Work satisfaction	2
Opportunity to meet interesting people	1

Since minimal capital was a very important criteria for Jane she gave it a weighting factor of 5, whereas the opportunity to meet interesting people, being far less important to her, was only weighted one.

Jane then gave each of her three business ideas a rating, in points (out of five) against these criteria. A secretarial agency needed capital to start so was given only one point. Back-up typing needed hardly any money and was allocated five points.

Her worked-out chart looked like this:

	Weighting Factor	**Secretarial agency** *points*		*score*	**Back-up typing** *points*	*score*	**Authors' manuscript** *points*	*score*
Criteria								
Minimal capital	5 x	1	=	5	5	25	4	20
Flexible hours	5 x	1	=	5	3	15	5	25
No new skills	4 x	2	=	8	5	20	5	20
Work satisfaction	3 x	4	=	12	1	3	3	9
Minimal paperwork	2 x	0	=	0	4	8	5	10
Meeting people	1 x	4	=	4	3	3	4	4
Total score				**34**		**74**		**88**

The weighting factor and the rating point multiplied together give a score for each business idea. The highest score indicates the business that best meets Jane's criteria. In this case, typing authors' manuscripts scored over back-up typing since Jane could do it exactly when it suited her.

The team approach

While starting a business can often be done by one person on their own, starting a substantial business or one that seeks to become a substantial business, calls for a team approach. Not surprisingly, an investor's ideal proposal includes an experienced and balanced management team, who have all worked together for a number of years. That will ensure management in depth, thus providing cover for everything from illness to expansion, and guaranteeing some stability during the turbulent early years. For this reason management buy-outs are a firm favourite.

At the other end of the scale is the lone inventor whose management skills may be in doubt, and who is anyway fully stretched getting his product from the drawing board to the production line. This type of proposal is unlikely to attract much investment capital. It has obvious risks beyond those every company expects to experience in the marketplace. In any case, without a management team in position the business is ill-prepared for the rapid growth required to service an investor's funds.

In practice, most business proposals lie somewhere between these extremes. Your business plan should explain clearly what the ideal composition of key managers should be for your business; who you have identified, or recruited so far; and last but certainly not least, how you will motivate them to remain with you and perform well for at least the first few all-important years.

> EXAMPLE: F International, set up by a group of technologically skilled women whose family ties made it impossible for them to work standard office hours, nearly floundered when six full-time staff left in 1982 to form their own business. They took with them many F International customers, as well as the business concept. F International's profits for the year up to this defection were £450,000. For the year 1982–83 profits slumped to £124,000 and it wasn't until 1984–85 that profits partially recovered to £340,000.

Certainly investors will look for reassurance in this respect and will expect to see some reference to the steps you will take to encourage loyalty.

What legal form should I choose?

Legal form for start-ups is as much to do with the personality of the entrepreneur as with the finer points of law and taxation.

At the outset of your business venture you will have to decide what legal form your business will take. There are four main forms that a business can take, with a number of variations on two of these. The form that you choose will depend on a number of factors: commercial needs, financial risk and your tax position. All play an important part. The tax position is looked at in more detail later, but a summary of the main pros and cons is set out later in this chapter.

Sole trader

If you have the facilities, cash and customers, you can start trading under your own name immediately. Unless you intend to register for VAT, there are no rules about the records you have to keep. There is no requirement for an external audit, or for financial information on your business to be filed at Companies House. You would be prudent to keep good books and to get professional advice, as you will have to declare your income to the Inland Revenue. Without good records you will lose in any dispute over tax. You are personally liable for the debts of your business and, in the event of your business failing, your personal possessions can be sold to meet the debts.

A sole trader does not have access to equity capital, which has the attraction of being risk-free to the business. He must rely on loans from banks or individuals and any other non-equity source of finance.

Partnership

There are very few restrictions to setting up in business with another person (or persons) in partnership. Many partnerships are entered into without legal formalities and sometimes without the parties themselves being aware that they have entered a partnership. All that is needed is for two or more people to agree to carry on a business together, intending to share the profits. The law will then recognize the existence of a partnership.

Most of the points raised when considering sole tradership apply to partnerships. All the partners are personally liable for the debts of the partnership, even if those debts were incurred by one partner's mismanagement or dishonesty without the other partner's knowledge. Even death may not release a partner from his obligations, and in some circumstances his estate can remain liable. Unless you take 'public' leave of your partnership by notifying your business contacts, and advertising retirement in *The London Gazette*, you will remain liable indefinitely. So it is vital before entering a partnership to be absolutely sure of your partner and to take legal advice in drawing up a partnership contract.

The contract should cover the following points:

- *Profit sharing, responsibilities and duration.* This should specify how profit and losses are to be shared, and who is to carry out which tasks. It should also set limits on partners' monthly drawings, and on how long the partnership itself is to last (either a specific period of years or indefinitely, with a cancellation period of, say, three months).
- *Voting rights and policy decisions.* Unless otherwise stated, all the partners have equal voting rights. It is advisable to get a definition of what is a policy or voting decision, and how such decisions are to be made. You must also decide how to expel or admit a new partner.
- *Time off.* Every partner is entitled to his share of the profits even when ill or on holiday. You will need some guidelines on the length and frequency of holidays, and on what to do if someone is absent for a long period for any other reason.
- *Withdrawing capital.* You have to decide how each partner's share of the capital of the business will be valued in the event of either partner leaving or the partnership being dissolved.
- *Accountancy procedure.* You do not have either to file accounts or to have accounts audited. However, it may be prudent to agree a satisfactory standard of accounting and have a firm of accountants to carry out that work. Sleeping partners may well insist on it.

A *sleeping partner* is a partner who has put up capital but does not intend to take an active part in running the business. He/she can protect against risk by having the partnership registered as a limited partnership.

Limited company

The main distinction between a limited company and either of the two forms of business already discussed is that it has a legal identity of its own separate from the people who own it. This means that, in the even of liquidation, creditors' claims are restricted to the assets of the company. The shareholders are not liable as individuals for the business debts beyond the paid-up value of their shares. This applies even if the shareholders are working directors, unless the company has been trading fraudulently or wrongfully.

The Insolvency Act, 1986, among other things brings into effect the notion that limited liability is a privilege rather than a right. Under these new rules incompetent as well as fraudulent directors may incur a measure of personal liability for debts incurred in the face of looming insolvency. Directors found unfit to manage can also be disqualified from holding office elsewhere.

Other advantages for limited companies include the freedom to raise capital by selling shares and certain tax advantages. The disadvantages include the legal requirements for the company's accounts to be audited by a chartered or certified accountant, and for certain records of the business trading activities to be filed annually at Companies House. In practice, the ability to limit liability is severely restricted by the requirements of potential lenders. They often insist on personal guarantees from directors when small, new or troubled companies look for loans or credits. The personal guarantee usually takes the form of a charge on the family house. Since the Boland case in 1980, unless a wife specifically agreed to a charge on the house, by signing a Deed of Postponement, then no lender can take possession in the case of default.

A limited company can be formed by two shareholders, one of whom must be a director. A company secretary must also be appointed, who can be a shareholder, director, or an outside person such as an accountant.

The company can be bought 'off the shelf' from a registration agent, then adapted to suit your own purposes. This will involve changing the name, shareholders and articles of association. Alternatively, you can form your own company, using your solicitor or accountant. The cost either way will be in the low hundreds of pounds.

Public limited company (PLC or plc)

This is not necessarily a company quoted on the stock exchange. Anyone prepared to back a venture to the tune of £50,000 worth of nominal shares can form a plc. The title adds a certain cachet above and beyond that of a plain limited company.

& Co

This title is one often used by partnerships and sole traders. The term '& Co' indicates unlimited liability, unless suffixed by the term, 'Limited'.

Co-operative

There is an alternative form of business for people whose primary concern is to create a democratic work environment, sharing profits and control. If you want to control or substantially influence your own destiny, and make as large a capital gain out of your life's work as possible, then a co-operative is not for you.

The membership of the co-operative is the legal body that controls the business, and members must work in the business. Each member has one vote, and the co-operative must be registered under the Industrial and Provident Societies Act, 1965, with the Chief Registrar of Friendly Societies.

Forms of business: pros and cons

Sole trader

Advantages:
- start trading immediately
- minimum formalities
- no set-up costs
- no audit fees
- no public disclosure of trading information
- pay Schedule 'D' tax
- profits or losses in one trade can be set off against profits or losses in any other area
- past PAYE can be clawed back to help with trading losses.

Disadvantages:
- unlimited personal liability for trading debts
- no access to equity capital
- low status public image
- when you die, so does the business.

Partnership

Advantages:
- no audit required, though your partner may insist on one
- no public disclosure of trading information
- pay Schedule 'D' tax.

Disadvantages:
- unlimited personal liability for your own and your partners' trading debts (except sleeping partners)
- partnership contracts can be complex and costly to prepare
- limited access to equity capital
- death of a partner usually causes partnership to be dissolved.

Limited company

Advantages:
- shareholders' liabilities restricted to nominal value of shares
- it is possible to raise equity capital
- high status public image
- the business has a life of its own and continues with or without the founder.

Disadvantages:
- directors are on PAYE
- full audit required if your turnover exceeds £350,000. (No audit up to £90,000 and a simplified report is required between £90,000 and £350,000.) Exemptions are automatic provided a company has assets of less than £1.4 million and approval from 90% of its shareholders. Trading information must be disclosed
- suppliers, landlords and banks will probably insist on personal guarantees from directors (except for government loan guarantee scheme)
- you cannot start trading until you have a certificate of incorporation.

Exercises

1 Carry out the self-evaluation check described in this chapter and see how closely you appear to fit the entrepreneurial style.
2 Review your motivations for getting into business to see how well they compare with typical entrepreneurs.
3 What legal form do you plan to use to set up and why? Are you sure the advantages of that form outweigh the disadvantages?
4 Your business should ideally suite your skills and criteria, i.e. lots of computing and no late nights. How well does your proposed venture meet those yardsticks?

NOTE

1 Coopers & Lybrand, Small Firms Survey, July 1991.

SUGGESTED FURTHER READING

Drucker, P. (1985) Innovation and Entrepreneurship, Heineman, London.
Golzen, Godfrey (1996) *Working for Yourself*, Kogan Page.
Hawkins, Barrie and Badge, Grant (1990) *Thinking up a Business*, Rosters.
Richardson, Pat and Clarke, Lawrence (1993) *Business Start Ups for Professional Managers*, Kogan Page.

Chapter 3

What is your marketing entry strategy?

The starting point for marketing entry strategy in your business plan has to be your customer. Everything has to be defined in terms of customer needs and how you will satisfy them. Customers want good quality photographs and may be less interested in the elaborate technology that is needed to produce them; they want coffee at home to taste just like it does on holiday in France, so how can products be designed to achieve this? Satisfying customer needs or solving customer problems are the keys to successful marketing strategy.

It may also help to shape your future business to distinguish between the needs of consumers of your product (e.g. children who eat the sweets) and the needs of customers who make the buying decision (e.g. parents who pay for the sweets, or distributors, wholesalers to retailers, in the distribution chain to end customer).

EXAMPLE: Autoglass, prior to setting up a skeleton network of depots to provide a quick windscreen replacement service to the motoring public, was concerned at the difficult task and cost of communicating the benefits of the service to millions of potential motoring consumers. Discussions with a major motor insurance company, which covered the cost of replacing windscreens for its insured motorists, indicated that the insurance company needed a reliable windscreen replacement company, with standard prices and credit payment terms, which would help the insurance company improve its service to motorists. In return for meeting this need, the insurance company 'customer' agreed to recommend Autoglass to all its insured motorists, at annual premium renewal time, solving the windscreen company's promotional problem and virtually guaranteeing customers for its new depots.

Your preliminary desk and field research ought to have given you some first feel for customer needs and even the segment of the market you wish to first attack, whilst your analysis of competitive offerings should have indicated weakness or opportunities which you may wish to exploit.

MARKET SEGMENTATION AND COMPETITIVE ANALYSIS

Market segmentation is the name given to the process whereby customers and potential customers are organized into clusters or groups of 'similar' types. For example, a shop or restaurant has regulars and passing trade. The balance between the two is a fundamental issue that affects everything the business does.

In addition, each of these customer groups is motivated to buy for different reasons and your selling message has to be modified accordingly.

EXAMPLE: David Sinclair's original Bagel Express business plan was to be focused on 'higher income earners, ABC1 demographic categories, under 45. Although they eat fast food less frequently than the equivalent C2DE income earners, they spend almost as much and are more likely to know what bagels are (although not necessarily to have tasted them)'. Segmentation might also be by geography, e.g. Robert Wright's original Connectair plan was aimed at 'business executives living in a 25-mile radius of Milton Keynes, who might consider an air taxi rather than ordinary taxi or train for connecting flights for Heathrow'.

The farming owners of the Hop Shop in Kent, in their business plan segmented the dried flower market in the South East in two ways:

1 By type of sales outlet, e.g. High Street flower shops, farm shops, garden centres, supermarkets, garages. airports and street markets.
2 By type of end use, e.g. commercial premises displays (pubs, hotels), shop window decoration, exhibition, display, educational courses at colleges, etc.

Such segmentation enabled Hop Shop to focus its selling efforts on specific outlets and users, which could be located and quantified, enabling the owners to set realistic sales tasks.

Industrial markets can be similarly segmented, by size and location of company (number of employees, turnover, geographic concentration), by category of trade (furniture, glass and ceramics), or by level of technology and production process (types of buyer, service requirement).

For example, one MBA student project, to provide creche services for working mothers, focused on computer software companies with under 500 employees in the Thames Valley. A building was converted to provide such facilities when four such companies had signed up for the project, as the creche facility promised to help companies solve their recruitment difficulties.

Here are some useful rules to help you decide on whether a market segment is worth trying to sell into:

- *Measurability*: Can you estimate how many customers are in the segment?
- *Accessibility:* Can you communicate with these customers? Just knowing 'they are out there somewhere' is not much help.
- *Size*: A segment has to have a 'large' number of customers, although exactly what constitutes large will be relative to your business.
- *Open to practical development*: Just being a large segment is not enough. The customer must have money to spend and be able to spend it.

EXAMPLE: One MBA student researching the nursing home markets completed an analysis of nursing homes in a 20-mile radius of Marlborough. This is shown in Table 3.1.

The information gathering process revealed that each nursing home had a lengthy waiting list of customers for rooms, encouraging the student to go ahead and develop a new property, matching some of the better facilities available for an assured customer market.

The purpose of your competitive analysis is, as Harvard's Professor Michael Porter has researched, twofold:

1 to determine where your competitor is weak
2 to help you define what should be your product's point of difference.

So, you must buy and analyse competitor's products, study competitive advertisements and visit trade exhibitions to learn all you can about competitor's offerings at first hand, and continue to do so, as competitors, like customers, change all the time. Never, ever, underestimate the opposition!

MARKETING ENTRY STRATEGY

Based on your market research, armed with the results of your customer and competitive analysis, you are now in a position to consider the primary thrust of your entry strategy to the market.

Professor Michael Porter has concluded that there are three distinctive marketing strategies for a company to pursue:

1 *Overall cost leadership*, often characteristic of large companies, able to achieve economies of scale by major capital investment, operating on low

Table 3.1 Competitor analysis: comparing nursing homes

Name of home	*Management*	*Nurses*	*Beds*	*Single*	*Age*[1]	*C or PB*[2]	*Price per week*	*Promotion*[3]
The Laurels	Owner	22	32	Y	1	PB	£270	n/a
Aldbourne Nursing Home	Manager	10	29	Y	1	PB	£350	n/a
Ashbury Lodge	Manager	26	18	Y	2	C	£290	7
Ashgrove House	Owner	23		n/a	2		n/a	n/a
Bethany House Nursing Home	Owner	16		n/a	4		n/a	n/a
Park View	Manager	15	15	Y	1	PB	£360	6
Station Court	Manager	32		Y	2	PB	£300	10
Weymuss Lodge	Manager	9	27	Y	2	PB	£275	6
Southdown	Manager	10	14	N	1	c	£260	5

[1]Age since registration
[2]Conversion = C; purpose built = PB
[3]Promotion = quality rating

margins by virtue of efficient control systems and to create barriers of entry through low pricing.

EXAMPLE: The major car manufacturers exemplify these traits; though Henry Ford lost money in his first year of operation with the model T, he raised his prices considerably above Buick in second year trading, and was subsequently able to trim prices, from a profitable basis, in a growing market, to the discomfort of his competitors.

2 *Differentiation*, characterized by quality, good design and image, with high margins, based on achieving brand loyalty and unique products.

EXAMPLE: If you think this is not possible for your company, just remember how Perrier has managed to sell a basic commodity, water, to the British, at the same price as Coca-Cola and even wine, and many small water bottling companies have been able to follow this example.

3 *Focus*, whereby a company serves one particular target market well, with low costs and high margins, creating barriers to entry by the very narrowness of the market and raising distribution barriers.

EXAMPLE: Autoglass Ltd focused simply on the replacement windscreen market in the UK (the average motorist would suffer only one broken windscreen every 20 years), too small to attract the attention of the major glass manufacturers, and by establishing a depot network was able to build a strong windscreen distribution network, able to supply garages, small tractor cab manufacturers, etc.

Our experience with new starters at Cranfield has emphasized the importance for the starter company of strategies 2 and 3. The temptation for new starts to follow strategy 1 is great; many correctly start their new businesses from a room at home and pay themselves minimum earnings. This comparative cost advantage however, combined with a simplified product or service, leads the owners to believe that under-cutting competitors prices will lead to rapid market penetration and growth. It may well lead to rapid, short-term sales, forcing the owners to consider adding the extra overhead (in the form of offices, employees or promotions) which slim margins cannot support. Even larger companies, with perhaps superior expertise and control systems, such as the late lamented Laker Airways, have to be extraordinarily efficient and swift in new product/service development to survive with their low margin strategies.

This is why for new starter companies with growth ambitions we emphasize concentration on focus and differentiation, a viewpoint shared in recent academic research[1], and as illustrated in the following example:

> EXAMPLE: Paul Howcroft, at the start of his Rohan clothing business, focused his attention particularly on the needs of outdoor hill walkers in the Yorkshire dales. Even in the mid-1970s there was little choice of lightweight walking clothes, other than ex-military gear, with material which allowed energetic walkers' perspiration to escape or which dried rapidly after showers. The special lightweight cloth which he discovered from a Scandinavian source, while working in a Yorkshire textile office, became the basis of his superbly designed lightweight trousers and 'hot-bags'. Sales grew by mail order from his tiny Shipton office to climbing clubs all over the country; climbers who travelled soon realized the advantages of easy packing and washing characteristics of the growing Rohan range (the unusual trademarked name coming from a Tolkien story). Business travellers became a second focus and the clothing became a fashion item with the opening of special Rohan retail shops in the 1980s, prior to acquisition and development of the business by Clark's Shoes, and Paul's untimely demise in a subsequent motor accident.

By clear focus on the needs of specific customer groups, and growing realization by different customer segments of the difference in Rohan clothing materials, skilfully promoted in a personalized mail order magazine, the business could grow with margins sufficiently attractive to support the subsequent development of expensive retail outlets. How do you use all the elements of the marketing mix (product, price, promotion, distribution and selling) to give yourself differentiation once you have an idea of your target customer focus? Some starting ideas would be as follows.

1 Define the product in customers' terms

Technical features are what a product has or is, benefits are, as we have noted, what the product does for the customer. Making your product or service different requires building in extra benefits for the customers, e.g. many small double glazing companies provide:

Features		*Benefits*	*Proof*
Two or three pieces of glass, in sealed frames	which means to me . . .	Saves heat from escaping	Lower fuel bills
Heavy Plastic frames		Low maintenance	Time saving
		Low noise and draughts	Able to live close to airport/ traffic

The customer pays for the benefit and the seller for the feature. So having a close understanding of your customer needs and product benefits, will enable you to focus your future advertising and promotional needs and to vary them as required, e.g. double glazing advertising in January and February emphasizes strongly the heat-saving economies of the product range. Low maintenance and leisure time saving can be promoted in mid-summer.

As we noted above, most customers value good quality photographs, not the technical features of the camera. This features/benefits exercise should help you to identify the benefits that matter most for your product/service and which should, therefore, be promoted accordingly. As we shall see later, the quality of your product offering is particularly important in your initial selling efforts.

Choose an appropriate business name

Your company name can, in effect, be the starting and sustaining point in differentiating you from your competitors and, as such, should be carefully chosen, be protectable by trademarks where possible (see below), and be written in a distinctive way. It is, after all, the visible tip of the iceberg in your future corporate communications effort, and will be used on all your literature and signs throughout the company.

If you have to use initials (and most companies in electronics do) try to make them into an acronym, to make recall easier, e.g. AMSTRAD stands for Alan Michael Sugar Trading.

Given all the marketing investment you will make in your company name, you should check with a trademark agent (see *Yellow Pages*) whether you can protect your chosen name (descriptive words, surnames and place names are not normally registrable except after long use).

Remember also that anyone wanting to use a 'controlled' name will have to get permission. There are some 80 or 90 controlled names that include

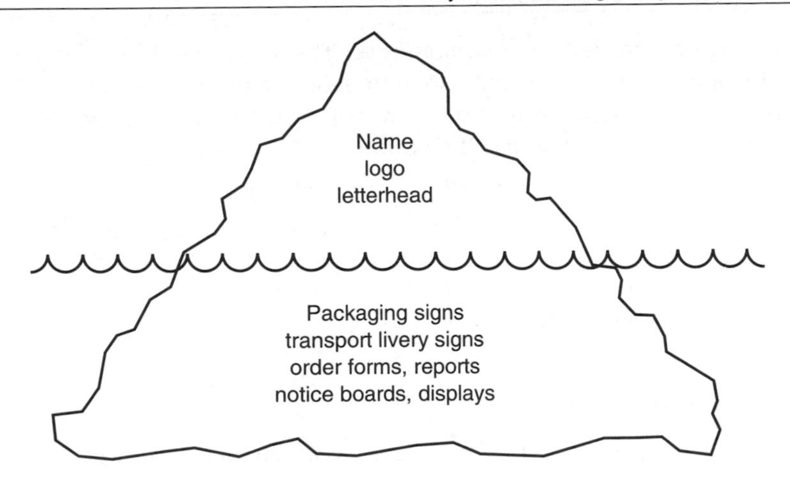

Figure 3.1 The corporate communications iceberg

words such as 'International', 'Bank' and 'Royal'. This is simply to prevent a business implying that it is something that it is not.

Second, all businesses that intend to trade under names other than those of the owner(s) must state who does own the business and how the owner can be contacted. So if you are a sole trader or partnership and you use only surnames, with or without forenames or initials, you are not affected. Companies are also not affected if they simply use their full corporate name. (A Guidance Note entitled 'Control of Business Names' is available from the Department of Trade and Industry.)

Finally, remember that Wally Olins, the corporate design expert, suggested that your business name should reflect:

- Who you are.
- What you do.
- How you do it.

A good name, in effect, can become a one- or two-word summary of your marketing strategy: Body Shop, Toys Я Us, Kwik-Fit Exhausts are good examples. Many companies add a slogan to explain to customers and employees alike 'how they do it'.

EXAMPLE: 'Solaglas' was the name chosen in 1984 by new owners to unify a group of some 40-plus, previously independent and family-owned glass and glazing merchants. The modest slogan, 'Glass with the world's best service behind it', was added to all company literature to communicate to both customers and employees alike how the new group was to be run and how it would be different from competitors. The improved brand recognition achieved by the unifying name and slogan was reflected in the ten-fold increase in the value of the company when the group was acquired in 1990 by St Gobain.

'Boots the Chemist', named after Jesse Boot, now uses the inscription 'Health and Beauty' after its name in shops, to describe its other activities. Changing your name, even marginally, can be very expensive so it is as well to try to get it right at the outset!

Protect your product properties

If you have a unique business idea, you should investigate the four categories of protection: patenting, which protects 'how something works'; design registration, which protects 'how something looks'; copyright, which protects work on film, paper or records; and trademark registration, which protects 'what something's called'.

Some products may be covered by two or more categories, e.g. the mechanism of a clock may be patented while its appearance may be design registered.

Each category requires a different set of procedures, offers a different level of protection and extends for a different period of time. They all have one thing in common, though: in the event of any infringement your only redress is through the courts, and going to law can be wasteful of time and money, whether you win or lose. (Some insurance protection can help in this process.)

Nothing adds more to your earlier credibility, however, than having protected your proprietary position.

EXAMPLE: Michael Gregson secured patent protection on the original mechanical presentation of his novel first-aid Gregson Safety pack. Not only did 'patent protection' count heavily in his early successful efforts at raising finance but five years later, on selling the company, it was the 15 years unexpired patent protection that the acquiring company was buying.

2 Set an appropriate pricing policy

As noted above, the most frequent mistake made when setting a selling price for the first time is to pitch it too low. This mistake can occur either through failing to understand all the costs associated with making and marketing your product, or through yielding to the temptation to undercut the competition at the outset. Both these errors usually lead to fatal results, so in preparing your business plan you should guard against them.

These are the important issues to consider when setting your selling price, within the context of prevailing economic conditions, when 'expansion' and 'recession' conditions clearly set an important pricing tone.

Costs

Make sure you have established all the costs you are likely to incur in making or marketing your product. Do not just rely on a 'guess' or 'common sense' – get several firm quotations, preferably in writing, for every major bought-in item. Do not fall into the trap of believing that if you will initially be working from home, you will have no additional costs. Your phone bill will rise (or you will fail!), the heating will be on all day and you will need somewhere to file all your paperwork.

You will need to know what your fixed costs will be (rent, rates, heating, marketing, etc.) and know what contribution your product or service will make from each sale, after deducting direct material and labour costs of each item. In this way you can calculate how many items you need to sell to cover your fixed costs (see Bagel Express, page 13).

Consumer perception

Pricing is an area of 'value judgement', but customers opinion of values may have little or no relation to costs. For example, in France, Perrier originally tied its price for a standard bottle of water to the price of the newspaper *Le Figaro*, as its target customers, health conscious middle-aged consumers, frequently bought the two items simultaneously. A later generation in the UK, concerned at tap water quality, was willing to pay the price of equivalent bottles of soft drinks for a basic product still simply being pumped from the ground, but now presented in an amusing French 'luxury goods' fashion format. A high relative price undoubtedly contributed to this new image for the same basic product (which should be boiled first, if used by under fives!).

The perceived image you wish to create for your company's product or service is, therefore, an important element in the pricing decision, as will also be your choice of channel of distribution (e.g. Harrods vs W. H. Smith), where your selling price will have to allow for the image and mark-ups of your retailers.

Competition and capacity

Clearly, you have to take account of what your competitors charge, but remember price is the easiest element of the marketing mix for an established company to vary. They could follow you down the price curve, within hours, not the months it might take to match your quality service, forcing you into bankruptcy, far more easily than you could capture their customers with a lower price.

Equally, your capacity to 'produce' your product or service, bearing in mind market conditions, will also influence the price you set. Typically, a new venture has limited capacity at the start. A valid entry strategy could be to price so high as to just fill your capacity, rather than so low as to swamp you.

EXAMPLE: Andrew Ingleston, in starting Dockspeed with one leased vehicle, was careful to price so that one major customer alone guaranteed that he would break even in his first year. Other, smaller customers, subsequently gathered with no discounts, guaranteed his profitability and future growth.

Margins and markets

According to *Management Today*, nearly 80% of UK companies price by reference to costs: either using a cost plus formula (e.g. materials plus 50%) or a cost multiplier (e.g. three time material costs). Whatever formula you use, as accountant Brian Warnes has pointed out, you should endeavour to ensure that you achieve a gross profit margin of at least 40% (sales price less the direct materials and labour used to make the article, the resulting margin expressed as a percentage of the sales price). If you do not achieve such margins, you will have little overhead resource available to you to promote and build an effective, differentiated image for your company.

Your competitive analysis will give you some idea as to what the market will bear. We suggest you complete the following Small Business Action Kit table shown in Figure 3.2 to give yourself confidence that you can match or improve upon competitors' prices. At the very least you will have arguments to justify your higher prices to your customers and, importantly, your future employees.

By pricing boldly, and justifying it, you will be different from most new companies. Price is, after all, the element of the marketing mix that is likely to have the greatest impact on your profitability. It is often more profitable for the new company to sell fewer items at a higher price while getting its organisation and product offerings sorted out (remember Henry Ford); the key is to concentrate on obtaining good margins, often with a range of prices and quality (e.g. Marks and Spencer have a tiered catalogue of three main price ranges: easy, medium and upper).

(Score each product factor from –3 to +3 to justify your price versus competition)

Rating score **Product attributes**	**WORSE** **–3 –2 –1**	**SAME** **0**	**BETTER** **+1 +2 +3**
Design performance			
Packaging			
Presentation/appearance			
After-sales service			
Availability			
Delivery			
Colour/flavour			
Odour/touch			
Image			
Specification			
Payment terms			
Other			
Total			

Figure 3.2 Product comparison with competitors

3 Decide launch material for advertising and promotion

You must certainly make the most of limited start-up means to promote your company to your target customers. Advertising is, after all, as Tim Bell, formerly of Saatchi & Saatchi has commented, 'simply an expensive way for one person to talk to another'. We recommend that you adopt a 'cost/benefit' approach to your early promotional efforts, i.e. use tear off reply coupons with your first advertisement, to measure the 100 or so replies to your first £1,000 advertisement, so that you know that if 10% of enquiries result in orders, and that your profit margin is £200 per item, then the extra £2,000 profit benefit generated more than covers the initial £1,000 cost.

In practice, press advertising, like radio and TV (all known in the media business as 'above the line' promotions) is not likely to be the new companies' main promotional area. There is, however, a vast array of 'below the line' specific items likely to be effective for targeted marketing by the starter company, ranging from business cards to entries in the *Yellow Pages* and including leaflets, brochures, press releases, giveaways, posters, promotional items. Some of the most effective promotional ideas from entrepreneurs at Cranfield have been the simplest, e.g. a business card for Sue Claridge, with a map on the reverse side showing how to find her restaurant. This is like the 'thank you cards' instead of letters, sent by Wally Olins showing the design company's recently completed assignments on the face of the card (e.g. new designs for Suttons Seeds packs).

We will concentrate briefly on the two we think most important for the starter company, leaflets and press releases.

Leaflets, brochures and letters

This is the most practical way for a new business to communicate with its potential customers. It has the merits of being relatively inexpensive, simple and quick to put into operation, it can be concentrated into any geographic area, it can be mailed or distributed by hand and, finally, it is easy to monitor results.

Sometimes, drawing up a new single-page sales leaflet for an exhibition can be a helpful way to rethink your marketing message: list the benefits of your product/service for your target audience and let the customer know where to contact you (with discount on return of leaflet to measure its effectiveness). Getting the leaflet right, after experimentation, can provide the basis for all future press and promotional advertisements. Quantum Cars, for example, drew up the following 'comprehensive' benefits list leaflet for their first Kit Car Exhibition, with technical details (engine, bodyshell drawing, dimensions, etc.) on the reverse side, not 'drowning out' the sales message to enthusiasts.

EXAMPLE: Introducing the Quantum

The Quantum has been designed to combine the best of both worlds: It is an exciting modern sportscar, built to out-perform and out-handle any mass produced car in the £10,000–£15,000 price range.

AND

It is a full 4 seater with a large boot. The Quantum is comfortable, refined and easy to drive whether visiting the local supermarket or motorway cruising.

At the centre of the design is an immensely strong and rigid composite monocque bodyshell incorporating modern hi-tech materials. There is no separate steel chassis so the body is totally rust free. The bodyshell has been fully computer stress analysed at a leading British university to give high strength at minimum weight. In addition crash protection and roll over protection have been built into the design. The front nose cone of the car is removable for ease of accident damage repair.

The Quantum uses standard Ford components which are highly reliable, cheap and easy to service. It will accept any Ford front wheel drive engine and gearbox up to the Escort RS Turbo unit.

The Quantum is about the same size as a Ford Escort, but is lighter and more aerodynamic, giving much better performance and economy. As an example, a Quantum fitted with a Fiesta XR2 engine has the same performance as an £18,000 BMW 325I but will return an average of 40 miles per gallon. The Quantum Turbo Plus is quicker than the £34,000 Porsche 944 S2.

Great attention has also been given to the suspension geometry which gives the Quantum the kind of handling expected from a supercar without sacrificing ride comfort.

Quantum Sports Cars is run by three partners, Mark, Harvey and Peter Wooldridge, all of whom have honours degrees in engineering. They pride themselves on being able to offer a very personalised and friendly service. There is always a Quantum available for a test drive so customers can experience for themselves the impressive performance and handling, and also the smoothness and quietness of the Quantum. Please note though that the company demonstrators are insured for 25 year olds and over. Those under 25 must bring proof of at least Third Party cover if wishing to drive. The company request that customers phone in advance to make an appointment which can be arranged at any convenient time, seven days a week.

Call Mark Wooldridge...

Public relations

This is about presenting yourself and your business at the outset in a favourable light to your various 'publics' – at little or no cost. It is also a more influential method of communication than general advertising because people tend to take editorials seriously.

EXAMPLE: The owners of the Hop Shop discovered that a *Times* special features writer lived near to their farm in the Darenth Valley, Kent. The journalist was invited to their newly converted dried flower farm shop (formerly a cart shed) and provided with a press release detailing the 48 different dried flowers, grown from seed and dried on the farm, together with photographs. A month later, a three-colour feature article in the Saturday *Times* leisure section appeared, which produced 200 immediate customer enquiries, air freight orders from as far away as Singapore and provided Hop Shop with excellent promotional material.

To be successful, a press release needs to get attention immediately and be quick and easy to digest. Studying and copying the style of the particular journals (or other media) you want your press release to appear in can make publication more likely.

- *Layout.* The press release should be typed on a single sheet of A4. Use double spacing and wide margins to make the text both more readable and easy to edit. Head it boldly 'Press Release' or 'News Release' and date it.
- *Headline.* This must persuade the editor to read on. If it does not attract interest, it will be quickly 'spiked'. Editors are looking for topicality, originality, personality and, sometimes, humour.
- *Introductory paragraph.* This should be interesting and succinct and should summarize the whole story – it might be the only piece published.
- *Subsequent paragraphs.* These should expand and colour the details in the opening paragraph. Most stories can be told in a maximum of three or four paragraphs. Editors are always looking for fillers, so short releases have the best chance of getting published.
- *Contact.* List at the end of the release the name and telephone number of a contact for further information.
- *Style.* Use simple language, short sentences and avoid technical jargon (except for very specialized technical magazines). Write in the style of the magazine to which you are sending the article.
- *Photographs.* They must be black and white, reasonably sized and well captioned. Don't staple them to the release (photographs with holes are unpublishable).
- *Follow-up.* Sometimes a follow-up phone call to see if the editors intend to use the release can be useful – but you must use your judgement on how often to do so.

Find out the name of the editor or relevant writer/reporter and address the envelope to him or her personally. Invite them to the 'opening' of your new business premises. The press release is not a 'sales message' but a factual story. Too many small companies, in their enthusiasm for their products, overlook this difference between the sales leaflet and PR release, which explains why a recent survey showed that only 6% of press releases are printed, 94% are not! With UK editors receiving an average of 80–90 press releases per week, make sure that you are making your latest newsworthy item public, but make sure it is free of puffery and jargon.

Exhibitions

As a means of gathering market research data on competitors, exhibitions are extremely valuable. They are also a useful way of establishing the acceptability of your product or service quickly and relatively inexpensively, and so provide a convincing argument in support of your case for financial backing.

EXAMPLE: Equinox, a designer furniture company, took part in their first national exhibition while on a Cranfield enterprise programme. The cost of their stand at Earls Court was £1,200. They secured £5,000 of new orders, which just recovered their exhibition costs, but more importantly they got 40 contacts to follow up. These eventually resulted in 10 further long-term customers. This whole process took two months, and transformed Equinox from the drawing board to being a bankable proposition.

There are hundreds of exhibitions to choose from. You can find a list of those forthcoming in the monthly publication *Exhibition Bulletin.*

Your business plan should indicate how you intend to use each of these promotional methods to reach your target customers.

4 Decide distribution and selling methods

Finally, your business plan should indicate how you intend to get your products to your customer. If you are a retailer, restaurateur or garage proprietor, for example, then your customers will come to you. Here, your physical location will most probably be the key to success. For businesses in the manufacturing field it is more likely that you will go out to 'find' customers. In this case it will be your channels of distribution that are the vital link.

Premises

The premises that you choose and decorate, just as the way you distribute (via Selfridges or via a corner shop) will all be factors in differentiating your service or product from your competitors, and should be in accord with each of the other elements of the marketing mix you have chosen.

EXAMPLE: Hop Shop could have chosen to sell dried flowers via a road-side stall, for passers-by seeking novel bargains; instead, concentrating on higher prices and margins, an individually styled farm shop was created opposite their attractive farmhouse, while Caroline Alexander chose to exhibit her displays only at the prestigious Chelsea Flower Show (where the Alexanders won the first Gold Medal for dried flowers).

Premises have to conform with planning and licensing requirements – will you lease or buy? Purchasing premises outright frequently makes sense for an established, viable business as a means of increasing its asset base. But for a start-up, interest and repayments on the borrowings will usually be more than the rental payments. Leasing itself can be a trap; e.g. a lease rental of £5,000 a year may seem preferable to a freehold purchase of say £50,000. But remember, as the law currently stands, if you sign and give a personal guarantee on a new 21 year lease (which you will be asked to do) you will remain personally responsible for payments over the whole life of the lease. Landlords are as reluctant to allow change in guarantors as they are to accept small business covenants. You could then be committing yourself, in these circumstances, to a minimum £105,000 outlay! Some financiers feel that your business idea should be capable of making more profit than the return you could expect from property. On this basis you should put the capital to be raised into 'useful' assets such as plant, equipment, stocks, etc.

Also, some believe that if you intend to spend any money on converting or improving the premises, doing so to leased property is simply improving the landlord's investment and wasting your money. You may even be charged extra rent for the improvements, unless you ensure that tenant improvements are excluded from the rent reviews.

In any event your backers will want there to be a lease long enough to see your business firmly established and secure enough to allow you to stay on if it is essential to the survival of your business. Starting up a restaurant in short-lease premises, for example, might be a poor investment proposition, but as Bob Payton proved (starting his Chicago Pizza Pie Restaurant on a tail-end six-month lease prior to moving to Hanover Square on a long lease when the concept was shown to be popular) it might be a sensible way to test your business at minimum risk. The ideal situation, which can sometimes be obtained when landlords are in difficulties, would be to negotiate a short lease (say one to two years) with an option to renew on expiry. All leases in Singapore and Malaysia are two years, with options to renew at prevailing rates, which might seem much more helpful to encourage new business start-ups. It may be best for you to brief a surveyor to help you in your search and negotiation (their charge is normally 1%, with payment only by result).

Channels of distribution

Individual retail stores will carry your goods if you make the personal selling effort necessary. Designer Victoria Richards, for example, following the successful exhibition of her textile designs at her college design show, secured appointments with buyers at Harrods and Selfridges and was rewarded with her first orders.

Sales volumes will need, however, to be built up before even small wholesalers will carry your range.

EXAMPLE: Dan Duncan and co-editors of *When Saturday Comes* spent Saturday after Saturday selling their monthly football 'fanzine' outside football grounds and built up 5,000 monthly sales before a local wholesaler agreed to distribute to local South London stores.

Mail order provides a direct channel to the customer and, as we noted above for Paul Howcroft at Rohan, is an increasingly popular route for small businesses. Mail order has the advantage that customers will pay in advance, but retailers can take up to 90 days.

Other direct 'producer to customer' channels include:

- *Door to door selling.* This is now used by insurance companies, cavity wall insulation firms, double glazing firms and others. Avon Cosmetics have managed to sell successfully door-to-door without attracting the stigma of unethical selling practices.
- *Party plan selling or 'network' selling.* A variation on door-to-door selling which is on the increase with new party plan ideas arriving from the USA. Agents enrolled by the company invite their friends to a get-together where the products are demonstrated and orders are invited. The agent gets a commission.
- *Telephone selling.* This, too, can be a way of moving goods in one single step, from 'maker' to consumer. Few products can be sold easily in this way, but repeat business is often secured via the phone.

Your business plan should clearly explain which channel and which selling method you have chosen, to help the differentiation and success of your business.

EXERCISES

1. List and describe your first target customers and the market segment they represent.
2. What are your main competitors' weaknesses and how will your product be different?
3. What is your company name and logo, and have you any proprietary protection on your business name or product?
4. How will your market entry strategy be focused and different in terms of
   - product or service features and benefits?
   - pricing policy?
   - launch promotional material?
   - distribution and selling methods?

NOTES

1 Smallbone, David and North, David (1995) Targeting established SME's, *International Small Business Journal*, April–June, 53: 'Strategy skills need to be tailored to particular sectoral guidelines, but they are likely to include ... great product differentiation and a more distinctive market focus.'

SUGGESTED FURTHER READING

Breckman, Malcolm (1992) *Running your Own Mail Order Business*, rev. edn, Kogan Page, London.

European Case Clearing House, *Hop Shop Case*, (595-001-1,595-010-1,595-011-1), Cranfield University, Cranfield.

Porter, Michael E. (1981) *Competitive Strategy*, Collier Macmillan, London.

Rosthorn, J., Haldane, A., Blackwell, E. and Whaley, J. *The Small Business Action Kit*, 4th edn, Kogan Page, London.

Warnes, Brian (1984) *The Ghenghis Khan Guide to Business Survival*, Osmosis, London.

Chapter 4

Can you make a profit?

Your big idea looks as though it has a market. You have evaluated your skills and inclinations and believe that you can run this business. The next crucial, question is – will it make you money?

It is vital that you establish the financial viability of your idea before you invest money in it or approach outsiders for backing. You need to carry out a thorough, workmanlike appraisal of the business's financial requirements. If these come out as unworkable, you can then rethink, without having lost anything. If the figures look good, then you can go ahead and prepare cash flow projections, a profit and loss account and a balance sheet, and put together the all-important business plan. (These procedures are covered in the following chapters.)

But first, you need to consider:

- the likely sales volume
- the costs associated with starting up and running the business from day to day
- what price the market will pay for the product or service
- what profit is required for the business not just to survive, but to thrive.

CALCULATING YOUR BREAK-EVEN POINT

Many businesses have difficulty raising start-up capital. To compound this, one of the main reasons small businesses fail in the early stages is that too much start-up capital is used to buy fixed assets. While some equipment is clearly essential at the start, other purchases could be postponed. This may mean that 'desirable' and labour saving devices have to be borrowed or hired for a specific period. This is obviously not as nice as having them to hand all the time but if, for example, photocopiers, fax machines, and computers and even delivery vans are bought into the business, they become part of the fixed costs.

The higher the fixed cost plateau, the longer it usually takes to reach break-even point and profitability. And time is not usually on the side of the small new business: it has to become profitable relatively quickly or it will simply run out of money and die. The break-even analysis is an important tool to be used both in preparing a business plan and in the day-to-day running of a business.

Difficulties usually begin when people become confused by different characteristics of costs. Some costs, for instance, do not change, however much you sell. If you are running a shop, the rent and the rates are relatively constant figures, quite independent of the volume of sales. On the other hand, the cost of the products sold from the shop is completely dependent on volume. The more you sell, the more it 'costs' to buy stock. The former of these costs is called 'fixed' and the latter, 'variable', and you cannot add them together to arrive at total costs until you have made some assumptions about sales.

BREAKING EVEN

Let's take an elementary example: a business plans to sell only one product and has only one fixed cost, the rent. In Figure 4.1, the vertical axis shows the value of sales and costs in £000 and the horizontal shows the number of 'units' sold. The second horizontal line represents the fixed costs, those that do not change as volume increases. In this case it is the rent of £10,000. The angled line running from the top of the fixed costs line is the variable cost. In this example we plan to buy in at £3 per unit, so every unit we sell adds that much to our fixed costs.

Only one element is needed to calculate the break-even point – the sales line. That is the line moving up at an angle from the bottom left-hand corner of the chart. We plan to sell out at £5 per unit, so this line is calculated by multiplying the units sold by that price.

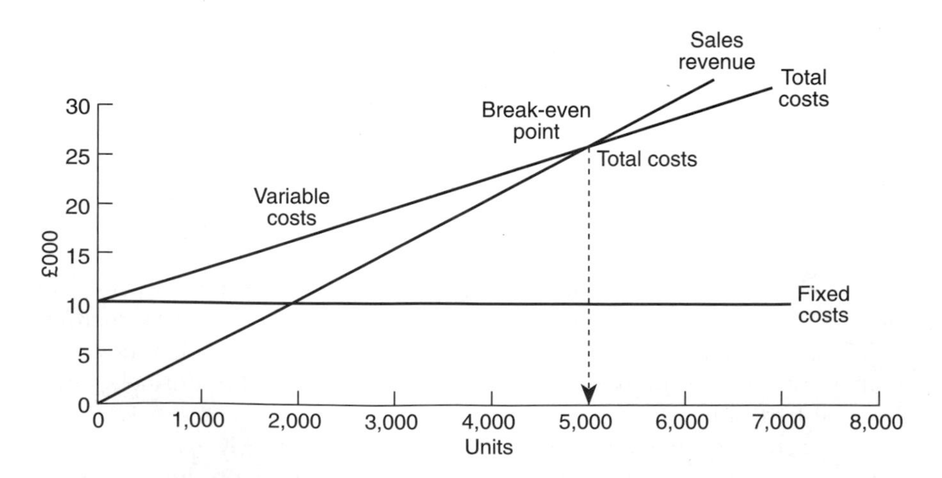

Figure 4.1 Breakeven chart

The break-even point is the stage when a business starts to make a profit. That is when the sales revenue begins to exceed both the fixed and variable costs. The chart shows our example break-even point at 5,000 units.

A formula, deduced from the chart, will save time for your own calculations.

$$\text{Break-even profit point (BEPP)} = \frac{\text{Fixed costs}}{\text{Selling price} - \text{Unit variable costs}}$$

$$= \frac{10{,}000}{£5 - £3} = 5{,}000$$

CAPITAL INTENSIVE vs 'LEAN AND MEAN'

Look at these two hypothetical new small businesses. They are both making and selling identical products at the same price, £10. They plan to sell 10,000 units each in the first year.

> The owner of Company A plans to get fully equipped at the start. His fixed costs will be £40,000, double those of Company B. This is largely because, as well as his own car, he has bought such things as a delivery van, new equipment and a photocopier. Much of this will not be fully used for some time, but will save some money eventually. This extra expenditure will result in a lower unit variable cost than Company B can achieve, a typical capital intensive result.
>
> Company B's owner on the other hand, proposes to start up on a shoestring. Only £20,000 will go into fixed costs, but of course, her unit variable cost will be higher, at £4.50. The variable unit cost will be higher because, for example, she has to pay an outside carrier to deliver, while A uses his own van and pays only for petrol.

So the break-even charts will look like those in Figures 4.2 and 4.3.

From the data on each company you can see that the total costs for 10,000 units are the same, so total possible profits if 10,000 units are sold are also the same. The key difference is that Company B starts making profits after 3,636 units have been sold. Company A has to wait until 5,333 units have been sold, and it may not be able to wait that long.

This is a hypothetical case; the real world is littered with the corpses of businesses that spend too much too soon. The marketplace dictates the selling price and your costs have to fall in line with that for you to have any hope of survival.

PROFITABLE PRICING

To complete the break-even picture we need to add one further dimension – profit. It is a mistake to think that profit is an accident of arithmetic

Company A: Capital intensive

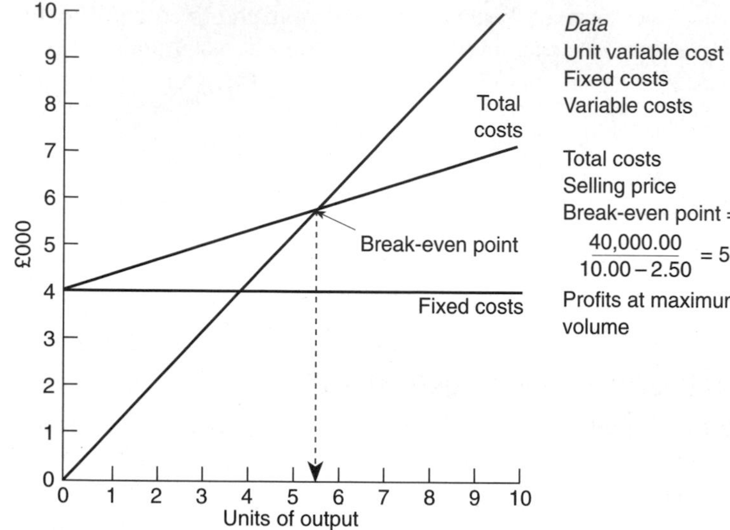

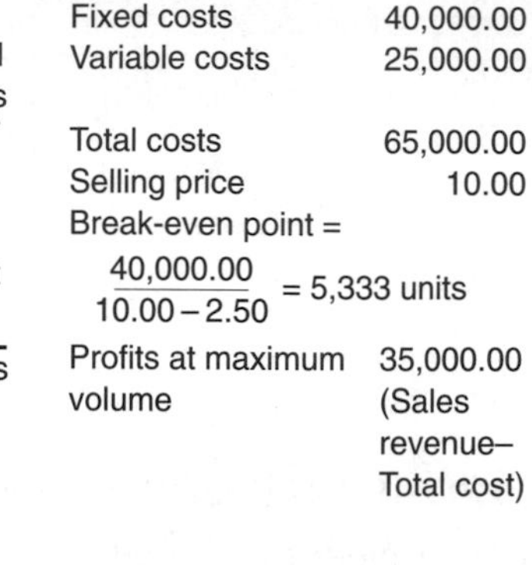

Data	£
Unit variable cost	2.50
Fixed costs	40,000.00
Variable costs	25,000.00
Total costs	65,000.00
Selling price	10.00

Break-even point =

$$\frac{40{,}000.00}{10.00 - 2.50} = 5{,}333 \text{ units}$$

Profits at maximum volume: 35,000.00 (Sales revenue– Total cost)

Figure 4.2 Company A: capital intensive

Company B: Lean and mean

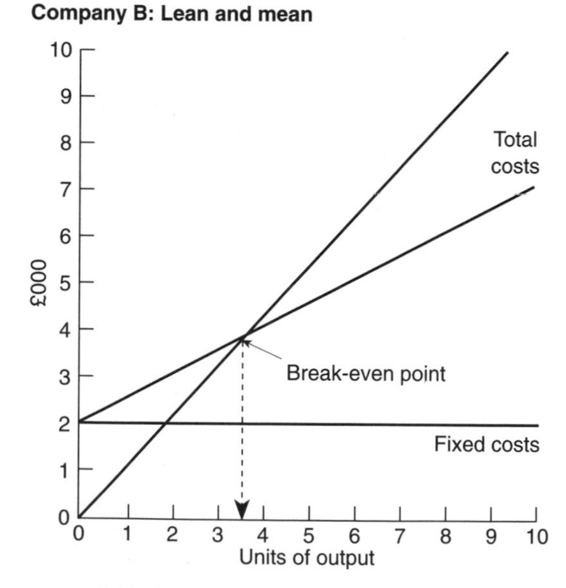

Data	£
Unit variable cost	4.50
Fixed costs	20,000.00
Variable costs	45,000.00
Total costs	65,000.00
Selling price	10.00

Break-even point =

$$\frac{20{,}000.00}{10.00 - 4.50} = 3{,}636 \text{ units}$$

Profits at maximum volume: 35,000.00

Figure 4.3 Company B: lean and mean

calculated only at the end of the year. It is a specific quantifiable target that you need at the outset.

Let's go back to our previous example. You plan to invest £10,000 in fixed assets in a business, and you will need to hold another £5,000 worth of stock too – in all say £15,000. You could get £1,500 profit just leaving it in a building society, so you will expect a return of say £4,000 (approximately to 27%) for taking the risks of setting up on your own. Now let's see when you will break even.

The new equation must include your 'desired' profit so it will look like this:[1]

$$\text{Break-even profit point (BEPP)} = \frac{\text{Fixed costs} + \text{Profit objectives}}{\text{Selling price} - \text{Unit variable costs}}$$

$$= \frac{10{,}000 + 4{,}000}{£5 - £3} = 7{,}000 \text{ units}$$

We now know that to reach our target we must sell 7,000 units at £5 each and have no more than £10,000 tied up in fixed costs. The great strength of this equation is that each element can be changed in turn on an experimental basis to arrive at a satisfactory and achievable result. For instance, suppose you decide that it is unlikely you can sell 7,000 units, but that 6,500 is achievable. What would your selling price have to be to make the same profit?

Using the BEPP equation you can calculate the answer:

$$\text{BEPP} = \frac{\text{Fixed costs} + \text{Profit objectives}}{\text{Selling price} - \text{Unit variable costs}}$$

$$6500 = \frac{10{,}000 + 4{,}000}{6{,}500} = £2.15$$

$$£x = £2.15 + 3 = £5.15$$

If your market will bear a selling price of £5.15 as opposed to £5 all is well; if it won't, then the ball is back in your court. You have to find ways of decreasing the fixed or variable costs, or of selling more, rather than just accepting that a lower profit is inevitable.

From the particular to the general

The example used to illustrate the break-even profit point model was of necessity simple. Few if any businesses sell only one or two products, so a more general equation may be more useful if your business sells hundreds of products as, for example, a real shop does.

In such a business, to calculate your break-even point you must first establish your gross profit. If you are already trading, this is calculated by deducting the money paid out to suppliers from the money you received from customers. If you are not yet trading then researching your competitors will give you some indication of the sort of margins you should aim for.

For example, if you are aiming for a 40% gross profit, your fixed costs are £10,000, and your overall profit objective is £40,000, then the sum will be as follows:

$$\text{BEPP} = \frac{\text{Overheads}}{\text{Gross profit margin}} = \frac{10{,}000 + 4{,}000}{40\%}$$

$$= \frac{14{,}000}{0.4} = £35{,}000$$

So, to reach your target you must achieve a £35,000 turnover. (You can check this out for yourself: look back to the previous example where the BEPP was 7000 units, and the selling price was £5 each. Multiplying those figures out gives a turnover of £35,000. The gross profit in that example was also two-fifths, or 40%.)

If you find that you need help transposing the facts and figures of your business on to a break-even chart or any of the other financial statements, contact a qualified accountant.

A worked example

Let us now look at how you could use break-even analysis and quickly evaluate the financial desirability of your own business idea.

The information on the facing page is on a hypothetical business, Luke's Plumbing. Luke's expected sales are £75,000 in the first six months. By using his knowledge of break-even analysis, Luke can see that he needs to achieve sales of £9,167 each month to cover all his costs. If he does reach his target of £75,000, then he can expect to make £6,000 profit over the six months. If this level of profit does not meet Luke's business objectives then he needs to review his pricing and costing strategies using the method described under the heading 'profitable pricing' above.

The first stage

These first three chapters are intended to show you how to assess a business idea relatively quickly before proceeding to write a business plan. The assessment procedure can be expressed as a model, laid out below.

You can drive any number of ideas through the model, both before you start up and afterwards when you are looking at opportunities for expansion.

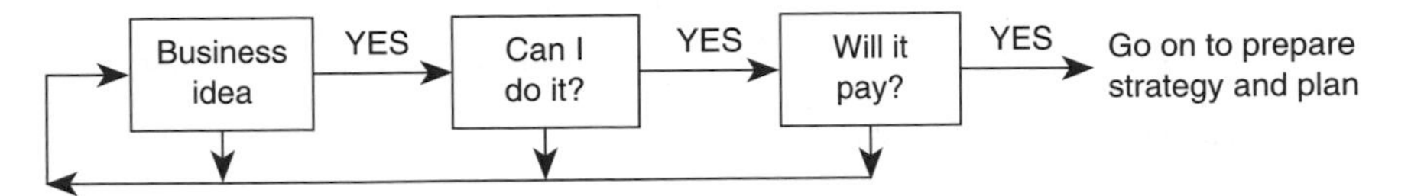

Figure 4.4 The initial evaluation model

Luke's plumbing: six-month financial projection

1 Calculate your gross profit

Projected sales	£75,000
Direct costs:	
Purchases(material costs)	£32,500
Labour costs	£20,000
= Gross profit	£22,500 (A)

2 Calculate your gross profit margin

$$\frac{\text{Gross profit (A) £22,500}}{\text{Sales £75,000}} \times 100$$

= Gross profit margin £30 (B)

Note: For simplicity all figures shown are exclusive of VAT

3 Calculate your overheads

Indirect costs:	
Business salaries (including your own drawings)	£ 6,000
+ rent	£ 2,000
+ rates	£ 500
+ light/heating	£ 500
+ telephone/post	£ 500
+ insurance	£ 500
+ repairs	£ 2,000
+ advertising	£ 1,500
+ bank interest/HP	£ 1,500
+ other expenses (e.g. depreciation of fixed assets)	£ 1,500
= Overheads	£16,500

4 Calculate your actual turnover required to break even

$$\frac{\text{Overheads (C) } \pounds 16{,}500}{\text{Gross profit margin (B) } 30\%} \times 100$$

= Break-even sales £55,000 (D)

5 Calculate the monthly target to break even

$$\frac{\text{Break-even sales (D) } \pounds 55{,}000}{6}$$

= Monthly break-even sales £9,167

6 Profits accumulate in favour of the business once the break-even point has been reached. As overhead costs have been provided for in the break-even calculation, profits accumulate at a rate of 30% (i.e. the gross margin percentage) on projected sales over and above the break-even figure.

In the case of the example, this is:

Projected sales	£75,000
– Break-even sales (D)	£55,000
× Gross profit margin (B)	30%
= Profit (for 6 months)	£ 6,000

These figures can be affected by:
- Actual level of sales achieved
- Increase/decrease in gross margin
- Increase/decrease in overheads

CASH FLOW vs PROFIT

Your business plan must show your clear appreciation that profit is not cash and cash is not profit. In the short term, a business can survive even if it is not making a profit as long as it has sufficient cash reserves but *it cannot survive* without cash even though it may be making a profit. The purpose of the cash flow projection is to calculate how much cash a business is likely to need to accomplish its objectives, and when it will need it in the business.

These projections will form the basis of negotiations with any potential provider of capital. Let us look at the following example to illustrate this point.

EXAMPLE: Kensington Quick Fit

The Kensington Quick Fit Exhaust Centre has just started up, employing a young apprentice. They have to stock a basic range of spares for most European and Japanese cars. In January they fit 100 exhaust systems at an average cost of £75 each to the customer, making total sales for the month of £7,500. These exhausts have cost Kensington on average £35 each to buy, and their total wages bill was £300. The company's position is as follows:

	£
Materials	3,500
Labour	300
Total direct cost	3,800

The gross profit in the month is £3,700 and, after making provision for other business costs of £500 for heat, light, rates, insurances etc., Kensington Quick Fit has made a profit of £3,200.

However, the proprietor is a little concerned that although he is making a good profit his bank balance is not so healthy; in fact it is worse than when he started. An examination of his operations reveals that when he buys in his exhaust systems his suppliers impose a minimum order quantity of 150 units, and since he needs two suppliers – one for the European car systems and one for the Japanese cars – he has to buy in 300 units at a time. He does, however, make sure that he has sufficient cash for his other outgoings before ordering these 300 units.

At the end of the month he has spent the following cash sums to meet his January sales:

	£
Materials	10,500
Labour	300
Total direct cost	10,800

During the month he has received cheques for £7,500 and made a profit of £3,500 *but* his cash at the bank has gone down by £3,300, and he still owes £500 for the other business expenses. He does have 200 exhaust systems in stock at a cost of £7,000, which accounts for his poor cash position, but these can only be converted into cash when they are fitted to customers' cars.

Kensington's proprietor was aware of the situation as he closely monitored the timing of the outflow of cash from the business and the inflow of cash from his customers, and he knew that the temporary decrease in his bank balance would not stop his business surviving. However, there was no escaping the fact that although his business made a profit in the month of January the most immediate result was that his bank balance went down!

The bare essentials

In practical terms, the cash flow projections and the profit and loss account projections are parallel tasks which are essentially prepared from the same data. They may be regarded almost as the 'heads' and 'tails' of the same coin – the profit and loss account showing the owner/manager the profit/ loss based on the assumption that both sales income and the cost of making that sale are 'matched' together in the same month; and the cash flow statement looking at the same transactions from the viewpoint that in reality the cost of the sale is incurred first (and paid for) and the income is received last, anywhere between one week and three months later.

Obviously, the implications for a non-cash business of this delay between making the sale and receiving the payment and using a service/buying goods and paying for them are crucial, especially in the first year of the business and when your business is growing quickly.

Pre-trading cash flow forecast

Cash flow projections are made on the assumption that the business is operating at optimum efficiency from the outset. This in all probability is a simplistic view. New businesses will have a period when set-up costs are being incurred but no revenue from sales is coming in. Under these circumstances your business plan should include a pre-trading cash flow forecast, as Frogurt did in theirs.

Frogurt: Pre-trading Cash Flow Forecast

£ Month:	1	2	3	TOTAL
Cash inflows				
Capital introduced	12,000	–	–	12,000
Loans	–	30,500	–	30,500
Total inflows	12,000	30,500	0	42,500

Cash outflows				
Fixtures and fittings	6,000	7,000	7,000	20,000
Stock	–	–	4,500	4,500
Machine purchases	–	17,000	–	17,000
Total outflows	6,000	24,000	11,500	41,500
Outflows/inflows	6,000	6,500	–11,500	1,000
Balance brought forward		6,000	12,500	
Balance carried forward	6,000	12,500	1,000	1,000

BALANCING FINANCIAL RISKS

Getting the money right – and the right money

According to an authoritative study carried out in 1992 by the 3I European Enterprise Research Centre, 58% of all small firms in the UK went into the recession that started in 1989/90 funded exclusively by bank overdraft.

The corresponding figure for Germany was 14%. In Germany 35% of small firms have long-term finance in their balance sheets, whereas in the UK only 18% have such funding.

Clearly it is wholly inappropriate for a long-term venture such as a business entity to be funded exclusively by short-term money. It is equally wrong for any business to be funded solely from one source.

From the different financial instruments, a small firm needs to select at least three, and more properly five available funding sources. (More on this in Chapter 12.)

Part of the problem in the UK has been the overemphasis on gearing as the primary means of reviewing funding in business.

External sources of funds

There are two fundamentally different types of external money which a growing company can tap into: debt and equity. Debt is money borrowed from outside the company, usually from a bank, and which one day you will have to repay. While you are making use of borrowed money you will also have to pay interest on the loan. Equity is the money put in by shareholders, including the proprietor, and money left in the business by way of retained profit.

What balance of debt to equity is right?

A company's gearing will be continuously changing depending on the growth opportunities it sees ahead, the current cost of money and the availability of equity and debt capital. At certain times it is hard to raise more money from shareholders, for example when the stock market is depressed, or if your profit performance is not up to the mark. Banks or other lenders may be your only hope. Conversely, when the conditions are right, companies frequently raise more share capital to fund growth, well in advance of needing the cash.

EXAMPLE: Vernon International, the West Midlands based machining manufacturer, raised £10 million of extra share capital via a rights issue in the summer of 1990. Mr Tim Kelleher, chairman and chief executive, said the issue, which would halve gearing to 53%, would give the group the flexibility to make further acquisitions in the next 12 months.

The board and the two venture capital organizations backing the management, which own about 63% of the equity, agreed to waive their rights to the issue. Their stake was pre-placed at a premium with institutional investors at a price of 43.5p.

The institutions were underwriting the remainder of the two-for-seven issue, made at 40p, about a 15% discount to the market. According to the annual report released with details of the rights issue, Vernon's order book has risen from £80 million to £94 million since May 1991.

Bankers generally favour a 1:1 relationship between borrowed funds and share capital, although the nature of the risks involved in your business strategy is a more important factor to consider than simply pursuing a symmetrical relationship of numbers. A more useful way to look at the debt-equity relationship is to compare money risk to business risk (Figure 4.6).

If the business sector you are in is generally viewed as risky – and perhaps the most reliable measure of that risk is the proportion of firms that go bust – then financing the business almost exclusively with borrowings is tantamount to gambling. Debt has to be serviced whatever your business performance, so it follows that in any risky, volatile marketplace, you stand a good chance of being caught out. Building firms are a good example of a high-risk business sector; they almost always use high-risk money. The fallacy is to believe that because houses were thought to be a relatively risk-free investment, building them was a safe enterprise too. It is no surprise that building firms top the bankruptcy rolls in both boom years and recessions.

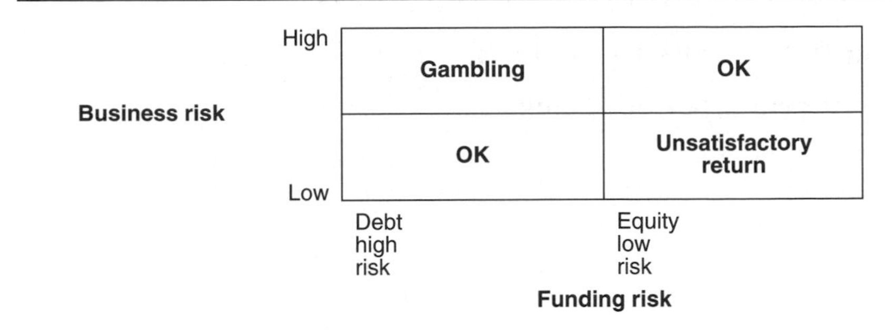

Figure 4.6 Business risk/funding risk matrix

If your business risks are low, the chances are that your profits are relatively low too. High profits and low risks always attract a flood of competitors, reducing your profits to levels that ultimately reflect the riskiness of your business sector. As venture capitalists and shareholders are looking for much better returns than they could get by lending the money, it follows they will be disappointed in their investment on low risk, low return business. So if they are wise they will not get involved in the first place, or if they do they will not put any more money in later. With the funding matrix in mind you can begin to work towards a balance of debt and equity that is appropriate for your business. Very often you will find it attractive to raise both sides of the equation at the same time, as Hélène has done.

EXAMPLE: Hélène, the clothing maker and textile merchant, has announced a £2.62 million rights issue to fund its expansion. The company plans to offer 14.4 new shares at 20p each on a one-for-four basis. The share price shed 1p recently to close at 24p.

Mr Monty Burkeman, chairman and joint managing director, said the company's sales had grown by 50% last year to £62 million – the pre-tax profit was £4.1 million. In the first five months of this year the turnover was 22% ahead of the comparable period. 'We need to finance it', he said. Mr Burkeman explained that Hélène needed to have the capacity to get orders ready for its retail customers, who would have arranged to take delivery at any time over a three-month period. The issue has been fully underwritten by Allied Provincial Securities. Hélène has also arranged a £5 million unsecured term loan with National Westminster.

SOURCES OF START-UP FINANCE

The different types of money

Your cash-flow projections will provide a good idea of how much money your business will need, when it is required and for how long.

The next step is where to go and find this finance. Before considering possible sources of finance, you should categorise your needs into fixed or working capital. Fixed capital is money tied up in things the business intends to keep over longer periods of time, such as property, equipment, vehicles, etc. Working capital is the money used to finance the day-to-day operations. The stock, for example, and any money required to finance your customers until they pay up, are elements of working capital, as are all other running costs and overheads.

Your own capital

Obviously the first place to start is to find out exactly how much you have to invest in the business. You may not have much in ready cash, but you may have valuable assets that can be converted into cash, or other borrowing. The difference between your assets and your liabilities is your 'net worth'. This is the maximum security that you can offer for any money borrowed, and it is hoped that the calculations below will yield a pleasant surprise (see Tables 4.1 and 4.2).

Table 4.1 Matching finance to business needs

Type of capital	*Business needs*	*Financing method*
Fixed capital	Acquiring or altering a property; buying equipment, such as cookers, ovens, photocopiers, or vehicles; the franchise fee and other 'start-up' package costs such as training	Your own capital; term loans; hire purchase; leasing; sale and leaseback; venture capital; government loan guarantee scheme; mortgage loan
Working capital	Raw materials or finished goods; money to finance debtors; dealing with seasonal peaks and troughs, loan guarantee scheme expansion or unexpected short-term problems; paying royalties	Your own capital; bank overdraft; factoring; trade credit; government

Table 4.2 Your net worth

Assets	£	*Liabilities*	£
Cash in hand and in the bank, building society, national savings or other deposits		Overdraft	
Stocks and shares		Mortgage	
Current redemption value of insurances		Other loans	
Value of home		Hire purchase	
Any other property		Tax due, including capital gains	
Motor car(s) etc.		Credit cards due	
Jewellery, paintings and other marketable valuables		Garage, local shop accounts due	
Any money due to you		Any other financial obligations	
Value of existing businesses			
Total assets		*Total liabilities*	

Net worth = Total assets = Total liabilities: £

External funds

There are a number of different types of external money which a growing company can tap into. Debt is money borrowed most usually from a bank and which one day you will have to repay. While you are making use of borrowed money you will also have to pay interest on the loan. Equity is the money put in by shareholders, including the proprietor, and money left in the business by way of retained profit. You don't have to give the shareholders their money back, but they do expect the directors to increase the value of their shares, and if you go public they will probably expect a stream of dividends too.

If you don't meet the shareholders' expectations then they won't be there when you need more money – or if they are powerful enough they will take steps to change the board. Cash-flow financing is a general title that covers overdrafts which are repayable on demand and receivables financing in its many forms. Receivables financing – factoring and invoice discounting – is a facility whereby funding is provided against sales invoices. As sales grow, so does funding.

Hire purchase and leasing are other ways to finance fixed assets. Franchising is another way to finance a growing business. People are invited to 'invest' in your business by paying you a fee to set up a branch in their own area. In this way you can expand the business across the country largely using their money.

Grants are also available in some circumstances to help the government of the day, or increasingly the European Union, achieve its own objectives. If their aims are in line with your own, their grants can be a useful help. But the strategy calling for the cash must be capable of standing of its own.

To most of us, raising money is synonymous with a visit to our local bank manager. Though not the only source of finance, the banks are a good starting point.

There are over a dozen clearing banks, as the high street bankers are usually called, and they are in serious competition with each other for new business. It is as well to remember that bank managers are judged on the quantity and quality of their lending and not on the deposits they take. If they cannot successfully lend, they cannot make a profit for the bank.

For most satisfactory new business propositions the clearing bankers would normally be happy to match pound for pound the money put up by the owner, i.e. 1:1 gearing. They will also recommend a 'package' of funds – part term loan, part overdraft and perhaps part government loan guarantee – that best suits the type of business you are interested in starting up. For example, if the business you are considering is a service, requiring few physical assets, serving cash customers and expecting to break even in the first year, then you may be advised to take a small term loan and a larger overdraft facility. This will give you the money you need to start, without upsetting the long-term security of the business. The converse relationship between loan capital and overdraft may be prudent if you are considering a 'capital-intensive' business such as a restaurant.

The banks offer a wide range of services in their own right. Through wholly or partially owned subsidiaries, they cover virtually every aspect of the financial market. For franchisees their services include overdrafts, term loans, factoring, leasing and the government loan guarantee scheme. As well as providing funds, the clearing banks have considerable expertise in the areas of tax, insurance and financial advice generally.

Overdrafts

Bank overdrafts are the most common type of short-term finance. They are simple to arrange: you just talk to your local bank manager. They are flexible, with no minimum level. Sums of money can be drawn or repaid within the total amount agreed. They are relatively cheap, with interest paid only on the outstanding daily balance. Of course, interest rates can fluctuate, so what seemed a small sum of money one year can prove crippling if interest rates jump suddenly. Normally, you do not repay the 'capital': you simple renew or alter the overdraft facility from time to time. However, overdrafts are theoretically repayable on demand, so you should not use short-term overdraft money to finance long-term needs, such as buying a lease, or plant and equipment.

There is evidence that many small firms are too dependent on overdraft financing and as a consequence are unnecessarily exposed to the mercy of their bankers. Midland Bank, however, claim the position is changing with over £4 billion of their £12.5 billion lent to small firms provided as overdrafts.

Term loans

These are rather more formal than a simple overdraft and cover periods of up to 3, 3 to 10 and 10 to 20 years respectively. They are usually secured against an existing fixed asset or one to be acquired, or are guaranteed personally by the directors (proprietors). This may involve you in some costs for legal fees and arrangement or consultants' fees, so it may be a little more expensive than an overdraft, but unless you default on the interest charges you can be reasonably confident of having the use of the money throughout the whole term of the borrowing.

The interest rates on the loan can either be fixed for the term or variable with the prevailing interest rate. A fixed rate is to some extent a gamble, which may work in your favour, depending on how interest rates move over the term of the loan. So if general interest rates rise, you win, and if they fall, you lose. A variable rate means that you do not take that risk. There is another benefit to a fixed rate of interest. It should make planning ahead a little easier with a fixed financial commitment; with a variable overdraft, a sudden rise can have disastrous consequences. The banks have been quite venturesome in their competition for new and small business accounts. One major clearer had a scheme which offered free banking to new businesses for one year – even if they were overdrawn – provided the limit had been agreed. The key innovation in such schemes is that the loan will be subordinated to other creditors, with the bank repaid before the shareholders but after all the other creditors if the company fails. In return for this risk they are likely to want to option on up to 25% of the company's capital.

Government loan guarantee for small businesses

Government loan guarantees for small businesses were introduced in March 1981 for an initial period of three years and were extended in the 1984 and later Budgets. To be eligible for this loan, your proposition must have been looked at by an approved bank and considered viable, but should not be a proposition that the bank itself would normally approve. You can be a sole trader, partnership or limited company wanting funds to start up or expand. The bank simply passes your application on to the Department of Trade and Industry, using an approved format. This is an elementary business plan, which asks for some details of the directors, the business, its cash needs and profit performance, or projection of the business. There are no formal rules on size, number of employees or assets, but large businesses and their subsidiaries are definitely excluded from the scheme. The other main exclusions are in the fields of agriculture, horticulture, banking, commission agents, education, forestry (except tree harvesting and saw-milling), house and estate agents, insurance, medical and veterinary, night clubs and licensed clubs, pubs and property, and travel agencies.

The loans can be for up to £250,000 (small loans up to £15,000 can be approved without reference) and repayable over two to seven years. It may be possible to delay paying the capital element for up to two years from the start of the loan, but monthly or quarterly repayments of interest will have to be made from the outset. The loan itself, however, is likely to be expensive.

Once approved by the Department of Trade, the bank lends you the money at bank rate plus 4% or 5% and the government guarantees the bank 85% of its money if you fail to pay. In return for this the government charges you a 0.5% to 1.5% 'insurance' premium on the 85% of the loan it has taken on risk. Borrowers would be expected to pledge all available business assets as a security for the loan, but they would not necessarily be excluded from the scheme if there were no available assets. Their personal assets should already be fully committed to the venture.

The rule certainly seems to be to ask for as much as you need, plus a good margin of safety – going back for a second bite too soon is definitely frowned upon. You do not have to take all the money at once. At the discretion of your bank manager, you can take the money in up to four slices, but each slice must be 25% or more.

There are now 30 banks operating the scheme, and 18,000 loans worth over £600 million have been made. The average loan has been fairly constant at £33,000. A number of franchisees have received funds under this scheme including franchise holders with household names such as Prontaprint.

Business angels

For small sums of money, from a few thousand pounds upwards, you could contact a business angel. An angel is a private individual who is willing to put their money and perhaps their efforts into your business. Various industry estimates suggest that upwards of £6.5 million of angel's money is looking for investment homes. Not only will angels put in smaller sums of money than conventional venture capital providers, they will be more prepared to back start-ups and riskier projects – if the chemistry is right.

So how do you get in contact with an angel? You will need to use an introductory agency or 'marriage bureau' such as LINC (Local Investment Networking Company), who circulate to subscribing investors a regular bulletin of abbreviated information on business projects. If you are seeking finance through LINC you should submit a business plan indicating the amount of finance required (sample plans and counselling services are available). Having once been accepted as a bona fide proposal you will be charged a small fee for as many bulletin entries (around 50 words) as are felt necessary. Also a longer, two-page summary business plan will be prepared to help any enquirers requesting further details. There are now 20 local enterprise agencies in the LINC Network, covering much of the country. You can obtain more details from: LINC, 4 Snow Hill, London EC1A 2BS (Tel: 0171 236 3000).

The whole angels sector was given a boost in the 1993 Budget with the introduction of the Enterprise Investment Scheme (EIS). The key features of the scheme, which is intended to raise £60 million a year for small firms, are:

- up-front tax relief at 20% in investments of qualifying unquoted equity
- no tax on capital gains
- income and capital gains tax relief on losses
- a maximum annual investment of £10,000
- companies may raise up to £1 million a year
- investors may become paid directors.

Angel Networks include:

- The Bedfordshire Investment Exchange, Bedfordshire TEC, 2 Railton Road, Woburn Road Industrial Estate, Kempston, Bedfordshire MK42 7PN (Tel: 01234 843100; Fax: 01234 843211). Contact: Jennifer Carley.
- Blackstone Franks Chartered Acountants, Barbican House, 26–34 Old Street, London EC1V 9HL (Tel: 0171 250 3300; Fax: 0171 250 1402). Contact: Vivienne Askew.
- Capital Connections, East Lancashire TEC, Red Rose Court, Clayton Business Park, Clayton-le-Moors, Accrington, Lancashire BB5 5JR (Tel: 01254 301333; Fax: 01254 399090). Contact: Business Development Manager.
- Daily Telegraph Business Network, 112 High Holborn, London WC1V 6JS (Tel: 0171 538 7171; Fax: 0171 831 2179). Contact: Gavin Wetton.
- Devon and Cornwall Business Angels Programme, Trevint Ltd, Trevint House, Strangways Villas, Truro, Cornwall TR1 2PA (Tel: 01872 223883; Fax: 01872 42470). Contact: Anyone within the organization.
- Enterprise Adventure Ltd, The Enterprise Pavilion, London Square, Cross Lanes, Guildford, Surrey GU1 1UG (Tel: 01483 458111; Fax: 01483 504675). Set up in June 1994 by Peter Benton, former deputy chairman of British Telecom. Through its venture list service they aim to build up a computer-based national data base that will act as a clearing house for 'angels' (investees) to be matched to small firms looking for money. Companies seeking funds pay £300 for a quality assessment by

a consultant. Individual investors pay £500 and intermediaries such as accountants pay £1,000.

- Gloucestershire Enterprise Agency, Enterprise House, Brunswick Road, Gloucester GL1 1HG (Tel: 01452 501411; Fax: 01452 305664). Contact: Mike Blackie.
- Hilling Wall Corporate Finance, 43 South Street, Mayfair, London W1Y 5PD (Tel: 0171 495 1302; Fax: 0171 495 1303). Contact: Andrew Wall.
- Informal Register of Investment Services (IRIS), Parkview House, Woodvale Office Park, Woodvale Road, Brighouse, West Yorkshire HD6 4AB (Tel: 01484 406297; Fax: 01484 400672). Contact: Geoffrey Sentance.
- Interim Management (UK) Ltd, 8 Bloomsbury Square, London WC1A 2LP (Tel: 0171 404 6772; Fax: 0171 405 1541). Contact: Alan Horn.
- Investors Forum, Portman House, Portland Road, Newcastle NE2 1AQ (Tel: 0191 261 4108; Fax: 0191 261 4108). An equity matching service for companies seeking funds between £10,000 and £250,000.
- Investors in Hertfordshire, Hertfordshire TEC, New Barnes Mill, Cottonmill Lane, St Albans, Hertfordshire AL1 2HA (Tel: 01727 852313; Fax: 01727 841449). Contact: Graeme Falconer.
- Local Investment Networking Company (LINC), 4 Snow Hill, London EC1A 2BS (Tel: 0171 236 3000; Fax: 0171 329 0226). Contact: Fiona Conoley.
- Milton Keynes Business Venture (MKBV), Medina House, 314 Silbury Boulevard, Milton Keynes MK9 2AE (Tel: 01908 660044; Fax: 01908 233087). Contact: Colin Offer.
- Principality Financial Management, 3rd Floor, Alexandra House, Swansea SA1 5ED (Tel: 01792 474111; Fax: 01792 474112). Contact: Peter Phillips.
- Techinvest, South and East Cheshire TEC, PO Box 37, Dalton Way, Middlewich, Cheshire CW10 0HU (Tel: 01606 737009; Fax: 01606 734201). Contact: Vivienne Upcottgill. Based in Cheshire and one of the DTI's five demonstration programmes, Techinvest is one of the more successful regional introduction services. Started in February 1993, it has 79 angels on its books and says it has raised more than £1 million for 20 deals in 12 businesses (£500,000 was provided in one deal by a venture capital group). The service offers companies seeking money a subsidized advisory service during which consultants put the proposal into shape. It also runs investor meetings and plans to open them to the public for a fee next month.

  Techinvest sends some of its proposals to VCR and some to LINC for inclusion in its national bulletin. Investors and companies pay £200 to join – £400 if their cases are published through VCR if cash is successfully raised. The source of future funding is uncertain.
- Venture Capital Report (VCR), Boston Road, Henley-on-Thames, Oxon RG9 1DY (Tel: 01491 579999; Fax: 01491 579825). Contact: Lucius Cary.
- WINSEC Corporate Exchange, WINSEC Financial Services Ltd, 1 The

Centre, Church Road, Tiptree, Colchester, Essex CO5 0HF (Tel: 01621 815047; Fax: 01621 817965). Contact: Claude Brownlow.

Venture capital providers

Over 50 providers of venture capital are members of the British Venture Capital Association, formed in 1983 to help to further the provision of such financing in the UK. In the decade to 1990, the UK venture capital industry has grown from a score of firms investing £66 million a year to over 200 who back new and growing firms to the tune of £1.65 billion. The UK venture capital industry is the largest in Europe and second only to the USA in world importance.

The largest player in this market is 3I's (Investors in Industry), formed in 1945, who account for around half of all this type of funding, with stakes in over 5,000 businesses. They are the only venture capital firm with a comprehensive UK regional office structure.

The British Venture Capital Association, 3 St Catherine's Place, London SW1E 6DX (Tel: 0171 233 5212), publishes an annual directory of providers, free each year.

Table 4.3 shows where venture capitalists put their money, in terms of the stage of the venture.

Accountants KPMG Peat Marwick, in conjunction with the journal *Venture Economics*, also maintain a comprehensive database of venture capitalists. This allows them to extract on a selective basis details of various capital sources as potential investment candidates. For further details contact: KPMG Peat Marwick, 1 Puddle Dock, Blackfriars, London EC4V 3PD (Tel: 0171 236 8000).

Table 4.3 Venture financing by stage of business

Stage	%
Pre-start-up	10
Start-up	25
Early stage development	28
Late stage development	26
Management buy-out	11
	100

EXERCISES

1 Calculate your expected break-even point using three different pricing strategies.

2 Prepare a pre-trading cash flow forecast and foreword until your cumulative cash flow becomes positive.
3 Prepare a profit and loss account for year one. If this shows either a loss or very small profit calculate future profit and loss accounts until you can show a satisfactory profit.
4 Work out how much money you need to get started. Which source(s) of capital do you think will be most appropriate for your needs and why?

NOTE

1 The UK average is around 18%; high-flyers aimed for 35%.

SUGGESTED FURTHER READING

Barrow, Colin (1995) *The Complete Small Business Guide*, BBC Publications, London.
Barrow, Colin (1995) *Financial Management for the Small Business*, Kogan Page, London.

Part 2:

The difficulties of staying in business

As Professor David Storey has noted 'the fundamental characteristic, other than size per se, which distinguishes small firms from large is their higher probability of ceasing to trade'. In the UK, Daly[1] has shown that the mortality rate, as measured by deregistration for VAT, is clearly related to business age, as the following graph shows:

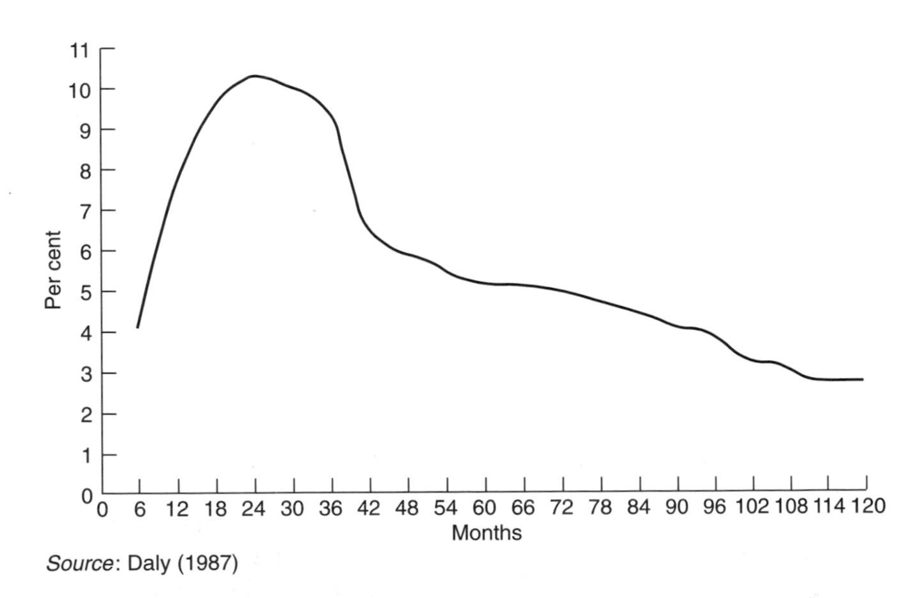

Figure PT2.1 Half-year VAT deregistration data by age

Nearly one-third of small firms cease to trade in the first three years, increasing to nearly two-thirds within 10 years. Getting to 10 years old is, at least, a goal to be desired, as failure rates are then similar for large and small! The reasons for failure are many and various, but have perhaps best been summarized by Hall who concluded:

> It would appear that the owners of young firms are more likely to suffer from inadequate funding, poor products and inefficient marketing. As their companies aged, however, they were more likely to be buffeted by strategic and environmental shocks for which they did not have the managerial skills to respond.

John McQueen,[2] secretary to the Association of Bankrupts, put it more bluntly: 'My own belief is that it is a dire lack of marketing abilities together with slack pricing and buying policies [too much stock] that is the real killer to business ... not the undercapitalisation myth.'

Those new start ups which had based their business plans upon the advice of Brian Warnes[3] will at least have avoided the low margins trap; but what were the characteristics of other surviving firms? Professor Storey found evidence to support two interesting conclusions:

1 failure rates were lowest amongst firms expressing a desire to grow, i.e were motivated to want to grow.
2 achieving real growth required 'active market development in terms of both the identification of new market opportunities and increasing the breadth of the customer base'.[4]

How to increase the customer base and broaden the product range are issues we will be examining below; 'motivation' to grow is, however, hardly within the capacity of a textbook. Participants in the Cranfield Business Programme were clearly all motivated to grow and willing to pay for the experience.[5] Hence, perhaps, their subsequent above-average performance in both sales and profits! Perhaps wide communication of the above statistics of failure, and the consequence of not wanting to grow, would – like hanging – concentrate a few more minds in a positive direction! Yet not all the participants in the 1995 Growth Programme had their minds set solidly on growth:

EXAMPLE: Richard Nye, with two equal partners, had successfully run for 25 years a printing and packaging business, focused particularly on the fragrance and perfumery business. With turnover static at around £2 million, and with one of the partners eager to take early retirement, Richard had enrolled on the programme with a view primarily of 'how to put the company in good order for a possible trade sale or at least to see how it could be run without the continued involvement of all the founding partners!' This in a company which typically had been founded by the partners leaving an advertising agency, taking with them an existing customer. A company in which the only planning characteristic was to meet once a year, when the auditors' annual accounts had been completed, in a luxury Mayfair hotel to discuss and reflect, after a good dinner, on the year ahead!

Despite initial scepticism at the beginning of the programme, four months later Richard had produced a written analysis of the three key strategy issues facing the company, with action oriented operating plans (for a diversification proposal, an equivalent investment proposition and a personnel succession plan) as well as finally agreeing to his auditors' by now annual request for regular monthly budgets and management account meetings![5]

We cannot be certain that Richard's company is now guaranteed a further 25 years of growth, but we do feel that he has established a process that reduces the business risks both for the existing partners and any interested purchasers. The key elements which we see as important for companies that have survived the initial years difficulties of 'getting into business' and now face the second stage difficulties of 'staying in business' are:

1 Determining the key factors for success in your business sector.
2 Developing a balanced management team.
3 Further developing your market differentiation.
4 Funding future growth.

Each of these key elements are examined in detail in the following chapters and can be included in annual operating plans, budgets and reviews, which grow naturally out of the early years business plans and which many successful business growth programme companies developed to control their growing businesses.

NOTES

1 Daly, M. (1987) Lifespan of Business Registration for VAT, *British Business*, 3rd April, p. 28–9. Also quoted in Storey, D. J. (1994) *Understanding the Small Business Sector*, Routledge, London, p. 93.
2 See Storey, D. J., *op. cit.*, p. 105.
3 Warnes, Brian (1984) *The Ghengis Khan Guide to Business*, Osmosis Publications, London.
4 Storey, D. J. *op. cit.*, p. 108.
5 Barrow, Colin (1995) *Training pays OK*, Cranfield Business Programme, Cranfield (cited in the *Financial Times*, 23 October, p. 15, 'Companies whose MD attended the Business Growth Programme at Cranfield grew more than four times as fast as did broadly comparable small firms in general, while at the same time doubling their return to shareholders'.
6 Barrow, Colin (1995), *op. cit.*

Chapter 5

Determine the key factors for success in your business sector

Successful companies on the Cranfield Business Growth Programme, while not necessarily having the most highly developed accounting and control systems, nevertheless were characterized by a keen sense of control on what management consultants typically call the 'key factors for success' in their businesses, i.e. those two or three key items of business performance which determine whether the business would prosper or not.

EXAMPLE: Robert Wright of Connectair had calculated that for his Bandeirante air taxi service to survive, he needed a minimum of nine passengers per flight, and accordingly devoted most of his energies to ensuring Connectair achieved such an 'occupancy rate'. For Richard Nye's printing and packaging company the golden rule was never to say 'No' to any request, however unreasonable, from their number one customer, L'Oreal, i.e. the 'service' to L'Oreal would be as near perfect as possible, even to the point of working all night to achieve 'impossible', next day, 9am deadlines and requests.

As businesses grow, however, and the number of customers and products offered increases, companies should verify on a regular basis that the 'key success factors' which helped establish the business, are still the most important, particularly from the customers' point of view. One way to do this is shown in Figure 5.1; owner/managers should list their company's main success factors, critical for the success of the company and rank their importance as shown in the example and attempt to do the same for two or three nearest competitors. The whole exercise should be done from the customers' point of view, as shown in the example. What customers require should then be translated into the internal tasks necessary for the company to satisfy these requirements and to monitor achievements. Measuring the performance on these key tasks is a vital factor, along with the company

Competitive position		**Score out of 10: Yourself and main competitors**			
Key success factors (KSF)	**Rank importance of KSF**	**Your own business Autoglass**	**Auto windscreens**	**Bridgewater Glass**	**Associated Windscreens**
KSF1 My insurance company recommends company	50%	9	9	5	5
KSF2 Quick service and friendly competent staff	25%	7	6	7	8
KSF3 Repair depot conveniently located to home	15%	7	6	6	7
KSF4 Good value for money	10%	5	7	7	6
TOTAL (weighted average, % x score)[1]	100%	7.8	7.6	5.9	6.2

[1] To calculate weighted average, multiply each score by KSF % e.g.

Autoglass KSF1 is 50% x 9 = 4.50
Autoglass KSF2 is 25% x 7 = 1.75
Autoglass KSF3 is 15% x 7 = 1.05
Autoglass KSF4 is 10% x 5 = 0.50
Weighted average 7.80

Figure 5.1 Autoglass windscreen replacements

accounts, in managing the growing company: showing where management action is necessary, highlighting areas of best practice, etc.

One problem with a quite open subjective assessment of your own and competitors' performance on key success factors (KSF), is that companies frequently rate themselves ahead of, or at least equal to, main competitors (as Figure 5.1 shows for Autoglass). Care should be taken through market research via questionnaires or focus groups, with customers, for example, to see if they agree with both your assessment of the key success factors and how your company and competitors compare in these areas. The internal tasks companies have to undertake to improve performance in each KSF, which become their core competencies, should now be listed, as for Autoglass.

EXAMPLE

1 KSF1 ensure we keep insurance company recommendation, locally and nationally, provide promotional material for distribution by insurance company. Verify via reception desk questionnaire 'how customer heard of service' to measure performance of promotional measures.

2 KSF2 Recruit, train and motivate competent staff (incentive payments, training school). Control stocks to balance availability to customers and cost of provision. Monitor stock and staff turnover.

3 KSF3 Ensure nationwide depot coverage, concentrating on main population and traffic movement areas. Measure % of population within 10 miles of a depot.

4 KSF4 Monitor prices vs competitors and key garage groups; provide added value services such as 24-hour call out.

Monitoring the achievement of the company on these key success factors is, we believe, one of the key requirements for the growing company. Monthly accounts, as we have stressed, are a key indicator of the overall health of the company; but they do not pin-point the areas where remedial action should be taken. Measuring occupancy rates (Connectair) customer service satisfaction (Nye) or in the case of Autoglass monthly stock levels and staff turnover ratios, would highlight, over time, places for remedial action. Each performance measure would focus management attention where specific action needed to be taken rapidly. Key measures will obviously vary from industry to industry.

EXAMPLES: Coldshield Windows, for example, in the early 1980s, after 10 years of explosive growth came under increasingly severe price competition from rivals Everest and Anglian Windows. With the economy in recession, one key indicator, cost per sales lead generated by press advertising, rose dramatically from under £10 to over £40. As the 500 or so Coldshield direct sales representatives depended entirely on a supply of low cost sales leads to support their sales efforts, and as on average only one lead in five was converted to a sale, the profitability of the company plunged dramatically. Uncertainty as to how to change the 'traditional methods' of running the company, via repetitive newspaper advertisements, in the face of new competitive forces (Everest with TV advertising and brand image; Anglian with extensive retail shop displays), led the group's owners, Pearsons,

to reluctantly dispose of the business. Subsequent owners were unable to reverse the decline in sales leads and had to bear closure costs of the company.
For Bagel Express, with five outlets providing snack hot and cold bagels, the key success measure in the 'fast food' industry had clearly to be the speed and quality of its service to its main lunch-time peak trade. Measurement by detailed observation revealed that at its loss-making Embankment shop, service levels were between two and three minutes per customer, compared with a nearby competitors' 15 seconds! Setting a new performance target of 95% of customers to be served within one minute was clearly vital to prevent losing queuing customers, as well as the provision of racks of ready priced cold bagels enabling customers to self-serve in as short a time as local competitors. Equally, recognition that at Bagel the average length of service of counter staff was only three months, resulting in little company loyalty or customer recognition, entailed re-thinking company hiring practice of recruiting mainly from visiting overseas students.

Companies, as they grow, need to continually reflect on their internal core competences, which provide customers with their product/service satisfaction, e.g. internal stock computer systems enable Kwik Fit to minimize stock levels, but maximize parts availability to customers, giving clear economies of scale and differentiation to the company. Larger companies, such as Disney with its training schools or McKinsey with skilled recruitment systems ensure continuous customer satisfaction by their internal management systems.

CONTINUOUS CUSTOMER RESEARCH

Performance measures which monitor the individual company key success factors and tasks required for their completion are therefore vital for the growing company. Continuing to keep in close touch with the customer is perhaps the most vital of all. How do the best growing companies do this?

EXAMPLE: For the Hop Shop's dried flower business, creation of a farm shop gave the farming Alexanders for the first time direct contact with end consumers themselves. Listening to shop customers requests led to planting of new flower species and to Caroline writing a book on dried flower gardening as well as setting up classes for regular customers on dried flower arranging. The shop also enabled the Alexanders to combine with other Darenth Valley farmers to produce joint promotional material (suggested walks with map trails, spots to visit, etc.) which successfully encouraged further visitors and potential customers to the valley. Caroline says 'by talking and listening to our shop customers and also to our main wholesalers, we have learned what flowers to grow and what quality is expected. Contact with other wholesalers, including overseas buyers, has also come from our attendance at Royal Horticultural Society annual exhibitions in Vincent Square, London. We became founder members of the British Dried Flower Association in 1988, which now numbers over 55 UK members and which has enabled us to cover the cost of commissioning market research showing that the EEC market in dried flowers is worth over £72 million and growing at an annual rate of 16%!'

Many hoteliers, retailers, and restaurateurs, for example, have taken advantage of their customer proximity by ensuring customer information cards are placed strategically near tills (see an example in Figure 5.2) or check-out desks.

However well designed the card (or screen), the need remains to motivate

SUPERDRIVE – Comments Card
– Help Us To Help You Please tick all appropriate boxes – Please return to address overleaf (reply paid)

Location Visited | Date of Visit | Have you used **SUPERDRIVE** before? Yes ☐ No ☐

How Did You Hear About Us?

Repeat Visit ☐
Recommendation ☐
Advertisement ☐
Passing By ☐

What Prompted You To Use Us?

Local Newspaper Advertisement ☐
National Newspaper Advertisement ☐
Leaflet ☐
Yellow Pages ☐
Previous Good Service ☐
RAC/AA/Fleet Advised ☐
Friend/Family Advised ☐
TV/Radio Advertisement ☐

How Did We Measure Up – Good, Fair or poor?

	G	F	P		G	F	P
Cleanliness of Centre	☐	☐	☐	Value for Money	☐	☐	☐
Appearance of Staff	☐	☐	☐	General Atmosphere	☐	☐	☐
Attitude of Staff	☐	☐	☐	Quality of Service	☐	☐	☐
Respect Shown to Car	☐	☐	☐	Quality of Work	☐	☐	☐

Finishing Touches

	Yes	No
Price/Estimate Agreed?	☐	☐
Were You Shown Finished Work?	☐	☐
Was The Job Completed in Reasonable Time?	☐	☐
Will You Use Us Again?	☐	☐

What Did You Buy?

Tyres ☐ Exhaust ☐ Shock Absorbers ☐ Battery ☐ Service ☐ Brakes ☐ Clutch ☐ Steering ☐ Puncture ☐ Others ____________

How Can We Improve Things?

Comments ....
....
....
What Was Best? .... What Was Worst? ....

Could We Have Your Details?

Name ....
Address ....
....
....
Post Code .... Tel ....

District Manager's ....
Report (for Office Use)

Thank You For Your Assistance

Figure 5.2 Example of a customer information card

the employee to ensure such cards are completed and collected (via some form of 'payment by results') while often customers are motivated to provide such information by promises of 'lottery' prizes, as witnessed, e.g. in a National Theatre card, offering participants who complete cards the opportunity 'to win a bottle of champagne in our monthly draw'.

Growing businesses have the advantage of existing customers to interrogate! Contact with such customers for a more profound enquiry can be established via focus groups, as the following short example for Bagel Express demonstrates.

EXAMPLE: CUSTOMER FOCUS GROUP, NOVEMBER 1993 – BAGEL EXPRESS

1 OBJECTIVES

- To identify Bagel Express strengths and weaknesses.
- To gauge customer sensitivity to price.

2 METHOD

A number of customers from the Fleet Street shop were asked to take part in a lunchtime discussion on Bagel Express. They were offered a free lunch in exchange for their views. Unfortunately none of those invited in advance turned up. However, 8 customers were persuaded on the day to give their comments. They were interviewed in small groups of 1 to 3 people for around 15 minutes. One of the interviewees also ate regularly at Villers Street.

3 SUMMARY

- Average spend: £2–£4.50. Seemed to vary according to how much people ate/drank (£4.50 was for hot bagel, drink and dessert).
- Sensitivity to price: customers rounded to the nearest 50p when discussing price per lunch, which suggests they would not be sensitive to small changes in price such as 5 or 10p per bagel.
- Reasons for choosing Bagel Express: close to work, reasonably priced, like bagels.
- Bagel: hot bagels very popular, fillings perceived to be generous.
- Manhattan: too difficult to eat.
- Service: staff helpful but too busy at lunchtime; seemed to get in each other's way.
- Delivery Service: of interest to limited number, but the person who did use did so very often.

- Competition: Prêt à Manger and Dillettos were mentioned most. Prêt à Manger seems able to justify higher prices by faster service, more exotic fillings, high quality food.

This short survey revealed the opportunity to improve margins, by modest 'rounding up' price increase, as well as focusing attention on the need to study closely the presentation and performance of Prêt à Manger as a major competitor.

Monitoring customer complaints is also a vital way of keeping in touch with customers. 'The customer who complains is our best friend', explains Stue Leonard of *In Search of Excellence* fame.[1] Why? Because the customer complaint is the 'last chance for you to complete the sale', to put things right. A recent McKinsey survey has shown that 'companies lose two-thirds of their customers not because of product quality or unsatisfactory price, but simply through indifference to customer complaints. Well over 80% of customers would re-purchase if their complaints were quickly resolved'. An adequate complaints recording and resolution system is thus important.

Whatever the method used, what is most important is maintaining a regular dialogue with customers, to ensure that products and services remain relevant and that the critical success factors in the supplier/customer relationship are well managed and at a satisfactory performance level.

CUSTOMERS AND COMPETITORS CHANGE

The need for continuous customer research is emphasized by the evident fact that customers and competitors change all the time. In an important book, *How to Handle Major Customers Profitably*, Alan Melkman[2] has provided a useful framework for classifying a company's existing customers (Figure 5.3).

Customers attitudes to your company will range from 'suspicious' at first, to trusting after satisfactory purchase experience, to 'disenchanted' if you fail to visit or improve your product/service offerings over time.

It may be a stimulus to action to broadly categorize your major customers by these stages. Clearly, re-launching the relationship by researching and re-analysing customer needs in the wedlock and deadlock stages, prior to

Objective	Courtship	Engagement	Honeymoon	Wedlock	Deadlock
Customer attitude	Suspicious	Moderately suspicious	Trusting	Boring	Disenchanted
Supplier objective	Get first order	Get repeat order	Increase sales volume	Maintain sales	Sell in new products

Figure 5.3 Customer dynamics

otherwise inevitably losing business to competitive suppliers, may be the quickest way to re-kindle sales! When in your company you begin to think of your older customers as 'debtors' rather than what they really are (the reason for your company's existence!) this is probably the warning signal that your 'marriage' is into wedlock. Melkman has several positive suggestions to make as to how to 'revive' the relationship (and sales!), including re-visiting, sharing market information, developing joint promotional activities with key customers, initiating computer buy/sell links, all aimed at building barriers to customers seeking alternative suppliers.

Equally, your competitors will not have been standing still and will need, as in the case of Bagel Express and Prêt à Manger, to be continuously studied. Customers who will have helped you with your KSF analysis will have had experience of competitors products and services. But not all competitors are obvious; the lunch-time gin and tonic is frequently now substituted by an iced Perrier in City bars. Reduced market share may not be the result of the activities of a direct brand rival, but through product offerings by substitutes.

The purpose behind your competitor analysis at this stage is the same as your customer analysis, i.e. to thoroughly understand the key factors for success in your industry. Are competitors successful through features of their product, or their after sales service? Is company image more important than payment terms? Professor Michael Porter, the Harvard expert on competitive analysis, sees competitive analysis as the way to making yourself different from your competitors; by identifying competitor's strengths and weaknesses, understanding your position in your industry (price-leader or price-cutter?), what their goals are and how they might retaliate to your offerings, all these make an important contribution to the continuing strategy you might pursue.

EXAMPLE: Perrier had built a 50% market share in the UK bottled mineral water market in the 1980s, using a humorous poster campaign (Eau-la-la!) to change a sleepy market sector into a vibrant one. Realizing the importance of image to its health conscious customer, Perrier had no hesitation in withdrawing all supplies from the market following a benzene scare at its bottling plant, prior to re-launching with 'new factory production'. Realizing also the difficulty of building further market share in the face of numerous new competitive British bottled waters, the company widened its competitive strategy by purchasing Buxton Mineral Waters, enabling the Company to challenge domestic producers and reach parts of the market previously denied to it on xenophobic grounds.

So, too, as the above example shows, competitors like customers, change all the time; hence the need for constant review. So how do you regularly keep track of your present and potential competitors? As noted in some of the examples above: buy and analyse their products and services; visit trade exhibitions; work with them, in trade associations, in pursuit of higher trade standards! This might, at least, not only serve the customer needs better, but by raising standards, build barriers to entry to new competitors in your market. For example, the Glass and Glazing Trade Association, in addition to serving customer needs by requiring members to adhere to strict British standards in terms of material, workmanship and insurance, only allows new members to join and use the GGF symbol after two years in existence! (Quite a long time for some double-glazing companies!) Stue Leonard, of the famous New England *In Search of Excellence* Store, actually organizes staff visits, by specially ordered buses, to major competitor openings!

Please remember, as you complete these checks, never to knowingly underestimate your competitors. General Wavell underestimated the fighting ability of Japanese city dwellers in the jungles in the Second World War just as much as General Motors underestimated the Japanese motor industry's ability to produce quality cars. Make new mistakes in finding out about your customers and competitors, but do not repeat old mistakes like these!

SUMMARY

By conducting regular customer and competitive research, to determine the key factors for success in your industry, by building a clear definition and way of measuring the management tasks in your company to fulfil customer needs, lies the healthy way to new product and market development. Your

Market	Existing product	Modified product	New product
Existing market	**No/No** Price War, e.g. 'Me Too' Product	**Yes/Yes** Low Risk, e.g. Humorous Cards	**Yes** Moderate Risk, e.g. Polaroid Camera
Identifiable market	**Yes/Yes** Low Risk, e.g. Clothes for smaller women	**Yes** Moderate Risk, e.g. Rohan Climbing Clothes	**?** High Risk/Reward e.g. Apple Computer
Unknown market	**Yes** Moderate Risk, e.g. Software Applications	**?** High Risk/Reward e.g. De Lorean Cars	**No/No** High Cost, e.g. Star Wars

Source: Stolze, W.J. *Start-Up* (1989), Rock Beach Press, Rochester, NY, p. 45.

Figure 5.4 The product/market matrix

customers can tell you what you should do; your competitors can inspire you to do it. All the while what you are striving to avoid is being 'fenced in' in the 'me too' box of the Product/Market matrix in Figure 5.4. Decide which box fits your product/service.

Learning from your customers, or from your competitors' example, how to modify your product/service performance (like Bagel Express) or how to exploit a new sector of the market (like Perrier) are vital for a healthy growing company. Performance measures on your critical success factors (e.g. occupancy rates, stock levels, etc.), will give the clue to action priorities and provide purpose and substance to visits to outlying parts of your company and focusing new managers' attention.

EXERCISES

1. List, from your customers' point of view, the three or four main reasons they buy from your company.
2. What is your company's KSF score compared with your main competitors?
3. List the two or three main internal performance measures, coming from your KSF analysis, which you check regularly to ensure the health of your company.
4. How do you research, or keep in touch, with your major customers and their changing needs?
5. Can you name and classify your major customers under the following categories: *courtship, engagement, honeymoon, wedlock, deadlock.*
6. What market segments are still open for you to exploit?
7. How do your major competitors' products and services satisfy customers needs?
8. What do you see as your major competitors' principal weaknesses?
9. What changes have your major competitors made in the last 12 months in their competitive approaches?
10. How are you regularly tracking major competitors' activities?

NOTES

1 Peters, T. and Waterman, R. (1982) *In Search of Excellence*, Harper & Row, New York.

2 Melkman, A. (1979) *How to Handle Major Customers Profitably*, Gower, Basingstoke, Ch. 2.

SUGGESTED FURTHER READING

European Case Clearing House, *Bagel Express Case*, (595-032-1,595-033-1,595-034-1), Cranfield University, Cranfield.

Melkman, Alan (1979) *How to Handle Major Customers Profitably*, Gower Press, Aldershot.

Peters, Thomas and Waterman, Robert (1982) *In Search of Excellence*, Harper & Row, New York.

Stolze, William J. (1989) *Start Up*, Rock Beach Press, Rochester, NY.

Chapter 6

Can you develop a balanced management team?

The essence of leadership is the activity of orchestrating the resources of others towards solving problems, not in being the hero oneself. Unfortunately, many entrepreneurial chief executives learn this lesson the hard way. They like to keep on being the hero. That is one reason why successful MDs often have to leave at a certain point. They have to leave because there is a dependency on them which they can't shift, and they can't let go. Most entrepreneurs will have to learn the transition from the 'meddler' to 'strategist' if they are to avoid being a constraint on the growth of their own organization. The essence of visionary leadership lies in two aspects: first articulating the vision or direction of the business, second in mobilizing the energies of all the employees towards the vision.

The managers of Innovex have a clear expectation of their chairman, whom they regard as a visionary leader: 'His role should be to lead ten paces ahead, like a magnet, grabbing us after him and challenging our way of doing things'.

Leadership can be best described not as a quality, nor as a combination of technical skills demanded by particular situations, but as an activity. This is why John Adair's 'action-centred leadership' model has proved so successful, both in training the officers of Sandhurst and in many walks of business life. The leader must satisfy three distinct but interrelated sets of needs.

Lao-Tzu said quite a few years ago: 'When the best leader's work is done the people say we did it ourselves.' The idea of leader as hero has been replaced by the concept of leader as conductor of an orchestra of players.

ACTION CENTRED LEADERSHIP

We do not all have the same potential for getting results through people, nor do all organizations require the same sort of leadership behaviour. However, when we are concerned with developing the competence to lead we might more appropriately ask 'What does a good leader do?' rather than what qualities does he have.

The essence of the functional approach is that the leader must satisfy three distinct but interrelated sets of needs:

- the needs of the *task*
- the needs of the *team*
- the needs of the *individual*

Task needs

The difference between a team and a random crowd is that the team has some common purpose or goal. Without this common objective, it would not stick together as a group. If a work team does not achieve the required result or output, it will become frustrated. Organizations have a task: to provide a service, to cover costs, or even to survive. So anyone who manages others has to achieve these results.

Team needs

To achieve these objectives the group must be held together. People need to work in a co-ordinated fashion in the same direction; team work will ensure that the team contribution is greater than the sum of its parts. Conflict within the team must be used effectively, arguments can lead to ideas, or to tension and lack of co-operation.

Individual needs

Within working groups individuals also have their own set of motivational needs. They need to know what their responsibilities are, how they will be judged, how well they are doing. They need an opportunity to show their potential, take on responsibilities and receive recognition for good work.

The leader's job must be to satisfy all three areas of need by achieving the task, building the team and satisfying individual needs. If leaders only concentrate on tasks, for example, in going all out for achieving output whilst neglecting the training and motivation of their people, they may do very well in the short term. Eventually, however, those people will give less than they know they are capable of. Similarly, neglecting the task will not get the maximum contribution from employees. They will lack the real sense of achievement which comes from accomplishing the task. Examples of *task*, *team* and *individual* behaviours are:

1 Task orientated behaviour:

- agree objectives
- plan and allocate resources
- make decisions
- control progress
- review and evaluate.

2 Team orientated behaviour:
- select the right people
- communicate with them
- encourage
- harmonize
- use humour
- co-ordinate.

3 Individual orientated behaviour:
- trust and respect
- listen
- identify training needs
- appraise
- delegate
- develop
- motivate
- recognize and praise.

The young, entrepreneurial business needs to give a little attention to its internal communication. Its people tend to be highly motivated small teams who spend a lot of time together at work and socially. As the business grows in numbers, sheer size will start to crack the foundations of this camaraderie; the introduction of new people without the original motivation will change the flavour of relationships. It is at this point you will find yourself consciously having to introduce ways and means of getting the team together and keep them facing the right way. Involving your team in preparation and presentation of the business plan can, in itself, be a good way of providing co-ordination to a growing business.

It is amazing how many business people expect a team to work as a team without any practice. After all it (presumably) doesn't work this way for football teams. The way to build a team is to find many formal and informal ways of bringing them together: cascade briefings, state of the nation addresses, lunches, social events, special project teams, happy hours. Fun is actually quite compatible with profit. The importance of informal contact between people, as a way of building productive networks, cannot be overemphasized, but again it will not happen without the mechanism to make it happen.

It is absolutely clear that the more you are trying to grow and change the business, the more you will have to communicate. Briefing groups are an excellent discipline for downward communication but there is a lot more to it than that. You need processes to ensure upward communication and especially to co-ordinate across the barriers which your organization will establish as it grows. There are plenty of examples to help here and plenty of ways of building your team: for example, outward bound programmes, internal team-building events. The Belbin team role profiles (see Figure 6.1)

Co-ordinator
Stable, dominant, extrovert
Concentrates on objectives
Does not originate ideas
Focuses people on what they do best

Plant
Dominant, high IQ, introvert
A 'scatterer of seeds', originates ideas
Misses out on detail
Thrustful but easily offended

Resource investigator
Stable, dominant, extrovert sociable
Contacts with outside world
Salesperson/diplomat/liaison officer
Not original thinker

Shaper
Anxious, dominant, extrovert
Emotional, impulsive
Quick to challenge and respond to challenge
Unites ideas, objectives and possibilities
Competitive
Intolerant of woolliness and vagueness

Implementer
Stable, controlled
Practical organizer
Can be flexible but likely to adapt to established systems
Not an innovator

Monitor evaluator
High IQ, stable, introvert
Measured analysis not innovation
Unambitious and lacking enthusiasm
Solid, dependable

Team builder
Stable, extrovert, low dominance
Concerned with individuals' needs
Builds on others' ideas
Cools things down

Completer finisher
Anxious, introvert
Worries over what will go wrong
Permanent sense of urgency
Preoccupied with order
Concerned with 'following through'

Figure 6.1 Belbin's team role profiles

are a particularly useful way of identifying individual preferred team roles; differences are essential for effective team-working and for learning to live with each other. Belbin (1984) suggests a successful team needs a mix of eight roles.

RECRUITMENT AND SELECTION

Recruitment is perhaps the biggest worry for growing businesses. It can be a major constraint on development plans. A survey in February 1990[1] identified the problems of small businesses (see Figure 6.2).

Getting the right people is a difficult, time-consuming and costly business. Getting it wrong is even more expensive and can be extremely painful. Few growing businesses can claim not to have fallen into this trap. However, you can increase the odds on success by putting in place some basic processes and disciplines. This is what they should include:

- Deciding on the numbers and skills mix you are going to need over the next one to three years;
- Preparing job descriptions covering job title and purpose, to whom responsible, limits of accountability and main tasks.

Key priorities	Percentages of respondents
Recruiting key staff	83
Finding customers	59
Raising new finance	31
High interest rates	27
Red tape	21

Figure 6.2 The key problems of small business

- Preparing a person specification, outlining the sort of person you think is likely to be effective in the job (the seven-point plan covers physical make-up, attainments, general intelligence, special aptitudes, interest, disposition, circumstances).
- Sourcing your requirements creatively, through networks of contacts, employment and search agencies, newspaper advertisements, hotel wine evenings, etc.
- Weeding out application forms or CVs of those who don't fit the job description and person specification.
- Using psychometric tests to supplement your interview process. A huge range of tests covering aptitude or ability are available, tests of general intelligence, test of attainments, personality inventories.

Forty-five seconds, it is claimed, is the time a typical manager takes between meeting an applicant and deciding whether or not he or she is the right person for the job. True or false, fears that the interview can be very subjective – and thus a biased way of selecting staff – are promoting the trend for companies to use standard measurement principles when recruiting.

Aptitude and personality tests (called psychometric tests) are among the battery of techniques that are being adapted into industry and commerce from the worlds of educational and clinical psychology. Once the preserve of big companies, the techniques are being used increasingly by small companies to help improve the selection of new employees and those in line for promotion, and for self-development by owner-managers themselves.

There are hundreds of different types of tests – not all necessarily reliable (there is no policing body for psychometric testing at present) – which test for different things. If you are considering psychometric tests, make sure you and the testing organization share the same priorities where aptitudes are concerned.

Job profiling

There are growing numbers of psychometric tests that help you decide if a particular person is suited for the job you are trying to fill. It is reasonably self-evident that being a successful salesperson or a successful librarian call for different types of people. They may well be equally intelligent, but their abilities and aptitudes will almost certainly be poles apart.

Fortunately, that is exactly what job profiling tests set out to measure. There are usually self-administered, computerized tests, custom-designed for the job in question, covering the field from secretaries to sales managers. The tests usually take around an hour to complete and they can assess both whether the mental aptitude and the personality are suitable for the post. The feedback comes in a computer produced report, which can then be used to help with shortlisting.

When administering a test do give the poor candidate an even chance. Don't put him or her in a noisy place, when peace and quiet are essential for concentration.

A huge range of tests covering aptitude or ability are available: tests of general intelligence, tests attainment, personality inventories. You can locate suitable tests through the British Psychological Society (01162 549568) or the Institute of Personnel and Development (0181 971 9000).

Dismissing people

Small firms hang on to people long after they should have been fired. No one pretends firing is easy or fun – but sometimes it is essential. If people who don't perform are seen to get the same job security and rewards as those who do, you will be sending the wrong signals to everyone.

It is a most painful experience, reaching the decision that one of your team is going to have to leave, and then dismissing either him or her. Especially so if the member is, as so often happens, one of your founding team. You may have to reach this decision very suddenly – discovering, for instance, that the person has done something quite unacceptable. Or more likely, it has gradually become clear over time, for one reason or another.

There may be a temptation to fire someone on the spot, in the heat of the moment. Or, the fear of the legal consequences, and of facing a claim for unfair dismissal, may make managers nervous about taking any action at all. Your own reasons for deciding that you want to dismiss someone will probably fall into one of the following categories:

- the employee is unable to do the job properly;
- there is no longer any need for the business to continue to employ someone in that particular role;
- he or she has done something unforgivable or even criminal.

Whatever the reason in your own mind, pause for thought, and plan your line of action carefully.

Unable to do the job

This can include such reasons as certain kinds of permanent disabling illness or simply being insufficiently skilled to carry out the tasks that you need the person to do. A key rule here is to satisfy yourself absolutely that you are right to conclude that the person is unable to do the job. For instance, you cannot safely assume an illness will be long-lasting and disabling, unless you have asked the employee for permission to talk to their doctor, and the doctor confirms this.

On the other hand, if it is a question of level of performance, you need to track and record output if you can, and to offer the employee time and opportunity to improve in the specified areas – by providing special training if appropriate.

Not needed

If someone's job is being abolished, then technically this is called redundancy. Separate rules and regulations then apply, of course. But often things are not so clear cut. For example, a firm may grow, and find that it now needs a proper finance director, and so wish to replace the current accountant's role with someone of higher calibre, doing a much bigger job. This is probably defensible as redundancy following reorganization, provided a new accountant is not then appointed in a similar role to the old one. And provided the current person is offered any relevant suitable vacancy – such as a new post being created underneath the new finance director. And provided you have reasonable proof that your present accountant is not up to assuming the role of finance director.

Misconduct

The contract of employment, drawn up when the employee began working for you should cover this area to some extent. To take some examples, a violent and unprovoked physical attack on a colleague at work is a reason for dismissal unlikely to be challenged in law, provided there are good witnesses. You will want to be certain of the event's real character – that it hasn't been exaggerated in the telling. Likewise, if you find that someone is stealing from the till – provided that you are absolutely certain you have proof of who the culprit is, and do not jump to conclusions without first asking for explanations.

But misbehaviour at work leading to dismissal can take many much less grave forms, right down to repeatedly wearing the wrong clothes, if for instance it has clearly been a condition of employment, from the start, that employees should wear a uniform.

Procedure

How you go about dismissing someone is almost as important in law as your reasons for doing so. By now, most employers know that it is safest to meet formally with the person concerned, to explain fully, to give the employee the fullest possible chance to state his or her case, to keep agreed notes of the meetings, and to give at least two written warnings with full reasons. Do give the proper period of formal notice, when it finally comes to terminating the employment.

Classic errors

To keep the threat of industrial tribunals at bay, whatever you do, don't dismiss anybody on the basis of information you have had by hearsay from a third party. Don't dismiss anybody just because they have got married or become pregnant. However personally provoked you may be by someone, as can sometimes happen in small teams working at close quarters, stand back and calm down before figuring out your grounds for dismissing them.

If someone's behaviour or performance at work goes into long-standing decline, you must seek out the reasons and possible cures, and involve them in the process. No more can one say: 'Pull your socks up, or you're out!' Don't try to sack someone for being late, if it's the first time you have even mentioned the subject to them.

Handling the termination

No matter what the circumstances, all employees are entitled to a high level of consideration and compassion, and the benefit to the company of treating dismissed employees well maintains morale and your image as a caring employer. It avoids making unnecessary enemies and causing unavoidable stress and pain to departing employees. Termination planned and carried out in a professional way helps to ensure this.

Plan the interview in advance

Decide the best time and place. Don't fire on a Friday – the dismissed employee needs time to adjust before facing his or her family. If possible choose neutral ground for the task – a private place, quiet and free from interruptions. Rehearse the interview if necessary, and decide in advance how to direct the individual after termination.

Don't procrastinate

Once the decision to let someone go has been made, get on with it, otherwise word of impending action might reach the employee's colleagues causing them to shun him/her. Procrastination is not only the thief of time but also of the individual's self-confidence and future job prospects.

These are the 20 questions most commonly asked by the employee being dismissed. Make sure you have your answers ready.

1 Why me?
2 Are the terms negotiable?
3 Do I have the right to appeal?
4 I intend to take the matter further!
5 What about my car?
6 What about my life cover and health care?
7 What about my pension?
8 Why wasn't I given prior warning?
9 What help will you give me to find a new job?
10 Are there any alternative jobs I could do even at a lower grade?
11 Can I apply for, or will you consider me for any future vacancies?
12 Can I work my notice?
13 Who's going to do my job?
14 I think this is totally unfair especially given my service and ability!
15 Am I the only one affected?
16 Can I return to my office?
17 What have my colleagues been told?
18 Can I tell my staff?
19 Who will supply me with a reference?
20 When does this come into effect?

Tell them the truth

Explain the clear, specific and precise reason for the dismissal, without being brutal, preferably backed up by documentary evidence. Many employees cannot believe that they are being fired and will look for any sign of uncertainty as an indication that the job is still negotiable. If the reasons are held back it may cause unnecessary worry and loss of self-esteem.

Don't be emotional

The emotional manager will either plunge in too quickly, without sensitivity, trying to get the whole thing over and done with, or hedge about, failing to make the point and leaving the employee unsure about the situation. Diffusing an emotional situation is one of the most immediate goals of a termination from the company's point of view, and one of the main reasons terminations go disastrously wrong is the emotional state of the manager as well as of the employee.

Don't prolong the agony

The initial interview should last no longer than 15 minutes. There is no point in going into a great deal of detail at this stage – the person may be in a state of shock and unable to take in much of the conversation. Give them a chance to respond, though, and make a subsequent appointment to discuss details of severance pay, and perhaps references.

Sanders and Sidney are one of the new breed of 'outplacement consultants', an idea from the US which is now being used by companies here. Outplacement consultants take over as soon as the firing is done. Executives are immediately wheeled in to see the outplacement expert who provides aid and assistance to the dismissed employee until they find another job. It is good PR for the company doing the dismissing and allays the worries of other staff – but it is not cheap.

Guidelines on Handling the Termination Interview is a free publication from Sanders and Sidney, 28 Dover Street, London W1X 4AE (0171 491 0491).

The exit interview

The exit interview is a means of arranging for anyone leaving the company to be questioned by an impartial person who can establish the reason why. For example, is that person leaving for more money, because of a better opportunity, or because they feel frustrated? Most people in these circumstances are quite happy to talk freely and you can learn a great deal. Attitude surveys, particularly if you carry them out year on year, will benchmark levels of employee morale and highlight problem areas.

Dismissing a partner can be a particularly painful process. Many of the same rules apply, but here a partnership agreement can be particularly helpful (see Chapter 2).

TRAINING

Training people, on a regular basis, in all aspects of their jobs, is a sure-fire way to reduce mistakes and get costs down and customer satisfaction up. This is doubly important with the high staff turnover that is all too common today. Some short-sighted employers say: why train them when they stay for such a short time? Answer: it costs 2% of salary to train them, which is less than 10% of the costs of their mistakes. And once trained who knows, they may even get enough job satisfaction to want to stay – just think how much you'll save if that happens.

Training can be one of the fastest payback routes to cost reduction. One study carried out by a major American corporation concluded that its productivity was improved by 5–20% simply by explaining to people why their jobs matter. This single action saved it a net $9 million, after training costs, over the past three years.

EXAMPLES: In the Summer of 1989, ACE/Chem-Resist, which employs 36 people and produces a range of industrial process plant in plastics, found that it was the victim of its own success. Its order book had grown substantially and the current workforce was fully stretched. Meanwhile the market, both in the UK and elsewhere in Europe, was becoming very complex.

Recruitment difficulties were looming and the management realized that its internal communications needed to improve. It was recognized that the company needed to develop a complete range of training and management systems to cope with the challenges ahead.

Contact was made with a Sheffield based consultancy. With its help the company identified its training and systems' needs and also applied for a grant under Option 3 of Business Growth Training. The business plan for BGT included some tough targets in terms of improvements in turnover and in gross margins. Central to the achievement of the business plan objectives however was the development of management skills at the senior level. Working in conjunction with ACE/Chem-Resist's Managing Director the consultancy produced a suite of training sessions covering the mainstream management skills including leadership and delegation, time management, staff appraisal, negotiating skills and recruitment. These training sessions were delivered during 30 training days spread over a period of one year and timed so that all members of the management team could participate.

All the goals set in the business plan were substantially achieved (or in most cases exceeded). There was a 44% increase in fabrication turnover; the gross margin on material sales went up by 50%; and there was a 47.8% increase in technical sales. As a result senior managers now feel confident of being able to cope with the increasing demands being made upon them and they now have a keen appetite for learning and further self-development.

Frank Baines Saddlery was started eight years ago with the aim of producing high quality saddles mainly for the export market. Success was achieved at an early stage with 90% of output going to Sweden. But as demand from Scandinavia grew, it became necessary to recruit more people in order to cope with demand. It was decided, in conjunction with the principal customer in Sweden, to develop a three-year training programme for young people.

The trainees were recruited through the Walsall Chamber of

Commerce and the training was delivered partly on the job through working alongside experienced saddle and bridle makers and partly in conjunction with the Walsall Leathergoods Training College. National Skill Assessment and Qualification Scheme awards were available and assessments were devised in conjunction with the Society of Master Saddlers and the Worshipful Company of Saddlers. Attachments have been arranged for the trainees with leather factories in both Sweden and Germany.

The firm now has double its original staff of five and output has trebled within three years. At the same time the quality of the saddles and bridles has been maintained.

Exports continue to grow and the firm has won commendations and recommendations from both Europe and North America.

J.V. Murcott and Sons Ltd is a family-run, 60 year-old business employing 140 people in Aston, Birmingham. They specialize in the manufacture of aluminium pressure diecastings. Continuous growth has increased the calls on management and supervisors and as the demands intensified the need for training became apparent.

Managers and their supervisors were given the responsibility for creating and implementing departmental training so that their teams could meet the goals and objectives laid down in the company's recently issued business plan. Before the company could tackle departmental and organizational issues, however, it was necessary to resolve individual weaknesses. Personalized training plans were drawn up for managers, supervisors and chargehands. It was recognized that there were problems over poor communications and a lack of trust, and programmes were drawn up specifically to deal with this. For individual supervisors a course leading to NEBSM standards was devised while for departmental and team training there were outdoor adventure programmes. Departmental training was developed to improve quality assurance, and to enhance the product and the overall skill base. Training was also implemented for a variety of technical departments using NVQ standards.

Turnover has gone up by 46% in the last two years while gross margins are up by 7%. There has been a reduction both in finished stock and work in progress as well as in customer arrears. There is now much greater all-round commitment to the future of the company.

Technical/job related	• For example accounting or sales skills • Negotiating skills • Computer skills
Management skills (existing and potential managers)	• Leadership and motivation • Team building • Appraising, counselling and disciplinary interviews • Managing change • Recruitment and selection • Training and developing staff
Business	• Basic finance • Principles of marketing • Putting together the business plan • Understanding strategy

Figure 6.3 An example of a training menu

The training plan

Unfortunately, when asked what training they need, most people find it difficult to answer. It is therefore essential to find time to identify the training needs of your team, for each key individual and also yourself. Training needs are the gap between performance now and the performance you would like in the future. For example, Innovex pharmaceutical company has historically employed managers with a sales and marketing background; what it needs for the future is strong all-round business people who can run parts of the growing business. The appraisal interview provides a good opportunity for identifying training needs, another approach is to carry out a training needs analysis. Interviewing members of staff to determine key issues such as their background, role, skills needed in the job, strengths and weaknesses, career aspirations. A good survey will also include a discussion of changing business requirements, and the gap between these demands and present capabilities (see Figure 6.3).

Business Links operate on a local basis and can provide up to 50% of the costs of management training (Business Links are a combination of the former Training and Enterprise Councils, Chambers of Commerce and Department of Trade and Industry schemes – they are charged with assisting and advising small firms in their area.) They will form an agreement with your business, and approve an appropriate training consultant who, typically over a 12-month period, will:

- Phase 1: Carry out a training needs analysis.
- Phase 2: Prepare a plan for change to include a training and development programme.
- Phase 3: Provide the agreed management training.
- Phase 4: Complete quarterly progress reports, document all the programmes and prepare a final report.

EXERCISES

1 What major task, team and individual needs have to be satisfied to ensure your business can succeed?
2 How well do you think the proposed members of your team will be able to work together and what makes you confident of that?
3 Draw up a job description and recruitment plan for the first two key appointments that you expect to have to make.
4 What training do you think you and your team may need during the first year of trading?

NOTES

1 Key Staff Recruitment in Small Firms, Cranfield School of Management, 1990.

SUGGESTED FURTHER READING

Belbin, M. (1984) *Management Teams: Why They Succeed and Fail*, Butterworth Heineman, Oxford.
Hayes, Nicky (1996) *Successful Team Management*, International Thomson Business Press, London.
Reay, David G. (1994) *Planning a Training Strategy*, Kogan Page, London.

Chapter 7

Further developing your market differentiation

While Professor Michael Porter has noted 'there is no formula for achieving competitive advantage, only approaches that are tailored to individual companies',[1] the growing business, as its product/service life-cycle develops, needs to concentrate on developing the differentiation and customer focus that enabled it to start and grow. In developing a marketing plan, which the Cranfield/Kellock survey found was a feature of more than 75% of companies with sales over £10 million (compared with under 50% of companies with turnover under £5 million!) the emphasis must be on:

1 developing customer segments and product/service quality
2 price and margin optimization
3 planned promotional activities
4 distinctive distribution
5 improving the sales team.

These elements can then be combined in developing regular sales forecasts for the company's annual planning cycle.

DEVELOPING CUSTOMER SEGMENTS AND PRODUCT/SERVICE QUALITY

Further analysis and segmentation of your customers may well suggest new product offerings, attractive for existing as well as new customers, which will facilitate business growth.

EXAMPLE: The Association of MBAs (Masters of Business Administration), in reviewing its services to ensure they remain relevant to membership, segmented their MBA market as follows:

- current students
- recent graduates
- mature MBAs

- self-employed MBAs
- MBAs: the public and private sectors
- MBAs working for multinationals.

The insights inspired by this customer segmentation encouraged additional and specialist service offerings by the Association, leading to renewed growth in membership.

Equally, it should be remembered that there are no such things as 'pure' products or 'pure' services; each product has a service element (e.g gaming machines need servicing) and each service has a product element (e.g. management consultancy relies on quality written and presented reports). In an increasingly competitive world, the way in which some 'mature' products are 'differentiated' from each other, which is how your company initially succeeded, may be in their service terms.

EXAMPLE: All kitchen white goods, for example, are strictly comparable. Philips, however, provided distinctive service terms for customers and retailers. Customers were allowed to replace any machine in the first 12 months which cannot be repaired; all parts were guaranteed for 10 years. Additionally, Philips provided a 24-hour call 'care' line for customers and would pay £12.50 if its repair engineers did not arrive within two days of call. All retailers were provided with dealer support for advertising, finance for display stock and inventory, together with extended payment terms.

'Service' businesses can be more difficult to differentiate because services, being intangible, are often seen as a 'commodity' and are certainly difficult to taste or test in advance! The customers even play a role in determining the quality and delivery of a service, e.g. in an English restaurant a complaint can lead at best to an improvement, or at worst, a complete withdrawal of service! Marketing a service, therefore, requires strong, consistent branding; the company name is frequently the brand (e.g. 'I'm with the Woolwich'). Making the company name synonymous with good quality is making the 'service' more tangible. At the end of the day, your company name and reputation may be the only difference between you and your competitors.

Achieving differentiation therefore entails an endless battle or trade-off against cost, quality and service level. In this battle you have to seek improvements along two or even all three dimensions, simultaneously! In the 1960s, British manufacturers, particularly in the automobile industry, appeared to have neglected the quality dimension, largely in the mistaken belief that 'dynamic obsolescence' (the marketing flavour of that moment) was almost good for that industry. The Japanese car manufacturers, in changing their image within 20 years from 'cheap and cheerful' in the 1960s to reliability and performance in the 1980s (which proved quality could be brought back!) showed that quality need not be neglected while fighting costs and the rising service levels expected by customers.

Product quality is clearly vital for the growing company.

> EXAMPLE: James Koch, in developing the Boston Beer Company, noted that the biggest problem for the new and growing company was in creating in customers' minds an image of product quality. 'You can't sell a product you don't believe in and in cold calling the only thing standing between you and the customer's scorn is the integrity of your product.'
>
> Equally, those people making pasta, as at Pasta Masters, who believed it was the freshest and best around, are likely to be the long-run winners. Getting up at four each morning to bake fresh bagels gave Bagel Express a quality winning start.

Product differentiation is important for profits as the matrix in Figure 7.1 shows.

High costs with low differentiation is clearly the box to avoid, confirming again the importance of working with and controlling suppliers' costs, seeking good design and image (that people buy with their eyes is as true for industrial products as for High Street goods), ensuring features and benefits match customers needs. But, above all, you must ensure that quality is not lost while you integrate these functions. Quality is not, of course, just what you do, but also how you do it, as Jan Carlson of Scandinavian Airways

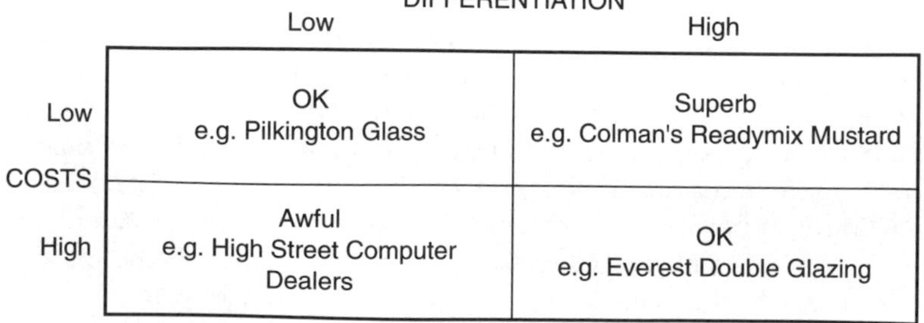

Figure 7.1 Differentiation

noted in listing these 'moments of truth' in customer contacts:

Customer contact point	*Customer expectation*	
Sales	Reliability	What does customer think of you at each contact point, at each 'moment of truth'
Invoices	Responsiveness	
Telephone	Competence	
Reception	Courtesy	
Packaging	Credibility	
Delivery	Security	
	Tangibles	

So, quality is hearts and minds, attitudes and standards, and your product marketing plan must include some quality targets and indications as to how you will audit your performance. Achieving British Standard 5750 (ISO 9000 equivalent) might be expensive for the growing company, in terms of extra personnel and procedures, but it is now firmly on the agenda of many growth companies, particularly given the quality discipline and assurance it gives to customers at home and abroad.

> EXAMPLE: Ian Hinton turned an old co-operative meat processing factory, York House, from a quarter of a million pound turnover in 1979 into £10 million business within 10 years, by listening to the quality requirements of major buyers at Tesco and Sainsbury's. Expansion of the factory, in accordance with strict EEC quality requirements, was the foundation of his success.

You must find out what are the procedures and requirements for BS5750 in your sector (your local Training and Enterprise Council will help) and once you decide to go this route, make sure you take full marketing advantage of your accreditation. A study by Manchester Business School[2] found that in 1994, only 28,000 UK small businesses had registered for BS5750, and only half of these had found it to be of financial benefit. Knowing the cost and then ensuring maximum use of the standard as a marketing tool, to improve quality and win new customers, is the key. Being able to prove customer satisfaction with the consistent quality of your goods and services, is vital, if you have not yet achieved the standard.

PRICE AND MARGIN OPTIMIZATION

Price and quality are closely linked in the minds of most customers. Concentration on good quality should provide greater flexibility in your pricing plan. Differentiation can be achieved by careful focus on the needs of different target groups of customers. Paul Howcroft's Rohan clothing company, achieved 'take off' when business travellers as well as hill walkers and climbers began to purchase the lightweight, easily packed trousers and shirts. Prices and margins improved immediately. Above all, attention has to be paid to the gross margins (i.e. sales less direct variable costs, such as materials and labour) on each of your product groups. As Brian Warnes has explained in his Ghenghis Khan guide:[3]

> Ignoring cash and service companies like banks and supermarkets, most manufacturing companies achieving less than about 25% gross margin are likely to fail sooner or later. Companies begin to achieve real strength, cash flow and financial durability once margins get over about 40 per cent. The real high fliers, like properly structured electronics companies, begin to get into their stride at over 60 per cent.

Typically, the growing company, having started with a good price and gross margin, will find prices falling with growth. What is important is trying to retain net margins (i.e. the margin after deducting overheads from gross margin):

> EXAMPLE: Andy Ingleston's Dockspeed company saw prices fall 25% in the first five years of development, partly occasioned by the 1990–92 UK recession. With growth, however, Andy was able to retain net margins (and operating profits) close to 20% by better bulk buying of diesel, tyres and ferry spaces, and better fleet utilization. Empty lorry return journeys were eliminated by new trade in refrigerated yoghurt to the UK and toast and sliced bread on return trips to Marks and Spencers in France and railway companies in Germany.

Many companies survive on smaller margins by ruthlessly pruning overheads at the same time as lowering prices, e.g. Archie Norman helped Asda to give 'value for money' by scrapping all directors' Jaguar cars and offering them for one month at a time to employees who achieved outstanding sales performances. Without a good margin there is no overhead room for building further differentiation by extensive promotion, research and development, or distribution experimentation.

Yet thriving retailers, even in depressed times, concentrate on margins and different target groups of customers by using price and quality across the range:

> EXAMPLE: Marks and Spencer used a 'tiered catalogue' with three main price ranges for St Michael brands: easy, mid and upper, to suit different customer groups. Ratners offered

customers jewellery at prices they could afford, rather than quality they could not: in many stores you could find a one carat diamond ring at £1,600, a silver plated tray and decanter at £14.99 and 9 carat earrings at £2. As a result Ratner's doubled H. Samuels' turnover per square foot from £32 to £62 a year.

Unfortunately, Chairman Gerald Ratner jokingly 'rubbished' his own product quality at a CBI conference, which took an enormous toll on his company. Try not to talk your company's quality down, especially in jest!

The pricing decision has to be revisited regularly, even in low inflationary times; margins, like quality, must be maintained by constant attention to cost, quality and competition.

EXAMPLE: Paul Henderson spent 15 years developing Gidleigh Park in Devon into one of the leading English country house hotels. Gidleigh's clientele, mainly wealthy businessmen, were attracted by the hotel's excellent restaurant and quality image; Paul was concerned, nonetheless, that lunches at £40 a head attracted only one or two regular diners. Adapting the successful *Financial Times* formula of 'lunch for a tenner', Paul offered mid-week lunches at £15 a head, rising to £20 on Fridays and £25 at weekends. This appealed, via the *Good Food Guide* recommendations to new customer segments of discerning diners, without detracting from existing clientele, and led to improved bottom line performances.

Price increases can be combined with improvements in quality or service:

EXAMPLE: Rabone Tools commissioned a new corporate design for its wide range of hand held tools. Featuring a single logo, distinctive colour schemes for product groupings, and highlighting new product features, permitted the company to relaunch its existing product range with a 5% price increase, leading to a 60% increase in profits.

Knowing, via continuous customer research on key success factors, which product/service attributes matter most to customers, and aiming to provide these benefits, can enable companies to be 'high benefit/higher price players' rather than the reverse. Equally prices can also be improved by close examination of all the elements of 'price leakage', i.e. order size discounts, payment terms discounts – especially when the payment is not timely. Regular re-examination of discounts and determining if they are still justifiable, can lead to profit improvement.

EXAMPLE: Autoglass offered introductory discounts on 'new' pop-up sunroofs in the early 1980s, but remembered to remove them when the line became established!

PLANNING PROMOTIONAL ACTIVITIES

The economist J. K. Galbraith has commented on the power of advertising: 'In great measure, wants are now shaped by advertising ... the individual product or service has little consequence.'[4] Good advertising and promotion is a powerful way to differentiate products and services. But advertising, being expensive, must be rigorously controlled. Thus procedures to follow include those recommended by Tim Bell, formerly of Saatchi & Saatchi:

- set specific campaign objectives (building sales, market share)
- decide strategy (budget, media choice, geographical profile)
- target audience (market segment, demographic profile)
- decide advertising content (specific product/service benefits to highlight)
- execution and style (humour, hard sell?); ask yourself, if your product/service was a car or a newspaper, which kind of car (Rolls or a Mini), which kind of newspaper (*The Sun* or *The Times*) do you want to be seen as?

Leaflets and brochures for exhibitions have to be written with the specific exhibition visitor in mind; press releases are written for professional editors, as Hyde and Partners, advertising agency, explain:

> It is the Editor who decides to print, not you, as when you supply and pay for advertisements. You must, therefore, attract the Editor's attention, with a snappy headline and a stimulating first paragraph. British Rail did it when their PR release entitled their new rail–airport link as 'Gatquick'. Your release must be short, it must be factual. It is not a 'sales message'. Print always in double space, to allow the Editor to make changes.

Issue targeted press releases regularly, including photographs, personality and performance quotations, and write in the style of the journal you have chosen.

EXAMPLE: Quantum Cars, after three years existence, began to issue press releases on a monthly basis, directed at the four major kit car magazines. These generally contained 'stories' about Quantum, such as a diesel version of the car, right up to a £17,000 model, complete with Wilton carpets. Editorial was seen as much more effective than the limited amount of expensive advertising undertaken, with a good press review of the car worth several advertisements.

Good newspaper or trade journal coverage can provide good copy to help improve the normally low, typically 2.5%, response rates on direct mail, if you include them in your mailing.

Above all, monitor carefully the cost effectiveness of each campaign undertaken; either by comparing tear-off coupon replies against the cost of the advertisement, or ensuring customers are questioned, at the till or on the invoice, as to how they came into contact with your company.

EXAMPLE: Autoglass, from its earliest days asked each customer when paying bills in their depots 'how the customer had heard of the service'. A form beside each till recorded each of the company's promotional activities, from depot sign, to *Yellow Pages* advertisement, insurance company recommendation, press adverts, etc. In the early years, *Yellow Pages* reference was by far the highest, so the company sought representation in all regional *Yellow Pages*. Later, when insurance company recommendations increased, expenditure on *Yellow Pages* coverage could be dramatically reduced. Equally, later experimentation with local radio could be monitored within days and weeks to judge its effectiveness.

In this way, Autoglass could not only judge the effectiveness of budgeted advertising expenditure, but could also ensure that specific planned increases would be likely to increase sales. Working with an advertising agency may also be easier, for both parties, if the mechanism is in place to judge the results of their efforts and recommendations! Agencies paid by media rebate (10–15% discounts on advertising spent) will, not surprisingly, rarely recommend reductions in media expenditure. Hence the need for accurate information on response rates (costs per lead, conversion rate per lead) to judge advertising and agency effectiveness. Nevertheless, the achievements of an agency like Leo Burnett in turning a commodity (water) into

Perrier, shows how the support of such agencies should not be underestimated.

Determining the most effective below-the-line promotional expenditure is just as important, given the higher expenditure most early growth companies are likely to have in this area. More money is actually spent on sales promotion techniques than on agency advertising. Yet both must work in harmony, as the objectives are the same: advertising campaigns are aimed at building long-term custom, while sales promotions are typically short-term activities to keep your company going. So, effective sales promotion can speed up stock movement, encourage repeat purchases, get bills paid on time, induce trial purchases. The variety and target customers for such schemes is immense. For example, your target customers may be trade or even your own employees and you may be offering money (prizes, bonuses) goods (gifts, vouchers) or even services (free training, free services).

However, for the growing business, promotional opportunities that stimulate interest and awareness among new and existing purchasers, at lowest cost, are the most important. While discounting to move discontinued or slow moving lines may be necessary from time to time, the main positive promotional activities would include:

1 Ensuring all company 'small items' are co-ordinated and effective (business cards to Christmas cards!).
2 Participating in exhibitions (with new leaflets and brochures).
3 Experimenting with direct mail (data-bases) and tele-marketing (direct response).

Business cards that are memorable (Gregson Pack cards contain a promotional photograph of the first aid pack) and commercial Christmas cards that are not blasphemous and help sales, may perhaps not seem worthy of a chief executive's attention, but they cost thousands of pounds and are perhaps the tip of the iceberg for your corporate identity programme. If they don't excite attention, perhaps your corporate communication package as a whole is unappealing!

EXAMPLE: What makes a good corporate Christmas card is highly subjective. The *Financial Times* judged Ratners, the jewellers, card (Roy Lichtenstein cartoon of young lady on telephone saying 'So this is what he meant by giving me a Ring for Christmas'!) to be the most memorable British card in 1990; the worst to have been Lancaster Kind, property consultants, announcing 'A babe is born', meaning themselves, the previous year. Clearly humour rather than blasphemy in reinforcing your company name and service is more likely to be favourably remembered!

Exhibitions are often used at the start of a life of a company, but later neglected. Given the expense and fatigue they can generate, this is not perhaps surprising: exhibitions are not free, a tiny stand for four days in the Spring Gift Exhibition at Birmingham NEC will cost at least £1,500. For the Ideal Home Exhibition in Earls Court, you are looking at 10 times this sum; lighting, display stands and manning costs will then more than double these amounts. Yet similar outlays on newspaper advertisements are visible by customers for a few seconds on one day only, whereas with exhibitions you are at least guaranteed eye to eye contact with committed trade and retail buyers for as long as you can stimulate their interest! Because each exhibition is specific, both costs and sales benefits arising from it can be easily determined; each time you exhibit you have an opportunity to re-focus your company by being forced to produce new exhibitions leaflets, to re-think your personal selling messages and to re-listen to what your key customer groups tell you about your company!

Finally, there are exciting (or alarming!) direct marketing media channels. Alarming, for Europeans who already believe we are deluged with junk mail, to discover that in the USA 65% of advertising expenditure is in direct mailing (20% in UK in 1988) and while UK citizens receive 29 direct mail items per annum, in the USA each person receives 300 items per annum. Is it worth it? Well, for the Royal Mail it is (representing a £7 billion market) and 62% of UK recipients are claimed to read their direct mail! Telemarketing is also growing rapidly, taking advantage of customer data-base lists provided by list brokers; so much so that 60% of company purchasing managers receive a minimum of five calls a week. Again, is this effective?

EXAMPLE: Paper-Safe sought the help of a telephone marketing company (UK Connect) early on to help launch their shredding service. Managing Director, Glen Fayolle comments: 'We could have done the work ourselves, but they did it faster, contacting 270 companies in two weeks, where we could only contact a maximum of ten companies per week. They encouraged two companies which were interested in our services immediately, and the cost was easily offset by the number of positive leads fed immediately to our salesman.

DISTINCTIVE DISTRIBUTION

The pricing and the distribution channels you operate are clearly closely related, particularly in terms of the trade or quantity discount structure you will need, to ensure your products or services are adequately represented in the marketplace. Prices are all too readily blamed for poor performance by management, when in fact poor distribution may be the key to low market share.

EXAMPLE: Dan Duncan, MD of the fast growing football magazine *When Saturday Comes*, had been delighted when a specialist distributor had agreed to deliver the magazine to newsagents throughout the South-East. Previously sales had been organized by an army of volunteers on Saturday afternoons outside football grounds. As sales climbed, however, and as major retail outlets such as Menzies agreed to handle the magazine, Dan reluctantly realized the excellent regional distributor would have to be replaced by a major national distributor.

If your product could potentially achieve a 50% market share, but only reaches 25% of the market through inadequate distribution channels, where only 50% of the public will buy it, it is not surprising that your maximum market share is only 6%! No amount of extra promotional expenditure or price changes can alter the result. Equally the way in which you distribute your products may be as significant as the products themselves:

EXAMPLE: Telford based TWS, a window systems manufacturer, faced with static sales, commissioned a customer survey on the merits of its German window profile system. The major surprise of the survey was to discover that 80% of actual and potential TWS customers did not have fork lift trucks, the result being all deliveries had to be handled off, depriving the fabricating customer of 'window-making' time. The solution was to commission the production of a new delivery vehicle, complete with its own fork lift. 'Now it just takes 15 minutes instead of 2 hours to unload 2 stillages and we don't use the fabricator's manpower', explained the MD of TWS.

The beneficial impact on TWS sales by this improved delivery service might be imagined! Even how you collect may also be a way of differentiating your business; Glen Fayolle, MD of Paper-Safe, a security paper-shredding company, grew his customer base by supplying them with special plastic containers, designed to take valuable (to paper merchants) grade computer print-out paper.

Whether or not to invest in retail property, rather than in the working assets of your business, is often a painful decision for businesses in securing

	Channel	Target group
Farm goods producers	Pick your own Farm shop Mail order Specialist shop Wholesaler/retailer Restaurants Health Farms	DIY Commuter, trippers Specialist interest groups (e.g. health, vegetarian, etc.) Variety of income groups Health/high income groups

Figure 7.2 Means of reaching target groups

adequate distribution for products and services. Increasingly, prudent businessmen balk at investment in 'safe' property, where money can be better invested in stock, which can perhaps be guaranteed to be turned over say five times per annum and earn 20% each time. Businesses 'protected' by freehold property from the market environment, witness Dunn & Co the gentlemen's outfitters in 1991, might, in turn, not adapt in time to the challenges of that changing marketplace.

Finally, monitoring of your own company's (and competitor's) product or service availability clearly requires frequent visits, inspection and interrogation of distributors and customers alike. Sometimes the results, as for TWS above, can be surprising.

In summary, the distribution plan must match the other elements of the marketing mix, noted above, to maintain the differentiation and focus sought by the company. If your product is of the highest quality, with price and promotion to match, it must be available in the major quality stores. Different channels must be used to reach different customer segments, as Figure 7.2 denotes.

IMPROVING THE SALES TEAM

Personal selling is the vital link in the communication process between company and customer, but Professor McDonald of Cranfield has noted:[5]

> Among European sales forces, there is an alarming lack of planning and professionalism. Sales people frequently have little idea of which products and which groups of customers to concentrate on, have too little knowledge about competitive activity, do not plan presentations well, rarely talk to customers in terms of benefits, make too little effort to close the sale and make many calls without any clear objective. Even worse, marketing management is rarely aware that this important and expensive element of the marketing mix is not being managed effectively.

Many studies have shown that if the average salesman's salary is £15,000 pa, the real cost to the company after travel, expenses and fringe benefits is frequently double or even treble, if sales support is added; while at the same time less than a third of the salesperson's actual time is spent in front of the customer. Hence the need for responsible sales management able to:

1 set and monitor sales target achievement
2 motivate, train and support the sales staff
3 recruit and organize competent staff.

Sales target setting at the simplest level may simply be in terms of ensuring minimum sales to recover the new salesman's costs; for example a minimum £50,000 extra sales, at 50% gross margin, to recover the average salesman's 'real' cost. It may also be in terms of unit sales volume, mix of products or even numbers of target customers to convert. Monitoring of sales achievement may not be simply in terms of these quantitative targets (to which may be added numbers of sales calls per day, letters written, exhibitions organized, etc.), but also in terms of qualitative achievement in terms of work planning and time spent in front of customers (see Figure 7.3).

Given such precise targets, the tasks of sales management in motivating and training sales personnel is made easier. Under-achievement may point the need to evaluate salesmen's call frequency and utilization.

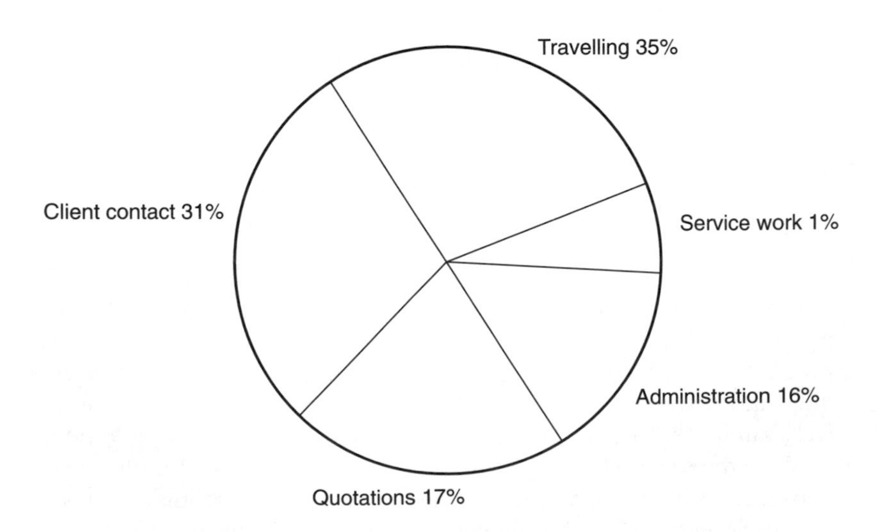

Figure 7.3 Analysis of salesforce time

EXAMPLE: JTM Business Consultants found in a customer survey that customers wanted the sales representative to call monthly, while their existing call pattern was fortnightly. This meant that salesforce time could be released to handle other work, such as new product introductions. Equally, another review found that the salesforce was calling on accounts too small to justify a call; it was decided to transfer small customers to the sales office and to use the telephone to make regular calls.

Sales targets should be mutually agreed between sales personnel and sales management, and motivation can be improved by judicious use of incentives. Analysts from Elton Mayo to McClelland have shown that all individuals have goals and aspirations and if their needs are met, they will work harder. A remuneration plan, with bonus or commission related to performance, remains pre-eminent, however, and often needed to encourage teamwork as well as accomplishment of specific sales targets.

EXAMPLE: At specialist hi-fi chain Richer Sounds branch managers get a cash bonus of 1% of total profits and sales personnel half of this. Employees are rewarded not just on the basis of sales but, as the quality of service is important, branches are assessed monthly on numbers of customer complaints, how swiftly staff answered 'phones, punctuality and efficiency in maintaining stocks of popular lines. Richer's package of staff incentives also includes the use of a country house near York and the loan of the boss's Rolls Royce for a month!

Excessively complicated bonus schemes should, however, be avoided! Quite often providing the sales force with information (e.g. sales by customer) and tools to make the selling task easier (e.g. sales brochures to route planning) are as important as any incentives that can be created. Sales and product training need to be repeated regularly. Businesses in particular which pay a bonus of less than 10% of basic salary might do better to spend their money on these aspects of salesman relations.

Good and motivating compensation packages will clearly assist companies in recruiting and staffing the sales function. The number of sales staff required and their specific functions derive from your listing of tasks required: e.g. opening new accounts, showing new products, servicing existing customers for orders and debts. Many of these functions can be handled by mail or telephone (repeat orders and debts); the number of personal salesmen will depend on workload involved in visiting, selling to and administering (record cards) your customers. Increasingly, information technology can help reduce this workload, e.g. customer ordering terminals, switching in to supplier stocking displays. Supplying customer data base information to sales personnel can also reduce their administrative tasks. These developments are important for the growing business, where competing with major companies for good salesmen is always difficult.

Finally, recruitment by the small growing business has traditionally been among family and friends, if for no other reason that these are likely to have been cheaper and keener than the all too expensive professional! Yet the informality of this process has to be generally replaced by more formal procedures (job descriptions, formal interviews, telephone checking on referees, etc.), particularly when one realizes that one misfit could destroy a small business while only doing a relatively small piece of harm to a firm the size of ICI! At the same time it is important to remember that technical skills are usually less important than the fit of new sales personnel in your organization. It is no sin not to employ people you do not like, however expert!

By further developing your market differentiation in each of the above categories, you will be increasing the probability of expanding your customer base and developing extra competitive advantage for your business. The marketing 'plan' also provides the basis to construct an operation (people) and financial plan, the binding link for these elements being the sales forecast.

SALES FORECAST AND CONTROL

The sales forecast should be the natural outcome and quantification of the marketing planning process. It should reflect:

- Known industry or market segment growth rates (e.g. if your growth is to be faster than the industry average growth rate, say 5% versus 3% for the industry sector as a whole, it should reflect explanations why – such as investment or extra promotional support).
- Estimated own and competitive local market shares (with explanations as to why your market share is to increase at the expense of competitors).
- Your own targeted and costed plans to increase market share (for example, new depot openings will add 2% market share).
- Your own company actual and planned capacity.

Comparisons should then be made between the above and the short-term forecasts of your sales team, based on known customer contacts.

Inevitably, the smaller, growing business cannot always achieve total levels of precision in all of the above areas; particular attention must be given to making best estimates, nevertheless, and learning from experience.

EXAMPLE: In making growth plans, the Directors of Autoglass were hampered by lack of market information. Through discussions with leading windscreen suppliers it was possible to guess the total size of the UK windscreen replacement market. This was compared with the known average windscreen breakage rate (3% pa) applied to the total car population (17 million) to corroborate market size. The average car population was growing at 3% pa, so forecasts of the future replacement market could be made; own unit sales indicated Autoglass market share, and forecasts could be tied to a programme of new depot openings and market growth.

Attention must also be given to:

- Known industry production and distribution capacity, with the effect of planned additions or deletions.
- Allowing for both the impact of seasonality and the effect of economic trends on your business.
- Relating the timing of your promotional expenditures to planned sales increases and monitoring their impact closely.

Some companies produce both optimistic and pessimistic forecasts and steer a middle course; conservatism is always recommended, particularly where new products are involved, especially because, as a rule, less than 20% of your first customers will become repeat clients. Sometimes the recent past can be a poor guide to even the immediate future.

EXAMPLE: Coldshield Windows, as one of the first national double glazing companies, grew at annual sales rates of between 25% and 30% throughout the early 1970s, benefiting from customer concern with the first oil price rise and the rapid spread of central heating. Attempts were made to correlate the percentage of homes with central heating (60% by 1979) and the low percentage of homes with double glazing (under 10% in 1979), to show that growth could continue at these rates throughout the early 1980s. Depot expansion plans were developed and promotional expenditure committed on this basis. The sharp economic downturn of 1980–82 halted market growth completely, and only the more conservatively planned double glazing companies remained in the black!

So, do not let the natural optimism of the sales team outweigh the careful reasoning and logic of the marketing plan. This can best be done by ensuring that your control system regularly monitors the effectiveness of your marketing efforts, regularly recording, for example, the cost of promotional sales leads, or sales per salesperson, to give some early indication of market maturity or turn-down. Continuing the Coldshield example:

EXAMPLE: Recording promotional expenditure per sales lead was only introduced by the company in 1980 and showed an average cost of £40 per direct newspaper lead; this compared with under £10 cost per sales lead for Wallguard's new company in France. The disparity emphasized the growth of UK competition in double glazing as well as the maturity of the market, soon to be shown in static sales figures.

Armed with a sensible marketing plan and a conservative sales forecast, you are now able to develop your matching operations (people) and financial plan.

EXERCISES

1. Is your business still dependent on one product or service for over 80% of profits?
2. Do your top five customers still account for more than 50% of your sales?
3. How do you measure customer satisfaction with the quality of your products and services?
4. When did you last increase your prices and by what %?
5. How do your prices compare with your major competitors?
6. Describe the distribution chain between you and the customer?
7. Do your customers and target market segments have easy access to your goods and services? How do you monitor this?
8. Have you determined the most cost-effective advertising/promotions media for your business? Describe.
9. How much (£ pa) do you budget for advertising and how much (£ pa) for promotion activity?
10. When did you last have a press release and with what effect?
11. What targets are set for each salesperson and what incentive is there to achieve targets?
12. What was your achievement against sales forecast last year?

NOTES

1 Porter, M. (1990) *Competitive Advantage of Nations*, Macmillan Press, London.
2 Chittenden, F. Manchester, Proceedings of 17th Institute of Small Business Administration (ISBA), Manchester Business School, Sheffield., p. 137.
3 Warnes, B. (1984) *The Ghenghis Khan Guide to Business*, Osmosis Publications, London, p. 32.
4 Galbraith, J. K. (1985) *The Anatomy of Power*, Hamish Hamilton, London.
5 McDonald, M. (1990) *Marketing Plans*, Heinemann, Oxford, p. 159.

SUGGESTED FURTHER READING

European Case Clearing House, *Dockspeed Case*, (595-004-1,595-005-1,595-006-1), Cranfield University, Cranfield.

McDonald, Malcolm (1994) Developing the marketing plan, *The Marketing Book*, Butterworth-Heinemann, London, pp. 110–36.

Chapter 8

How do you fund growth?

Whatever strategic direction you propose to pursue it is almost certain to require money. By now you will have discovered that a healthy business has an equally healthy appetite for cash. For the first years of a business's life its strategic choices are invariably limited by the availability of funds. Once it gathers momentum and begins to plan its strategic direction, the corset elastic is usually the limited availability of good opportunities and the management to exploit them successfully.

The constant search for funds is not in itself a cause for concern. Businesses, after all, exist in part at least to turn money into goods and services, which can be sold on for a profit. It usually takes a while for the business cycle to move from strategic ideas to profit and so, as long as you are growing, more money will be needed.

What should concern you, however, is where that money comes from. There are two main sources of money: internal and external, with a number of sub-divisions of each sector. Getting the right balance of funds from these different sources is the key to profitable growth – and perhaps even to survival itself.

INTERNAL SOURCES OF FUNDS

Surprisingly enough, many businesses have much of the money they need to finance growth already tied up in the firm. It may require a little imagination and some analysis to uncover it, but a financial position audit should give some pointers to how this might be done.

The main way in which the Financial Position Audit is established is through the use of ratios. A ratio is simply something expressed as a proportion of something else, and it is intended to give an appreciation of what has happened. For example, a percentage is a particular type of ratio, where events are always compared with a base of 100.

In our everyday lives we apply ratios to tell us how well, or otherwise, something is performing. One measure of a car's performance is in miles per gallon (petrol consumption). If the mpg rate drops, say, from 35 to 1 to 20 to 1, it tells us the car is long overdue for a service – or worse.

In the financial field the opportunity for calculating ratios is great, for computing useful ratios, not quite so great. Here we will concentrate on explaining the key ratios for a small business. Most you can calculate yourself, some you may need your bookkeeper or accountant to organize for you. All take a little time and may cost a little money, but they do tell you a lot about what is going on.

One main value of the position audit using ratios is that it points to questions that need answers. A large difference between what actually happened and what standard was set suggests that something may be wrong. The tools of analysis (the ratios) allow managers to choose, from the hundreds of questions that might be asked, the handful that are really worth answering. In a small or expanding business where time is at a premium, this quick preselection of key questions is vital.

SQUEEZE WORKING CAPITAL

Working capital is a further area rich in possibilities for squeezing to release cash for expansion. Debtors and stocks are perhaps the most fertile areas to start. According to figures prepared by the credit management group, Intrum Justitia, British firms wait on average 78 days for bills to be paid while German, Swedish and Norwegian companies wait just 48 days, Danish firms wait 50 days, Dutch companies, 52 days. Italian and French companies wait 90 and 108 days respectively, but they quote 60-day payment terms rather than our normal 30 days, so they are still better off in relative terms.

Intrum Justitia calculates that the total cost of providing customers with the extra 48 days of credit is equivalent to 5.7% of the average business's turnover, and, assuming a net profit margin of 10%, more than half its net profit. Instead of companies being able to borrow to grow the business, they often need to borrow just to fund their sales ledger.

EXAMPLES

Holliday Chemical Holdings

Companies are turning increasingly to computers to provide them with the information they need to forecast likely demand and the stocks they must carry to meet it. Holliday Chemical Holdings, a Huddersfield-based chemicals manufacturer with UK turnover of £33 million, is spending £160,000 on a computerized materials requirements planning system which will allow it to plan production schedules in its two UK plants (employing 367 people). Michael Peagram, head of the new management team which bought into Holliday in 1985, believes tighter controls on purchasing and the computerized systems will allow him to cut £1 million from current stocks of £8 million. Stocks have been allowed to grow over the past five years as turnover quadrupled but there is now a need for tighter controls.

Sophisticated computer systems may be appropriate for a company the size of Holliday but smaller businesses can achieve considerable improvements by relatively simple changes in the way they purchase and monitor their stocks of raw materials. Holliday itself is buying in chemicals on a monthly rather than a quarterly basis where possible, to reduce its own stocks.

Mercado Carpets

Mercado Carpets, a Leeds-based carpet wholesaler, has computerized its stock control procedures but combines this with what John Wharton, joint managing director, calls 'gut feel' to decide on the types and volumes of carpets to be purchased. Wharton estimates he devotes five hours a week to stocks and purchasing.

Mercado normally carried between £4 and £5 million worth of inventory in its warehouse compared with an annual sales level of £26 million. Acquired by its present management by means of a buy-out in 1989, the company employs 168 people.

Wharton keeps stocks low by buying, where possible, from suppliers with short delivery times, though shipment delays mean he is forced to hold 12 weeks' stocks of carpets from his US suppliers. In the wake of the buy-out Wharton persuaded his major suppliers to extend their payment terms by one month.

For businesses which have failed to monitor stock levels closely, the introduction of tight controls can prove daunting. A 'quick and dirty' way of making improvements can be achieved by grading stock as A, B or C according to the value of individual items or of the total number held. Attention is then focused on items in the A category which can provide the greatest savings. These items can then be subjected to regular stock-takes; patterns of demand can be studied to see how frequently orders are placed, if there are peaks or troughs, or whether demand is seasonal. Managers can then decide the quantities they require and when to place their next order or start their next production run if they are making the item in-house. B and C items can be brought into this programme once it is well established.

Much of the cost of many products is incurred in the final stages of manufacture so big stock savings can be made by holding stocks of semi-finished items. Only put the finishing touches to an item when the customer wants it.

Companies frequently maintain larger stocks than are necessary because a new order is triggered automatically when stocks fall to a certain level. These trigger points should be re-examined for each product to see if lower levels can be set.

MAKE MORE PROFIT AND PLOUGH IT BACK

Another internal source of finance is to make your present business more profitable and plough that profit back to grow your business. Five steps you can take to unlock the extra profit potential in your business are:

Recognize the iceberg

Just as the small tip of the iceberg showing above water conceals an enormous mass below, the small(ish) percentage of profits the average business makes (typically under 10% of sales), conceals a great volume of money being used to arrive at that profit. It requires only a few percentage points reduction in costs to dramatically improve profits, as Table 8.1 illustrates.

In the example given in Table 8.1 the last profit-to-sales figure was 5%. Costs, the 'below the water line' mass, are 95%. By reducing those costs by a mere 2%, bottom line profits have been increased by a massive 40% (this is a simplified example from a real life case).

This extra profitability can then be used to finance extra investments, saved as a reserve for bad times, or be used to compensate for lower sales. In Table 8.1, when costs are reduced by 2%, turnover from sales can drop by over 25 per cent to £714,000 before profits will dip below £50,000. That should take care of even the worst recession seen since the 1920s and 1930s.

Now much of this will come as no surprise to you – after all most of this is your money, so naturally you are well informed as to where it goes. But the people who work for you have probably never considered (or been given the chance to consider) the phenomenal impact that relatively small

Table 8.1 The effects of cost savings on profits

Before		*After 2% cost saving*		*Extra profit*		*But if sales drop . . .*	
£000	*%*	*£000*	*%*	*£000*	*%*	*£000*	*%*
1,000	100	1,000	100	–	–	714	100
950	95	930	93	–	–	664	93
50	5	70	7	20	40	50	7

savings in costs can have on the bottom line. So why not tell them? You could start by giving your key employees a copy of the above table and inviting their comments.

Use the 80/20 rule

Obviously, you cannot leave the whole responsibility of reducing costs exclusively to the people who, after all, created the costs in the first place. Just as with any other business, task objectives have to be agreed and strategies adopted.

Fortunately, here you have the 80/20 rule working in your favour. This rule states that 80% of effort goes into producing 20% of the results. Look at Table 8.2, which was prepared for one company on a recent business training programme. This more or less confirms the rule, as 18% of customers account for 78% of sales.

A quick glance at figures in your own business will in all probability confirm that 20% of your customers account for 80% of your sales, and yet your costs are probably spread evenly across all your customers. Sales people tend to make their calls in a cycle that suits their administrative convenience, rather than concentrating on customers with the most potential.

Interestingly enough, when the salesman in the company used in the above example was asked where he thought his sales in two years' time would be coming from, (see column 3, Table 8.2) he felt that his top 18% of customers would account for 88% of sales (up from 78% of actual sales this year). And yet an analysis of his call reports showed that he spent over 60% of his time calling on his bottom 68 accounts, and planned to continue doing so. This 'activity' – rather than results-based – outlook was being used to make out a case for an additional salesperson. What was actually needed was a call grading system to lower the call rate on accounts with the least sales potential. So, for example, accounts with the least potential were called on twice a year and phoned twice, while top grade accounts were visited up to eight times a year.

Table 8.2 The 80/20 rule in action

Number of customers		*value of sales*		*Value of potencial sales*	
	%	*£000*	*%*	*£000*	*%*
4	3	710	69	1,200	71
21	18	800	78	1,500	88
47	41	918	90	1,600	94
116	100	1,025	100	1,700	100

This grading process saves costs, as phone calls are cheaper than visits; it eliminates the need for an additional salesperson, which at first glance the projected growth would have justified; and it even frees up time so the salesman can prospect for new, high potential accounts.

The 80/20 rule can be used across the business to uncover other areas where costs are being incurred that are unwarranted by the benefits. In some areas you just need to open your eyes to see waste. Did you know that the average executive spends 36 minutes a day looking for things on or around the desk? This can waste up to £6,000 a year for a fairly senior person – you, for example. The same survey conducted for the British Institute of Management revealed that a quarter of the 500 executives they questioned spent 11 hours a week in meetings – equivalent to 13 weeks a year. Few were satisfied with their investment.

The chances are, if you are anything like many other UK chief executives, you feel that you and your management team waste too much time on the wrong priorities. It is not that managers aren't working hard enough – on average they work 20% more hours than a decade ago. It is just that organizing time and daily priorities in a world in which there has been a 600% increase in business information, and the average manager is interrupted every eight minutes, is difficult to say the least. But the 'cost' of wasting time is very real in two senses. First, you end up buying more management than you need – and that cost has to be spread across your products. Second, people are too busy doing the wrong things to have time to do the right things.

Zero-based budgeting

The 80/20 rule is helpful in getting costs back into line – but what if the line was completely wrong in the first place?

When you sit down with your team and discuss budgets, the arguments always revolve around how much more each section will need next year. The starting point is usually this year's costs, which are taken as the only 'facts' upon which to build. So, for example, if you spent £25,000 on advertising last year and achieved sales of £1 million, the expense would have been 2.5% of sales. If the sales budget for next year is £1.5 million, then it seems logical to spend £37,500 next year. That, however, presupposes last year's sum was wisely and effectively spent in the first place, which it almost certainly was not.

Popularized in the 1970s by Robert McNamara, zero-based budgeting turns the cost argument on its head. It assumes that each year every cost centre starts from zero spending and, based on the goals of the business and the resources available, arguments are presented for every penny spent, *not just for the increase proposed.*

Cut out mistakes through training

According to Tom Frost, former Chief Executive of the National Westminster Bank, basic mistakes by employees account for between 25% and 40% of the total costs of any service business – and not just in banking. It is certainly true that people learn from experience, and the more often they do a job, the faster and better they get at it (up to the stage where indifference sets in of course)! What a pity, however, that so many of Britain's smaller firms let their employees practise on their customers, losing money and goodwill in the process.

Training people, on a regular basis, in all aspects of their jobs, is a surefire way to reduce mistakes, and get costs down and customer satisfaction up. This is doubly important with the high staff turnover that is all too common today. Some short-sighted employers say: why train them when they stay for such a short time? Answer: it costs 2% of salary to train them, which is less than 10% of the cost of their mistakes, if Mr Frost is right. And once trained who knows, they may even get enough job satisfaction to want to stay – just think how much you'll save if that happens.

Training can be one of the fastest payback routes to cost reduction. One study carried out recently by a major American corporation, concluded that its productivity was improved by 5% to 20% simply by explaining to people why their jobs matter. This single action saved it a net $9 million, after training costs, over the past three years. You can even get government help, through the Enterprise Initiative, to train your staff (contact the Department of Trade and Industry or your local TEC for details of Training for Business Growth).

Incentivize everyone around profit

Lots of companies have incentive schemes, but most end up rewarding the wrong achievement. Some firms actually reward people by how much they spend! So, for example, buyers with the biggest budget get the highest pay and perks. Production staff are paid for greater output and salespeople for more sales, whether or not either activity is particularly desirable at the time it is achieved. In one company (name withheld to protect the embarrassed) one of the largest creditor items on liquidation was sales people's commission.

There are always hundreds of reasons for giving people intermediate incentive, such as sales commission. But unless you build profit targets into your goals and incentives, nine times out of ten you'll end up with the wrong result. You get nothing if the company doesn't make a satisfactory profit, so rewarding others if they don't make money is only encouraging an illusion of reality.

Building incentives for everyone around the profit you make focuses the whole business around customers and costs, and that has to be good. It will make everyone look for: cheaper ways to do things, ways to eliminate waste; more effective ways to spend their time (and your money); and ways to get more money out of more satisfied customers – in short, all the ways to unlock the profit potential in your business.

EXAMPLE: Medic Aid
Figure 8.1 shows how one participant on a Cranfield Business Growth Programme managed to increase his profit per unit of output. Mark Kirby of Medic Aid, a company that grew from £2 million turnover per annum to over £4.5 million within 18 months of attending the Cranfield programme, took a detailed look at everything they did with a view to increasing the profitability of every hour they worked. Each process was examined and made the subject of a brainstorming session. For example, one part of the manufacturing process of their nebulizer products required several hundred plastic parts to be tipped on to a table. Invariably, 50 or so fell off the table and were either damaged or took valuable seconds to recover. By putting a 3″ high plastic rim around the table, at a cost of £5, the company saved two hours' production time per week. Several hundred simple ideas like this reduced the total production time for one key product by nearly 40%.

The overall effect was quite staggering. At long last Medic Aid managed to grow both profit and sales. Unit profitability, which in the graph in Figure 8.1 is the difference between the sales line and the break-even line, got progressively bigger from December 1989 when the profit improvement programme (PIP) was introduced. By December 1990 the company was making six times as much profit as before.

One final thought on internal sources of finance: do you really need to do everything you do yourself? If you don't you could release all the working capital and fixed capital tied up in that process and use it for better things.

EXAMPLE: Mark Kirby of Medic Aid subcontracted his low value-added production processes to a subcontractor who could actually make them more cheaply. The subcontractor took on the commitment to buy raw material and hold stocks, and Mark used the factory space saved for better things.

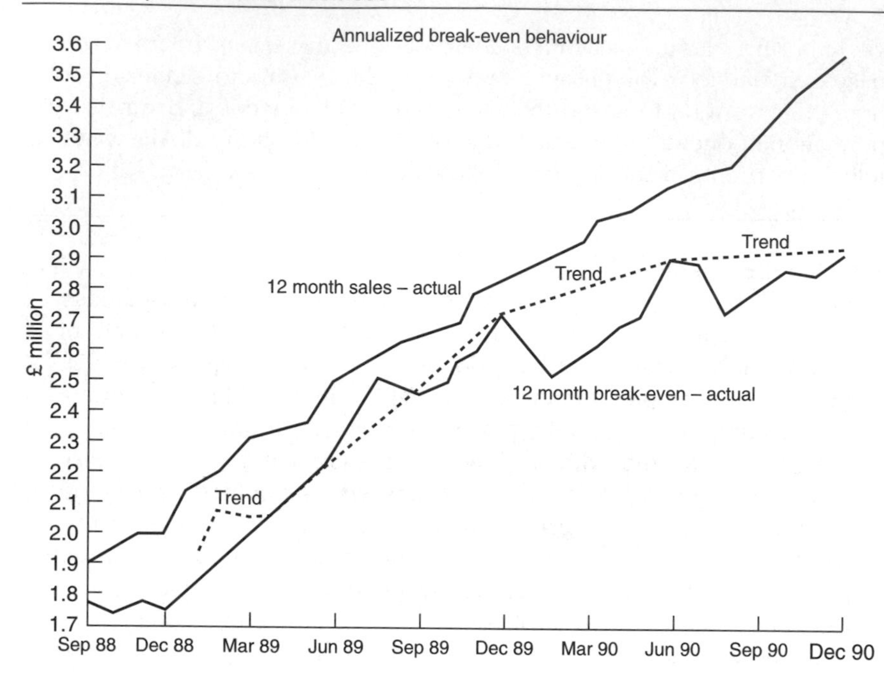

Figure 8.1 Reducing production time and increasing profits, Medic Aid Ltd

Here is another example of how this concept can work successfully.

EXAMPLE: No manufacturing. No salesmen. No research and development. Mrs Tina Knight has grown her company from a £4,000 launch five years ago to a turnover of £2 million a year as much by deciding what not to do as by what she has to sell.

She is managing director of Nighthawk Electronics, based at Debden, Essex. The company supplies switches for computer equipment, the kind of gadget that, for example, allows half a dozen personal computers to use one printer between them.

She says: 'I didn't want to get into manufacturing myself, but I save myself the headaches. Why should I start manufacturing as long as I've got my bottom line right? Turnover is vanity, profit is sanity. I have run companies for other people and I do not have to grow big just for the kudos.' Instead Mrs Knight contracts out to factories in Derby and Bedford. She feels she still has control over quality, since any item that is not up to standard can be sent back. She also has the ultimate threat of taking trade away, which would leave the manufacturers she uses with a large void to fill.

'We would do so if quality was not good enough. Many manufacturers have under-utilized capacity.'

Mrs Knight uses freelance salesmen on a commission basis. She explains: 'I didn't want a huge salesforce. Most sales managers sit in their cars at the side of the road filling in swindle sheets. Research and development is another area where expenses would be terrific. We have freelance design teams working on specific products. We give them a brief and they quote a price. The cost still works out at twice what you expected, but at least you have a measure of control. I could not afford to employ R & D staff full time and I would not need them full time. Our system minimizes the risk and gives us a quality we could not afford as a small company.'

Indirectly, the tight knit staff of 12 at Debden control and provide work for about 380 elsewhere.

EXTERNAL SOURCES OF FUNDS

There are two fundamentally different types of external money which a growing company can tap into: debt and equity. Debt is money borrowed, usually from a bank, and which one day you will have to repay. While you are making use of borrowed money you will also have to pay interest on the loan. Equity is the money put in by shareholders, including the proprietor, and money left in the business by way of retained profit. You don't have to give the shareholders their money back, but they do expect the directors to increase the value of their shares, and if you go public they will probably expect a stream of dividends too. If you don't meet the shareholders' expectations, they won't be there when you need more money – or if they are powerful enough they will take steps to change the board.

Around 1,000 companies a year, out of the total population of 1.5 million, take on equitly finance. The principal sources were covered on pages 78–81. Going Public is covered in Chapter 12.

WHY IS BORROWING ATTRACTIVE?

High gearing is the name given when a business has a high proportion of outside money to inside money. High gearing has considerable attractions to a business which wants to make high returns on shareholders' capital, as the example in Figure 8.2 shows.

In this example the business is assumed to need £60,000 capital to generate £10,000 operating profits. Four different capital structures are considered. They range from all share capital (no gearing) at one end, to nearly all loan capital at the other. The loan capital has to be 'serviced', that

Capital structure		No gearing – £	Average gearing 1:1 £	Average gearing 2:1 £	Average gearing 3:1 £
Share capital		60,000	30,000	20,000	15,000
Loan capital (at 12%)		–	30,000	40,000	45,000
Total capital		60,000	60,000	60,000	60,000
Profits					
Operating-profit		10,000	10,000	10,000	10,000
Less interest on loan		None	3,600	4,800	5,400
Net profit		10,000	6,400	5,200	4,600
Return on share capital	=	10,000 / 60,000	6,400 / 30,000	5,200 / 20,000	4,600 / 15,000
	=	16.6%	21.3%	26%	30.7%
	=	N/A	10,000 / 3,600	10,000 / 4,800	10,000 / 5,400
Times interest earned	=	N/A	2.8X	2.1X	1.9X

Figure 8.2 The effect of gearing on ROSC

is interest of 12% has to be paid. The loan itself can be relatively indefinite, simply being replaced by another one at market interest rates when the first loan expires.

Following the columns through, you can see that ROSC grows from 16.6% to 30.7% by virtue of the changed gearing. If the interest on the loan were lower, the ROSC would be even more improved by high gearing, and the higher the interest the lower the relative improvement in ROSC. So in times of low interest, businesses tend to go for increased borrowings rather than raising more equity, that is money from shareholders.

At first sight this looks like a perpetual profit growth machine. Naturally owners would rather have someone else lend them the money for their business than put it in themselves, if they could increase the return on their investment. The problem comes if the business does not produce £10,000 operating profits. Very often, in a small business, a drop in sales of 20% means profits are halved or even eliminated. If profits were halved in this example, it could not meet the interest payments on its loan. That would make the business insolvent, and so not in a 'sound financial position', in other words, failing to meet one of the two primary business objectives.

Bankers tend to favour 1:1 gearing as the maximum for a small business, although they have been known to go much higher (a glance at the Laker accounts will show just how far the equation can be taken, with £200 million plus of loans to £1 million or so equity). Gearing can be more usefully expressed as the percentage of shareholders' funds (share capital plus reserves), to all the long-term capital in the business. So 1:1 is the same as saying 50% gearing.

All loans from banks take time to set up, attract an arrangement fee and it is generally frowned upon if you go back a few weeks later and ask for more money. The days when you could expect to cultivate a lifetime relationship with either a bank or a bank manager are long gone. Banks are into market segmentation and profit generation, so you need to be prepared to: a) shop around and b) manage your relationship with the bank carefully.

As a rough guide if you are with the same bank for over five years you haven't pushed them hard enough. There are a myriad of things to negotiate with your banker, and there is even a new breed of consultants who advise on banking relationships.

HIRE PURCHASE AND LEASING

Finance houses are the main providers of hire purchase funds. They were first formed in 1890 to supply credit to private traders, mainly colliery owners and coal merchants, to enable them to buy railway wagons to transport their goods. Hire purchase is now used to finance the purchase of most types of business asset and over £8 billion is currently lent in this way. Sixty of the 100 largest UK enterprises and 45% of all small firms are regular users of hire purchase facilities.

Leasing is also a major source of finance for new enterprise, providing over £4 billion a year of funding for everything from aircraft to typewriters. Operating leases are taken out where you plan to use the equipment in question for less than its full economic life – for example, a car, photocopier or vending machine. The lessor takes the risk of the equipment becoming obsolete and assumes responsibility for repairs, maintenance and insurance. As you, the lessee, are paying for this service, it is more expensive than a finance lease where you lease the equipment for most of its economic life and maintain and insure it yourself.

Leases can normally be extended, often for fairly nominal sums, in the later years.

The obvious attractions of leasing are that no deposit is needed, leaving your capital available for use elsewhere in the business. Also, the cost of leasing is known from the outset, making forward planning simpler.

Hire purchase and leasing companies have their own association which can provide details of suitable companies. (Contact: The Finance and Leasing Association, 18 Upper Grosvenor Street, London W1X 9PB. Telephone: 0171 491 2783.)

Long-term lenders, as a general rule, are mainly interested in:

- security and low risk

- 5–15 year horizon
- ability to pay back loan and interest immediately
- conservative growth
- small sums, with frequent top ups
- no share of future profits but a loyal, long-term customer
- no management involvement.

CASH FLOW FINANCING

The problem with both debt and equity as an exclusive source of funds for a growing business lies in the fact that the 'shape' of the money is not ideal.

Selling shares takes a long time to arrange and debt providers tend to frown on companies that return quickly or often for further funds.

Consequently, those seeking these types of funds are requested to bunch their calls for money, while in practice sales growth requires continuous funding.

It follows that using debt and equity only, a growing business can move from feast – where cash is idle and only earning bank interest – to famine – when good business opportunities have to be forgone for lack of funds.

Or more likely these days, the movement is from one level of famine to a worse one! Where cashflow financing comes into its own is where a company needs a continuous surplus of funds promptly provided to finance sales growth (see Figure 8.3).

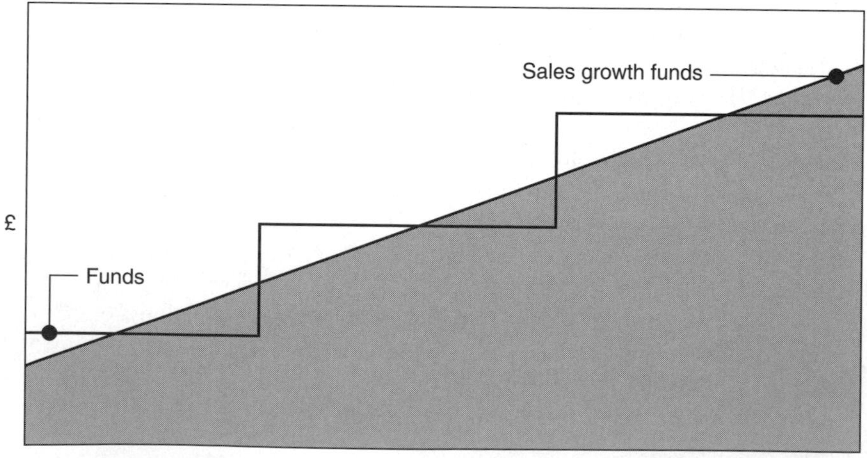

Figure 8.3 Funding growth

OVERDRAFTS

Bank overdrafts are the most common type of short-term finance. More than six out of 10 small businesses rely almost exclusively on an overdraft as their source of external finance. They are relatively simple to arrange; you just talk to your local bank manager. Sums of money can be drawn or repaid within the total amount agreed. They are relatively cheap, with interest paid only on the outstanding daily balance.

The overall limit is agreed usually each year, and you may be asked for an arrangement fee of several hundred pounds. Exceeding the agreed overdraft limit can be very expensive as a fairly punitive interest rate is levied on such 'miscreants'. For example C.H. Engineering Services of Cambridge went into an unauthorized overdraft of £798 in January 1992 which resulted in bank charges of £140 over and above the normal interest.

Of course, interest rates can fluctuate. So what seemed a small sum of money one year can prove crippling if interest rates jump suddenly. Normally you do not repay the 'capital'. You simply renew or alter the overdraft facility from time to time. However, overdrafts are theoretically repayable on demand.

EXAMPLE: Ted Bryant's Surrey and Hants (S&H) Financial Services Company went into liquidation at the beginning of 1991 and he was declared bankrupt on April 2nd 1991. Like many others in the financial services business he lived a high life in the 1980s and then lost it all.

Bryant had an overdraft limit of £100,000, but ran it up to £220,000 to enable him to open new branches. One of those was tied to Colonial Mutual, a life assurance company, which had agreed to clear S&H's overdraft with the bank.

The bank manager was enthusiastic about the deal, and agreed to give Bryant a working overdraft of £50,000 to continue his business. However, the week that Bryant paid in the last cheque to clear the £220,000 overdraft the bank 'pulled the rug' and immediately bounced four cheques and withdrew the £50,000 trading facility which the company had already partly spent.

But even when a bank doesn't actually pull the rug out from under your feet, it can quickly remind you that an overdraft is repayable on demand and subject to constant and sometimes expensive reviews.

EXAMPLE: The Brass Tacks publishing company started up in 1986 and was founded by five directors with about £30,000 of mostly borrowed money and bank lending of £70,000 under the Guaranteed Loans Scheme.

The company's first venture, *The Mortgage Magazine* (now called *What Mortgage*?) soon had sales of £45,000 a month and made a modest profit. Somewhat ambitiously Brass Tacks launched two magazines in its second year of trading and by April 1989 turnover hit £700,000 and profits were encouraging. Against this background the company launched *Stately Home*; the magazine was not a success and with the recession looming Brass Tacks saw its bottom line plummet. The founders held a crisis meeting in April 1990 and made substantial redundancies, shut or sold two titles and offered themselves to all and sundry as contract publishers.

To tide the company over until its new strategies bore fruit, the directors asked their bankers to provide a 40% increase in the overdraft. They were met with a £4,000 bill for a special audit, a 10% cut in facility and a request for personal guarantees. The company's accountants introduced Brass Tacks to another bank which provided the necessary cash, but insisted on personal guarantees. Within 18 months the company was making six figure profits – no thanks to their original bankers.

FACTORING

Factoring in its present form has been widely available for over 30 years (see Figure 8.4). In 1992, members of the Association of British Factors and Discounters, the umbrella organization for the 11 largest companies in the field, provided finance on around £16 billion worth of sales invoices. This represents a sevenfold increase over the last decade. Taking the industry as a whole, turnover grew by 200 times in the 22 years between 1970 and 1992.

At first business had reservations about using factors. Their arguments were usually clustered around the vague feeling that their customers would feel they were in financial trouble, or that they would lose control of the relationship with customers. As with leasing, hire purchase, venture capital and the Unlisted Securities Market, business people were naturally wary of new forms of finance. They wanted to be sure of the downside risk as well as recognizing the more obvious benefits that factoring has to offer in terms of releasing cash flow.

The reasons for these reservations have largely disappeared with the rapid growth of the service and many customers already have suppliers who use factors. It may even be that they are using a factoring service themselves. This broadly based exposure to factoring has done much to inform business people and to arrest their concern.

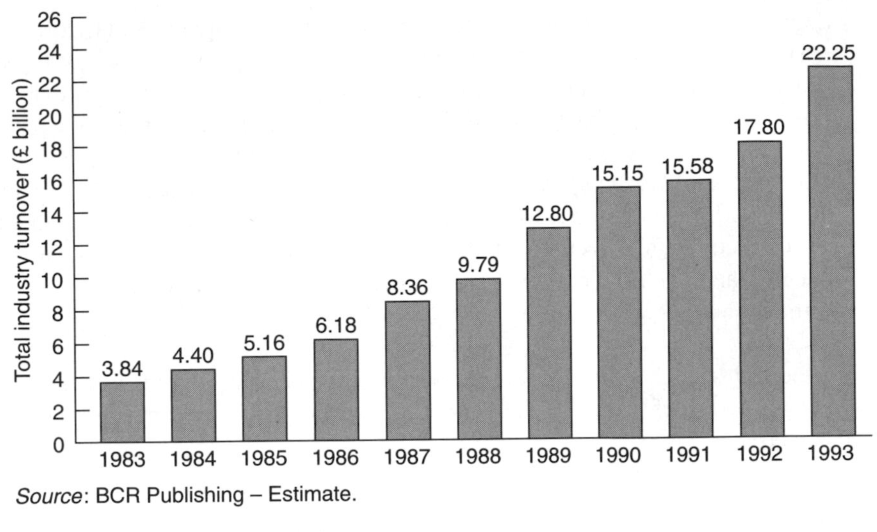

Source: BCR Publishing – Estimate.

Figure 8.4 Factoring's UK rise

Factors provide three related services:

- Immediate finance of up to 80% of the value of the client's invoices, with the balance (minus administration and finance charges) payable after a set period, or when the invoice is paid.
- Taking over a client's sales ledger; sending out invoices and ensuring they are paid.
- Advising on credit risks, and insuring clients against bad debts.

Full service factoring

At the top of the range comes the full service factoring agreement. Here the company issues invoices to its customers in the normal way. Within 48 hours it receives up to 80% of the invoice value from the factor.

The job of running the sales ledger and collecting the money from customers is now in the hands of the factoring company and its dedicated team. Working according to procedures agreed with the client, the factoring company will issue statements and chase up invoices as they become due. Effectively they take on the role of the client's own credit control department. When the money arrives, the factor will process the cheque and forward the proportion of the invoice value not already financed, less a deduction for its charges.

There are two main types of full service factoring agreement: recourse and non-recourse.

- *Recourse Factoring.* Under this type of agreement, the client retains ultimate responsibility (and control) regarding any unpaid debts from its customers. If an invoice remains unpaid after a set period (typically three months after the month of invoice), the factor ceases to provide finance on it and refers it back to the client. However, the factoring company continues to chase the payment on the client's behalf.

- *Non-recourse factoring.* With this arrangement the factor assumes liability for unpaid invoices – but only where they are credit approved. If payment is not received, the factor will automatically send the client the remaining balance at the end of a set period. The clients often pay more for this form of factoring.

For the full service you will pay between 0.5% and 2.5% of turnover and an interest charge of between 2% and 3.5% over base rate on the money advanced.

Export factoring

With export factoring, businesses can be paid up to 80% of the value of exports as soon as the invoice has been raised and the goods shipped. And just as with domestic full-service factoring, the balance is paid once payments from the customers has been received. Payment may be made in sterling or in the currency of the invoice.

Similarly, the factor will look after the client's export sales ledger and collect payments from overseas customers. This is done either direct from the factor's UK offices, or through a correspondent organization in the country concerned. The factor will also be able to provide its client with export credit insurance and credit information on overseas customers.

In its international services, the factoring industry is just as competitive a form of finance as in the domestic market. Finance charges for export factoring are around 3% above bank rate for sterling. Administrative charges, at around 1% to 1.5%, compare favourably with the extra costs for a business of running its own export credit control and sales ledger operation.

Charges for credit insurance vary from country to country, but are typically between 0.5% and 1% of export turnover. In addition to their services for UK exporters, factors also can provide similar services for businesses based overseas and selling into Britain.

Invoice discounting

Invoice discounting is the service for companies who want the cash advance facilities offered by the factor and little else. The service costs range between 0.2% and 0.7% of turnover, much lower than for the full service. The company has to chase up customers for the money and usually assumes responsibility for any bad debts. Invoice discounting is the fastest growing service in the factoring business, accounting for over 60% of all business – up from 20% in 1981.

Confidential invoice discounting

Larger companies with turnover in excess of £1 million and a net worth of typically more than £50,000 can arrange a confidential discounting service. Customers are not informed of the arrangement and send their cheques to the company in the normal way.

So factoring and invoice discounting are on the increase. But exactly what benefits could these services bring your business?

Helps avoid over-trading

Unless you are in a service industry, and you are lucky enough to have your clients pay up front, the faster you get new orders the more cash you consume. You have to pay for raw materials and labour to put products on the market before your customers pay up. If you are not careful the eager pursuit of new business can lead to the cash-flow disaster known as 'over-trading'. By factoring your debts you can get the cash to finance growth as quickly as you can find credit-worthy customers and deliver products or services to them.

Balances cash requirements

The classic source of short-term funds for a small business is an overdraft. Unfortunately, overdrafts seem to be very much a feast-or-famine affair, with facilities being increased when you don't need funds, and the supply restricted sharply when you do.

This paradox is not caused exclusively by the bloody-mindedness of short-sighted bank managers – though that surely must play its part. Rather, the problem arises because overdraft limits are usually determined by using historical balance sheet ratios. Hence bankers are always examining the entrails of the past for guidance, while entrepreneurs are extolling the opportunities for the future.

In situations of rapid growth the banker's advice is often 'consolidate', while the factor will say 'go for it'. The factor is able to respond in this way because he is in daily or weekly contact with his client and sees the flow of invoices and payment cheques, in contrast to the banker who often works from out-of-date audited accounts, and only a hazy recollection of what you do and for whom.

Improves your operating margins

By being able to match the cash available to the level of your business activity you can get two important benefits that should have an immediate

Table 8.3 Cost of extending credit

£000	*Assumed interest rate 10%*			
Debtor days	*30*	*60*	*90*	*120*
250	£2,055	£4,110	£6,164	£8,219
50	£411	£822	£1,233	£1,644
20	£164	£329	£493	£658
1	£8	£16	£25	£33

and positive effect on your operating margins. First, you can negotiate the finest terms from your suppliers – a luxury usually only available to those who can pay up promptly. Otherwise you have to buy what you need, wherever you can, when you can afford it – not a recipe for great economy.

Second, with a predictable cash flow, you can plan production schedules and stockholding in a manufacturing business to optimize plant efficiencies. This is in sharp contrast to those whose cash shortages force them to move labour and materials around in a haphazard way which inevitably results in more down-time, higher unit labour costs and more material wastage.

You can concentrate on what you do best – running the business

Once you start to view your customers simply as debtors, your marketing focus will become blurred. In any event, the chances are that you are better at making and selling than you are at playing policeman chasing up late payers. Factoring allows you to concentrate on what you do best, leaving them to their field – collecting cash.

One company used to take 90 days to collect money from customers. Factoring has reduced this to, on average, 50 days a year. This can result in a very large saving as Table 8.3 shows. Factoring also leaves your salespeople's relationships with customers intact, rather than damaged through constant pestering for payment, and allows them to spend more time on selling which should pay handsome dividends. These figures reflect what you could be paying in interest, in order to offer extended credit to your customers – your debtors.

You can trim overheads

Not only can factoring allow you to spend more time on managing the business rather than the sales ledger, you can save the overhead cost currently incurred in running your own credit control department. One company we know gets a factoring service for £12,000 per annum, less than the cost of employing a credit controller and finding a desk for him to sit at!

Factoring will also allow you to optimize the resources needed to collect cash, rather than using the blitz approach that is common to so many small firms. In other words, the effort put into cash collection is always maintained in proportion to the amount of cash to be collected – a feat near impossible to attain when you run your own credit control. The chances are you will get a more professional service into the bargain when it comes to such matters as assessing credit risk and insuring against bad debts.

Can anyone use a factor?

The popular mythology is that only big manufacturing companies can make use of factoring services. Nothing could be further from the truth. Less than half the users of factoring services provided by members of the Association of British Factors and Discounters, the main trade organisation for the industry, are in manufacturing. Nearly 70% of users have a turnover below £1 million and only 5% have a turnover greater than £5 million.

Nevertheless, it is undoubtedly true that providers of relatively uncomplicated goods, services and raw materials are the most attractive type of client from the factor's point of view. This is simply because invoices in this arena are not usually open to dispute in the same way that more complex plant, equipment and major project invoices are.

When it comes to invoice discounting – where the factor is more exposed to his clients' competence at assessing risk and collecting cash – more stringent criteria apply. Here the factor will be looking for companies with a minimum net worth of around £50,000; turnover in excess of £1 million: goods and services being sold on terms no greater than net 30 days; an efficient sales ledger and credit assessment system in place and a good spread of debtors with no one customer accounting for more than 30% of debts outstanding.

Before being taken on as a customer for invoice discounting you can expect a visit from the factor's auditors to assess your credit control systems and verify debts. They will examine your credit control systems in great detail and on the basis of their findings agree to provide one of three levels of financial facility: all invoices on selected customers, as and when agreed. You can expect your factor to keep in close contact with you thereafter – monthly at least, and weekly, perhaps even daily, at the outset.

(Contact: Association of British Factors and Discounters, 1 Northumberland Avenue, London, WC2N 5BN. Telephone 0171 930 9112.)

OTHER WAYS TO FUND GROWTH

Industry backers

EXAMPLE: Safetynet, is a company that specializes in providing back up computer services for companies whose computer systems are put out of action short term by fire, flood or human error.

Set up five years ago by two former IBM salesmen, the company now has 230 subscribers, of whom only nineteen ever experienced a 'disaster'. The company's turnover is £3 million and pre-tax profits are around £1 million. Their 17 competitors are not doing quite so well. None make any money, according to Safetynet's founders.

Compatibility being all important in the computer business, Safetynet has had to specialize. It is only interested in disasters affecting the medium range IBM machines. The decision to concentrate on this area appears to have been influenced by the knowledge that IBM's AS 400 was going to prove a highly popular machine. There are at least five hundred of them in the City now.

Convinced that they had hit upon a sound proposition, they then had to convince others. Venture capitalists were not enthusiastic but another approach proved more rewarding.

Reasoning that their prime requirement would be equipment, they approached companies in the industry for support. Eventually United Computers provided hardware in exchange for a 14% stake. Bluebird Software, now IBM's largest agency in the mid-range but then a relatively new company which had bought its first computer from Safetynet, agreed to cover all the business's variable costs, and took a 26% stake.

As Safetynet has grown, the founders have been able to buy out their early backers for more than £600,000. The two founders are now the sole owners of the company and seem happy to keep it that way. Talk of a flotation has stopped. 'We feel very cool about going public', says Paul Hearson, founder.

Franchising

Have you ever wondered why Steve Bishko's Tie Rack is surviving in this turbulent economy and Sophie Mirman's Sock Shop has gone to the wall? Both are (or in Mirman's case were) niche retailers; both need small high street locations; both came from Marks and Spencer's and knew all about their product; neither product is essential for survival such as food – indeed, if anything socks seem more essential than ties!

One of the key differences lies in the way these businesses were funded and managed. All the Sock Shop outlets were funded by the company itself and in the last year of its life this was largely provided by the banks. In Tie Rack's case the situation is rather different. One hundred and seven of their

135 outlets are effectively owned by the people who manage them. These franchisee's, as Tie Rack's 'managers' are called, have stumped up at least £60,000 each for the privilege of following the Tie Rack formulae for business success. That is a fairly staggering £7 million of new money which is completely risk and cost free to Tie Rack. For Mirman a similar sum would have cost her £1.25 million a year in interest charges alone – and it probably did as £2 in every £3 in the Sock Shop was put up by the banks.

EXAMPLE: Miles O'Donovan's franchise, Material World (named after the Madonna hit record, Material World), is a good example of how to turn a successful conventional business into a franchise. He is an up-market version of a market stall trader, buying up manufacturers' ends-of-lines and seconds and selling them to an apparently appreciative public. 'It is a very simple business', he says. And he never doubted that it would succeed because, the way he looks at it, it is providing a service at both ends of the equation. Not only is he helping out those people who would love to make their home 'very Sanderson' but currently find themselves strapped for cash; he is also helping out the manufacturers who have to rid themselves of their surplus stock somehow.

This mutually beneficial system is already well established in the clothing business, where disposing of chain store cast offs is the basis of several retail chains. O'Donovan, however, operates with goods from rather further up-market. Much of what he stocks would normally sell at £15 to £20 per metre but he has a blanket price of £7.95 per yard. The fact that he sticks to yards is not just hankering for days gone by, it gives him a 10% price advantage.

O'Donovan woke up one morning about 18 months ago and decided that with nine of his own shops he was about as exposed as he would like to be. Watching Coloroll and Lowndes Queensway sink without trace he decided the time had come to share the risk with others. After a brief flirtation with the idea of venture capital, he plumped for franchising and has never looked back. His new franchisees have helped lift turnover from £1.8 million to £3 million in the present year and his business is now expanding fast both in the UK and Europe. Best of all, he can sleep easy at night with the comfort of knowing his franchisees are as exposed as he is to the consequences of failure, something no Queensway store manager ever was.

Grants

The EC, the government and many local authorities give grants for one purpose or another. Various estimates put the total figure of grant aid available at between half and two billion pounds a year. *Government Funding for UK Business and European Community Funding for Business Development*, Kogan Page, London.

Before you rush off and search for this 'free money' do remember that anyone giving a grant wants you to do something that very often doesn't make much commercial sense. There may be millions available to encourage you to set up your satellite production facility in an area that is currently mainly populated by sheep. The grant may or may not compensate you for being miles from markets and potential employees.

The golden rule is to decide what you want to do and know it makes sound business sense – then see if anyone will pay you to do it.

EXERCISES

1 How much money can you squeeze out of your business by:
   a) greater working capital efficiencies, i.e. getting paid faster, reducing stock holding, etc?
   b) by reducing the amount of fixed assets tied up?
2 How much extra capital is required to fund each 1,000 of growth in sales?
3 So how much new capital is required to meet your growth objectives and which sources of funds would be most appropriate?

SUGGESTED FURTHER READING

Buckland, Roger and Davis, Edward (1995) *Finance for Growing Enterprises*, International Thomson Business Press, London.
A Guide to Financing Growth (1995) The Institute of Directors, London.
Zairi, M. (1996) *Effective Benchmarking*, Chapman & Hall, London.

Part 3

Difficulties in deciding whether to re-invest or to sell the business

While there has been much academic and government attention on the high numbers of start-ups and closures each year in the small business sector, less attention has perhaps been focused on the number of new companies which achieve the ultimate accolade, of 'coming to the market' each year, i.e. achieving a public listing for the stock of their company, producing therefore a reward for both the owners and investors as well as providing the company with access to further fund raising possibilities by issue of new equity shares.

With only 100 or so new companies per annum coming onto the market in the UK in the early 1990s, thus perhaps explaining the lack of academic interest in the area, many more owners chose to arrange 'trade sales' of their businesses as a way of 'harvesting' their efforts, rather than face the costs and responsibilities of a public listing. (Professor Sue Birley, in a research project with Grant Thornton, found that 'the consequences of bringing in outside shareholders was more likely than anything else to keep owner-managers awake at night'.)[1] Robert Wright's Connectair company was a classic example of this early exit route.

EXAMPLE: From first business plan concept in 1982 to first actual operations in early 1984, Connectair started to provide a twice daily flight from Gatwick to Rotterdam, as a feeder service for British Caledonian, thanks to a £200,000 investment mainly from 3I. After first year start-up losses of nearly £200,000, Connectair made tiny operating profits of £47,000 and £67,000 in succeeding years. Further capital investments from external investors followed in 1987/8 to permit second and third airport connection routes to be established. By 1988, founder and former BA pilot Robert Wright, backed by £800,000 venture capital, had achieved his original mission of creating and running a profitable feeder airline employing 60 personnel. He could declare himself 'happier than ever before'. At the height of the Thatcher/Lawson boom he found himself contesting extra route applications with Harry Goodman's Air Europe; following prolonged negotiations, Air Europe, with its fleet of 747s bid £6.25 million for the 6,000 take-off and landing slots belonging to Connectair's 20-seater Bandeirante fleet. Despite his 'happiness' with his company and team, and doubtless encouraged by his outside investors, Robert Wright found this unsolicited increase in value of his still fledgling company irresistible. After five short years of intense and sometimes frantic activity, acting as MD, pilot, steward, etc., the financial rewards for selling, in an industry littered with unsuccessful start-ups, were very great indeed.

Thus Connectair became one of the many successful start-ups which did not 'make it' to the stock market. The additional interesting twist in the Connectair case history was that two years after the 'trade-sale', Air Europe International Leisure Group (ILG) was itself in difficulties with the onset of recession. Robert Wright, once again backed by the now admiring UK venture capital institutions, led by 3I, was able with £2 million venture capital to re-acquire his former airline, now consisting of a fleet of four new ATR42s, a French Italian 48-seater twin turbo prop, plus four Short 360 aircraft. A plan to build turnover from £8 million to £20 million on three commuter routes was quickly put into effect and in 1992 profits of £150,000 on £15 million turnover were achieved, despite the recession. As *The Sunday Times* (13 June 1993) commented, 'City Flyer Express turned in financial results that should make some big operators blush!'

This achievement by Robert Wright and team no doubt explains the large influence his case history has had in influencing the structure of this book! As *The Sunday Times* further commented: 'As both a qualified pilot and an MBA, Robert Wright is very much a rarity in the industry ... his formal business training comes out continually and his message is relevant to any business, big or small: the need for focus, service, cost control, staff motivation and step by step expansion.' To which Robert Wright added, 'we will possibly expand by about a route a year'.

Apart from the fact that value is often in the eye of the beholder (value of 6,000 take off and landing slots was different for the owner of 747s than for the owner of 20-seater Bandeirantes), rather than necessarily on the balance sheet, one of the main learning points from the Connectair case was the importance of Robert's sense of timing, i.e. the ability to sell at the height of the economic cycle and to re-purchase two years later and to re-launch in the midst of the economic recession of the early 1990s. In the property market we are frequently told that location, location, location is all important; too often recently it has been timing,

timing, timing (e.g. London Docklands). Robert's sense of timing of the economic cycle, which certainly influenced his initial 'sell' decision, led us to conclude that in this 'maximizing value' decision stage of small business growth, where strategic planning skills are required, owner managers must regularly determine:

1 What is changing in your business sector environment?
2 Can you successfully change from owner to manager?
3 Can your differentiation and marketing strategy be optimized?
4 Can you withstand the financial pressures?

These key questions constitute for many growth companies a 'strategic planning review', often undertaken annually (e.g. in mid-year), before committing the company to detailed annual operating plans and budgets, usually completed in the autumn for the year ahead. When should you be considering such a review for your company? Perhaps not as infrequently as the following example provides.

EXAMPLE: The Boddington Brewery Group, founded in 1788, appointed a new chairman in 1989, Mr Dennis Cassidy. One of Mr Cassidy's first acts was to organize a two-day 'strategy review' for board members, apparently the first time this had been undertaken in the company's history. The highlight of the review was a presentation showing the remorseless downward trend in UK beer consumption in general since the 1960s, while within that declining market, lager sales had increased their market share against domestically brewed bitters from 4% in 1970 to 50% in 1988. The new chairman's revolutionary advice, feeling that in 10 years time there would be no room for regional brewers, was to sell the brewery and Boddington brand name, therefore giving up 210 years of history, and to re-invest the proceeds in refurbishing the company's network of public houses, hotels and, later, in nursing homes (the latter having had lesser competition and a rising market demand). Those actions over the next few years resulted in a five-fold increase in market capitalization for the company, subsequently realized in the 1995 acquisition by Greenalls.

Suffice it to say, we do not feel that you should have to wait 210 years for your first 'strategy review' of your operations! Companies under five years old, with turnover between £1 million and £2 million, have used the Business Growth Programme at Cranfield and elsewhere to effectively conduct such a review of their businesses. The elements for maximizing business value in such a review, we now examine below.

Notes

1 Birley, Sue (1994) *People in Business*, Grant Thornton, London.

Chapter 9

What is changing in your business sector environment?

In starting and growing a business, the owner-managers' concern in scanning the environment was initially to prove there was a market opportunity for the business and subsequently via customer research to keep products and services in tune with existing and new customers' requirements. As the company matures, and this might be within five years as in the case of Connectair or 'later, the same century' for the 10 or so English companies more than 300 years old (e.g. Tiffin Group PLC, with 'over 300 years of property care'), the need to conduct regular 'environment scans' as part of an annual or occasional strategy review by the company, becomes increasingly important.

EXAMPLE: Richard Nye and his two co-directors in their printing and packaging business had from their earliest days booked a Mayfair hotel for a weekend as soon as they received their annual accounts. Discussion focused on what the company was doing well and not so well; what was changing in their business environment and what their action points focus should be in the next 12 months.

For Robert Wright, after five short years of activity, it was the challenge posed by Air Europe, for their application for two new routes, that led him and his co-directors to take time out to reconsider the direction of their company. Their review focused on the growing airport overcrowding at Gatwick in the late 1980s, leading to CAA limitation in numbers of take off and landing flight slots; major capital re-financing would be needed for Connectair to purchase wide-bodied aircraft to improve their carrying capacity on limited slots. Air Europe already had such aircraft, while Robert feared new capital investment at a time when the economic cycle (1989) appeared set for a downturn. Negotiations for a 'trade-sale' to Air Europe seemed, therefore, appropriate.

PEST ANALYSIS

The purpose of environment analysis for the maturing company is, therefore, to determine what elements are changing in the marketplace which helped give birth to the company in the first place, and what the implications of these changes are for the future growth and direction of the company. One useful format for such scanning, to ensure consistency in approach and in order that no stone is left un-turned, is PEST analysis. For example, for the C.A. Lawrence Group, specialists in placing temporary engineering staff with government and civil contractors, the major environment trends were:

1. *Political.* Growth of privatization and 'compulsory competitive tendering', increasing company downsizing, means more skilled engineers in the marketplace, needing placement assistance.
2. *Economic.* Costs of employment rising, companies move more to 'outsourcing', means increasing opportunities for temporary placement of skilled engineering staff.
3. *Social.* Ending of 'jobs for life' and reductions in job creativity increase opportunities for placement agencies, 'head-hunters' such as C.A. Lawrence.
4. *Technology.* Constant improvements in technology and communications allow employer and employee to become more flexible in working environments.

Given these favourable trends, further recruitment for C.A. Lawrence would facilitate further growth.

SWOT ANALYSIS

PEST Analysis of this type can be usefully combined with SWOT analysis, where the OT (Opportunities and Threats) detected for the company in the environment can be combined with an analysis of the company's own SW (Strengths and Weaknesses).

> EXAMPLE: Autoglass, after five years existence in the early 1980s and with a basic 12-depot network in place, adopted a mid-year strategy review procedure to enable directors and managers to agree priority actions, which could later be translated, with help from accountants, into the following year's budgets. The review centred around a day long meeting of senior management to agree the basic opportunities and threats facing the company (see Table 9.1).

Table 9.1 Summary of Autoglass opportunities and threats analysis

Area	*Opportunities*	*Threats*
Market	Growing steadily at real 3% in line with car population	Slow market growth does not favour rapid expansion
Political	Government favours changing MOT regulations to include windscreen inspection	Entry into EU is encouraging cheaper windscreen imports from France, disrupting our traditional UK suppliers
Technology	Energy crisis encourages motor manufacturers to fit lighter bonded laminated windscreens (fovours specialist fitters)	Switch by motorists to laminated windscreens threatens to make our stocks of toughened windscreens obsolete
Competition	Shows no signs of becoming organized enough to approach insurance companies	Our market share would be threatened if car accessory company (e.g. Kwik-Fit) diversified into windscreens

This was subsequently followed by an analysis of company strengths and weaknesses in internal systems, the core competences of the company, (see Table 9.2), which could thus be addressed in a series of planned actions for incorporation in the following year's budgets (see Table 9.3).

SOURCES OF ANALYSIS

The emphasis throughout these analyses, for the growing company, has to be on pragmatic, realizable assessments. The future cannot be forecast with any great deal of accuracy, and alternative forms of analysis, such as 'scenario analysis' as practised by major companies, such as Shell, require staffing and resources beyond most growing companies' capacities (note that in 'scenario analysis' alternative 'what if' situations are imagined, e.g. oil prices rise or fall 50%–100%, and strategies to deal with such situations are constructed and tested). Many of the key trends affecting growing companies can, nevertheless, be monitored:

1 In politics, approximate election dates and cycles are usually known, political programmes are announced and publicized.
2 In terms of economic forecasts, we are frequently asked 'who can we trust'? One answer is to take an average of the averages, e.g. the second weekly *Economist* of each month, inside last but one page, summarizes all major economic forecasts for the UK and major European countries for

Table 9.2 Summary of Autoglass Strengths and Weaknesses

	Strengths	*Weaknesses*
1 Customers	We have a unique position with UK insurance companies	We are weak in the garage repair sector
2 Product	We provide a unique 24-hour, 7 days a week service to motorists	We lose some customers because answerphone system not alive
3 Place	We have a strong depot representation in South	We are weak in depot representation in North
4 Promotion	Insurance companies give us good coverage to all insured motorists	We do not have representation in all Yellow Pages throughout country
5 Price	Our prices, with our fast service, are competitive with garages	We are a price follower not leader
6 Finance	Our Southern depots are earning a minimum 25% return on assets	Our new start-up depots in the Midlands are losing money
7 Operations	We have well-motivated managers through profit sharing scheme	Employee turnover is high because of irregular hours

Table 9.3 SWOT action plan

SWOT area	*Action*	*Target date*	*Who actions*
SWOT 3 Improve Depot coverage in North of England	Investigate opening two new depots in main population centres, Manchester and Leeds:		PJB/RJB
	• Contact estate agents	Nov. 15	PB/RB
	• Visit suitable sites	Dec. 20	
	• Cost and prepare plans	Jan. 15	
	• Select and train staff	Jan. 30	
	• Open 2 depots	Mar. 1	
SWOT 7 Reduce employee turnover by recruiting YT staff and providing suitable training	Approach Training Centre, Birminghan to:		PS/CB
	• Draw up approved training programme	Oct. 1	
	• Obtain Training Centre approval	Nov. 1	
	• Fit out one depot (Neasden) as training centre; cost and approve	Nov. 30	
	• Recruit suitable applicants	Jan. 30	
	• Post trainees to 2 new Depots	Mar. 1	

the next two years, and provides an 'average' forecast. This should give most businessmen an idea as to where we are in terms of stages in the economic cycle (knowing the direction of the cycle is perhaps more important than the precise growth figure).

3 In terms of social trends and technology, population trends and demographic details are widely available and the technology that will most affect us in the next 10 years has already been invented! Some time and effort, therefore, must be spent to make sure you are aware of the most significant factors likely to impinge on your business and to securing regular updates of this information.

Much of this information can be gathered not simply from published sources (e.g. in business libraries) but also from regular contact with major suppliers and membership of industry associations.

EXAMPLE: One of the major reasons for creating the Dried Flowers Growers Association was to enable market research to be commissioned for members to determine the approximate size of the dried flower market in Europe and annual market growth rates. Equally, market research undertaken and shared by members of the Glass and Glazing Federation in the mid-1980s enabled companies to understand, at last, whether it was the overall market that had slowed down or whether it was the fault of their own managers! Equally, Pilkington Glass made available to Federation members, as a way to build further relations with customers, their views on future economic forecasts and likely impact on the glass and construction industry.

Remember also in these searches for information Professor Porter's Five Force Model, which included research for information not just on competitors, customers and suppliers, but also suggests scanning for possible substitutes for your product (e.g. Perrier water replaces soft and alcoholic drinks) as well as identifying potential new competitors, if barriers to entry to your sector are not significant (which explains, for example, why many trade and industry associations require companies to exist for a minimum of two years before being allowed to join the association!)

REVISIT STRATEGY AND VISION STATEMENT

Having completed these environment analyses, you should be well placed to answer what Strategist Cliff Bowman of Cranfield University has termed 'the five essential questions which determine whether you have a competitive strategy', i.e. do you know:

1 Where you should compete (market segment)?
2 How you can gain sustainable competitive advantage?
3 What competencies and what kind of organization do you require to deliver the strategy?
4 What do you look like now?
5 How can you move from 4 to 3?

In other words, if you know which market segment you are competing in, and could define a clear competitive advantage, you could then define your organization to deliver the strategy. Clearly, the most important of these from a strategy point of view is number 2; are the factors and the strategy still in place that enabled your company to start and grow?

EXAMPLES
For Robert Wright, the early encouragement by British Caledonian and a supportive climate for new entrants had begun to be overshadowed by the late 1980s by increasing competitive pressure on his search for new routes, as his competitors began to take Connectair seriously. The sheer scale of the new investment required in wider bodied aircraft, to build upon his competitive advantage in take-off and landing slots, made him vulnerable to takeover bids.

Autoglass, on the other hand, by the mid-1980s could see that its unique position as the sole windscreen replacement company recommended by major insurance companies needed to be protected by an aggressive programme of new depot openings and employee training. Both of these could be financed by its 'high margin, high quality service' backed by strong internal cash flow.

Re-visiting and re-editing your original mission statement, in the light of your environment analyses and experiences to date, is one clear way to ensure that your competitive strategy is in place and is feasible. Mission statements can and do change and may indeed take many years to develop.

EXAMPLE: Thomas Cook took 25 years from 1841 to 1865 to build an organization of three full-time employees and two offices in Leicester and London. In the next 25 years he built an organization of 1,714 full-time employees and 85 offices around the world! Starting as a jobbing carpenter, taking advantages of new technology (the train) to transport temperance friends to a conference, aided by the Great Exhibition in London, he could announce his mission statement after 21 years as being 'My constant aim has been to render excursion and tourist travel as safe and as pleasant as circumstances would allow.' Once clear in his aim he was able to make the Grand Tour possible for the masses.

As Coulston-Thomas has stated it is the role of the owner-managers and directors 'to provide a vision statement for the company, which defines the distinctive purpose of the company and describes why it exists – or should continue to exist'. At the current time mission or vision statements, when well constructed tend to be accompanied by 'Guiding Principles' or 'value statements', all of which aim to demonstrate how the competitive advantage of the company can be built. For example, management consultants McKinsey's mission reads:

> To help our clients make positive, lasting and substantial improvements in their performance and to build a great firm that is able to attract, develop, excite and retain excellent people.

Attached guiding principles include:

1 *Serving clients*: adhere to professional standards and follow the top management approach.
2 *Building the firm*: show a genuine concern for our people, foster an open and non-hierarchical working atmosphere.

McKinsey is thus still able to recruit the cream of MBA students, focus on major companies and grow as a worldwide firm. Lest this be perceived as simply the latest in a line of American management jargon, one of the newer but fastest growing English housing associations (New Progress HA) has produced and proceeded to justify, both a mission statement and a vision statement.

> MISSION STATEMENT
>
> Using a dedicated and well-trained workforce, New Progress Housing Association is committed to providing a range of affordable housing and associated services to help people with housing related needs to achieve a satisfactory quality of life.
>
> VISION
>
> To be recognized as a market leader in the efficient and effective provision of affordable housing and related services, and to be regarded as a model of excellence in all our dealings with customers and staff.

Renewed mission statements, reaffirming the existence of the firm (or in their absence, the need to find a buyer for the company!) need then to be accompanied by specific and measurable objectives and most importantly the people, marketing and financial strategies that will make them achievable, as we will examine in the following chapters.

EXERCISES

1 Complete a PEST analysis for your company's business sector. What are the key factors you need to regularly monitor?
2 Complete a SWOT analysis for your company. What are your key action priorities?
3 In which market sector are you competing?
4 In what way does your company have sustainable competitive advantage?
5 Do you have the right competencies to deliver your strategy? What are you lacking?
6 Revisit your original mission statement. In what way should it be re-written to reflect your current market strategy?

NOTES

1 Birley, Sue (1994) *People in Business*, Grant Thornton, London.

SUGGESTED FURTHER READING

Bowman, Cliff with Faulkner, D. (1994) Measuring product advantage using competitive benchmarking and customer perception, *Longe Range Planning*, **27**, (1), 119–32.

Coulston-Thomas, Colin (1993) *Creating Excellence in Boardrooms*, McGraw-Hill, New York.

Ingle, Robert (1991) *Thomas Cook of Leicester*, Headstart History.

Chapter 10

Can you change from owner to manager?

Essentially the personal decision on whether to stay with your own business and re-invest in its success revolves around these issues.

Can you make the transition from owner to manager – not an easy metamorphosis and one that most entrepreneurs either cannot or will not make?

Can you stand the financial heat? By the time you reach this stage in your company's development, your stake in the business will be considerable and getting out may be your only way to realize any capital in your lifetime.

In this chapter we will look at the management issues only. The financial issues will be examined in Chapter 12.

HOW MUCH MANAGEMENT DOES YOUR BUSINESS NEED?

Most large organizations today have grown up according to basic management principles. If you started your business career working for a bigger firm, or your present managers have worked in such enterprises, you will know the scenario. Managers in these organizations plan, organize and control in a way that produces consistent, if unexciting results. It is a formula that worked remarkably well for much of the twentieth century when all a successful company had to do to prosper was more of the same.

But management, which is all about maintaining order and predictability is ill-equipped to deal with change, which is the order of the day for the 1990s. To cope with it effectively you need to be a leader as well as a competent manager. Leadership and management are not the same thing, although many business people fail to make the distinction. A professor at the University of Southern California summed up the difference between leaders and managers thus: 'A leader challenges the status quo; a manager accepts it.'

Peter Drucker says that the first task of a leader is to define a company's mission. In a world where product life-cycles are shrinking, new technologies have an ever-shorter shelf-life and customers demand faster delivery and higher quality, this increasingly means defining and inspiring change within a company. By setting a company's direction, communicating this to its work force, motivating employees and taking a long-range perspective, a leader adapts the firm to whatever volatile environment it does business in. In short the leader becomes the change master in his own firm.

There are certain attributes you need to lead a growing business:

- *High energy levels and drive* – to overcome the inevitable setbacks and be able to work long hours.
- *High intelligence* – required to cut through complex information and get to the root of problems.
- *Good mental and emotional health* – which allows leaders to sustain good interpersonal skills.
- *Honesty* – managing people requires long term trust which can only be built up through honesty and integrity.

These personal characteristics sound very ordinary. But remarkably few people apparently possess all four, maybe one in 50. Still, that means that there are plenty of people around with the potential to lead a larger organization than the one they currently run.

Your business will need different amounts of leadership and management at different stages in its life and when the environment around you becomes more (or less) turbulent.

Use the matrix in Figure 10.1 as a guide to deciding how much leadership and management you need now. The vertical axis shows how much change your company 'needs' at present. This change can be either caused by external factors such as your competitors, customers, or the economic climate; or it can be self-imposed because you want to change from running a low growth to a high growth business. The horizontal axis is the complexity of your business. It can be complex because of its size, for example, the number of products or services offered or the number of locations in which business is carried out.

The top left-hand box is the typical profile for a start-up business. Here, the business is relatively simple, but the change required to create something from nothing is enormous. Leadership is the key skill needed and by definition there is little to manage at this stage. If the business grows very slowly and stays very simple doing much the same as when it started, only more so, then it will never need very much leadership or management. The firm will evolve and tick over until it is overcome by a calamity or its profits decline to the point where it would be more profitable to do something else. Edgar Watts, a firm making willow clefts for cricket bats since 1840, are a good example of this.

The company, one of only three in its field, announced its closure in July 1990, making seven staff redundant. Asked why the firm was to close, Toby Watts, 61, the third generation of the family to run the business said: 'scarcity of good willows caused by the 1987 hurricane'. But it is hard to

Amount of change needed (due to environmental instability, rapid growth, etc.)		Low complexity	High complexity
	High	Considerable leadership but not much management required (start up business)	Considerable leadership and management required (most big businesses and other organizations today)
	Low	Little management or leadership required (most very small businesses)	Considerable management but little leadership required (many successful corporations until lately)

Low — High: The complexity of the operation (due to size, technology, geographical dispersion, the number of products or services, etc.)

Figure 10.1 The leadership/management matrix

believe this is either the only or the principal reason for the firm's demise. Mr Watts did admit in a subsequent interview that: 'If I was 20 years younger, and prepared to spend five days a week on the road searching for the right trees we might have been able to save the business.'

However, if after three generations the firm still employed only seven people making the same product in a very stable environment, there was clearly neither the desire for growth nor the need for complexity. The company just had to wait long enough before it was overtaken by events.

More complex businesses which operate in relatively stable environments can usually prosper with lots of management and very little leadership. The problem here is that it is becoming increasingly difficult to locate friendly backwaters that will support a sizeable firm. These firms need to be sure-footed enough to inject sizeable quantities of leadership when the environment becomes unstable, or they too will be swept away.

ICL up to the early 1980s is a good example of a company that was over-managed and under-led. Its main customer, the government, was determined it should stay in business. This created an artificial backwater in the turbulent computer world for ICL, an over-complex company, to survive in. Margaret Thatcher's attitude to government purchasing threw ICL's management into the competitive arena, where leadership was more important than management. Fortunately, a strong leader emerged and the company just survived.

If you want to achieve rapid growth and not unnaturally expect to have to do different things to achieve that growth, your business will need management and leadership in depth. The myth of the solitary hero leader attached to popular entrepreneurs of the last decade has largely been exploded. An army in peace-time needs good leadership at the top and good management below. In war-time it needs competent leadership at all levels.

The business world today is undoubtedly at war and clever companies must learn how to find and recruit people with both leadership and management potential – small firms cannot afford leaders and managers so the skills must often be combined in one person. Decide from the leadership attributes given above which of your managers have leadership potential, and give those that have it challenging assignments as quickly as you can. This will stretch them and allow them to grow. Keep them in each job for a reasonable amount of time so they can learn from both success and failure. Don't make the mistake of promoting too rapidly – this means people are not around long enough to see the impact of their actions and encourages that scourge of strategic thinking, short termism.

Move your potential leader/managers sideways as well as upwards. Assignments which broaden their base allow people to build relationships across the whole business and encourage them to develop the full range of interpersonal skills and empathy needed to motivate the whole business, not just the part they are currently responsible for.

WHAT KIND OF LEADER ARE YOU?

Are you a 'hero' or a 'meddler'? The dividing line might be thinner than you think according to research being carried out at the Cranfield School of Management. And your answer may reveal whether your company will grow or stagnate. Cranfield has been studying the behaviour of owner-managers and their relationship with key staff in some 200 growing UK companies. They have concluded that owner-managers can be clustered into four dominant types of relationship with their staff; heros, meddlers, artisans, or most desirably, strategists. Strategists give their managers the tools to do the job and let them get on with running today's business, while they plan for the future.

This present research project follows on from an earlier study which uncovered the alarming fact that 60% of senior staff in small firms leave within two years of their appointment. Poor recruitment is one of the reasons for these premature departures – half of all key staff in small firms are recruited via personal contacts, a notoriously variable method at the best of times. But unsatisfactory relationships between key staff and the owner/managers of the business is another important reason.

The researchers studied two key elements of this relationship. First, how much time the owner-manager spent at marketing, selling, analysing figures, reviewing budgets or arbitrating between senior staff. On average, with the exception of the group of entrepreneurs who were still preoccupied with basic non-management functions such as delivering their

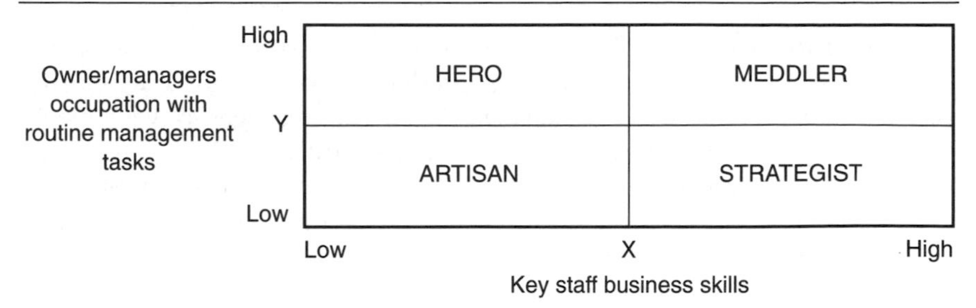

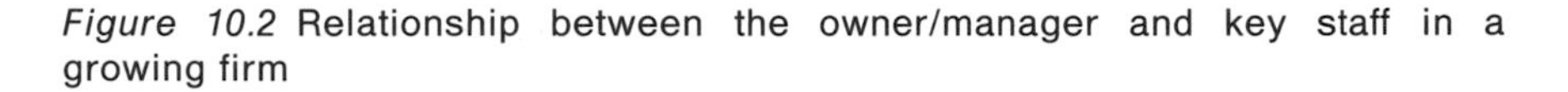
Figure 10.2 Relationship between the owner/manager and key staff in a growing firm

service or making their product, e.g. architects, small builders, retailers, etc., over 85% of the entrepreneur's working day was spent on these routine management tasks.

The owner's behaviour can be more easily understood by showing this graphically, as set out in Figure 10.2. A low score on the 'y' axis indicates either that most time is spent on basic non-management functions, or that most time is spent on strategic issues such as new product or market development, improving market share, acquisitions and divestments or diversification. A high score indicates that the owner-manager is still largely pre-occupied with routine management tasks.

The second element examines what level of business skills has been attained by key staff and this is plotted on the 'x' axis of the graph. Here a low score would be where most of the management team were relatively new to their tasks or largely untrained for their current job. An example (true, believe it or not) of this would be an unqualified book-keeper trying to produce the management accounts for a £5 million business. A high score would be where people were mostly either specifically qualified or trained for their current job. If, for instance, we had replaced the unqualified book-keeper with a fully qualified accountant.

Types

The artisan

The artisan in the Cranfield model is typified by low occupation with routine management tasks, because most time is spent producing a product or delivering a service. Every hour that can be sold, is sold and little time is left over to improve the quality or profitability of today's business or to consider strategy for tomorrow.

The level of business skills in the company are also low as most of the artisan's staff are employed helping on 'production' or carrying out primary tasks such as book-keeping or selling. The owner-manager is very much 'one of the boys' still. Artisans can encompass professional firms such as architects and surveyors, manufacturers, sub-contractors or small building firms; owners of small retail chains such as chemists, video stores and proprietors of hotels and restaurants.

The artisan has low growth prospects, relative to his market. Training and development is needed to raise awareness of the importance of management as a business task of equal importance with daily revenue earning.

The hero

The hero by contrast probably heads up one management function such as sales or production. But if, for example, the hero heads up sales he/she will do little selling except for handling some key accounts. Time is now spent on managing the business. As the level of business skill among employees is still relatively low, such a hero will take the lead initiating routine management procedures. Typically he/she will read up or attend one-off courses on topics such as Value Added Tax, accounting business ratios, market segmentation, sales management and staff appraisal systems. He/she will introduce them to the firm, and be the only person who really understands them. To a managerially illiterate team he/she will consequently be seen as a hero.

Unfortunately the hero has a Herculean task on his or her hands. Shedding the day-to-day tasks is relatively simple as working skills in most businesses are either readily available in the local community, or people can be trained up via YTS or other on-the-job schemes. But passing out routine management tasks will almost invariably require the owner-managers to train up their own management team.

There are relatively few well-trained managers available to the small company, for two main reasons. First, the overall pool of such people is small as training in the small business sector has, until recently, been almost exclusively concentrated on the entrepreneur. Second, well-trained managers usually seek jobs in larger firms with more opportunities for advancement and more resources to practise the 'art of management'. The hero has a high capacity for improving the performance of the firm but still has low growth prospects relative to his market. There is no time for strategic thinking and no depth of management to handle growth effectively.

The need is for training and development to help raise the general level of management skills in the business, while at the same time increasing his/her own grasp of motivation, leadership, organization design and development and of strategic management issues in general. If the hero fails to do this, as many do, the hero becomes a meddler.

The meddler

The meddler raises the firm's level of management skill either by training or recruitment, but then fails to let go of routine management tasks. At this stage, the owner-manager probably has no functional responsibilities and has assumed the role of managing director. Typically, much time is spent second-guessing subordinates, introducing more refined (but often unnecessary) management systems. The meddler also goes on courses or reads books that make him/her even more knowledgeable, but sometimes better at routine management tasks than subordinates, who anyway are doing a perfectly satisfactory job of managing today's business. He/she gets in early, and leaves late and practises 'management by walking about'.

The meddler's problem is he/she has been used to a 70–90 hour week, with only 10 days holiday each year and is scared his day will feel empty if he relinquishes responsibility. Once the management team is in place and trained, he/she is out of a job. Until involvement with routine management tasks is reduced, the meddler will limit the growth capacity of the firm for two reasons. First, the management team won't take on more responsibility if the reward for taking on the last lot was being nagged and criticized. Second, he/she is too busy checking on people to develop sound strategies for growth.

The strategist

The strategist is the best type of entrepreneur to develop a growing business. The management skills of the team are developed to the highest appropriate level and depth. He/she may introduce staff to help line managers in such areas as personnel and market research. This will free-up key managers to think strategically too.

He/she will devote roughly a third of working time to management tasks such as monitoring performance, co-ordinating activities, resolving conflict, and helping manage today's business. Another third of time will be spent developing strategic thinking to form the shape of the future business. The strategist's training needs are to update constantly the core leadership and motivation skills to increase depth of knowledge on strategic issues, acquisition/divestment activity, financing sources and the City.

The natural path of development for the relationship between owner-manager and the team is to progress from artisan to hero and, if possible, to strategist (hopefully by-passing meddler), so that energies can be directed to making 'new business for a new tomorrow', to borrow Peter Drucker's phrase.

GROWING INTO LEADERSHIP

To grow into the leadership role requires a fundamental shift in attitudes for many owner-managers. One of the most profound of these shifts lies in appreciating why people work at all. Most owner-managers – indeed most managers for that matter – believe that people work largely for money. However most of the research shows money ranking third or even fourth in order of importance as to why people work.

Theory 'x' and theory 'y'

These theories were developed by Douglas McGregor, an American social psychologist, to try to explain the assumptions about human behaviour which underlie managerial action.

Theory 'x'

1 The average human being has an inherent dislike of work and will avoid it if possible. So management needs to stress productivity, incentive schemes and a 'fair day's work'; and to denounce 'restriction of output'.
2 Because of this human characteristic of dislike of work, most people must be coerced, controlled, directed, threatened with punishment to get them to put forth adequate effort toward the achievement of organization objectives.
3 The average human being prefers to be directed, wishes to avoid responsibility, has relatively little ambition, wants security above all.

Theory 'x' has persisted for a long time, because it has undoubtedly provided an explanation for some human behaviour in organizations. There are, however, many readily observable facts and a growing body of research findings which cannot be explained on these assumptions. McGregor proposes an alternative.

Theory 'y'

1 The expenditure of physical and mental effort in work is 'as natural as play or rest'. The ordinary person does not inherently dislike work: according to the conditions it may be a source of satisfaction or punishment.
2 External control is not the only means for obtaining effort. Man will exercise self-direction and self-control in the service of objectives to which he is committed.
3 The most significant reward that can be offered in order to obtain commitment is the satisfaction of the individual's personal business needs. This can be a direct product of effort directed towards organizational objectives.
4 The average human being learns, under proper conditions, not only to accept but to seek responsibility.

5 Many more people are able to contribute creatively to the solution of organizational problems than do so.
6 At present the potential of the average person is not being fully used.

Delegation – a remedy for overwork

Overwork is a common complaint of the small business owner. Too much hard work and never enough hours in the day to do it. However, it is a problem that could easily be remedied by some effective delegation.

Delegation is simply the art of getting things done through other people. And if you show any of the following symptoms you should consider building delegating into the management of your business. Do you:

- have problems with deadlines for jobs that you do?
- have to work late regularly?
- take work home regularly?
- avoid accepting help with jobs?
- devote a lot of your time to details rather than planning and managing?
- feel insufficiently confident about your employees' ability to take on greater responsibility?

Delegation will help to keep the work flowing smoothly and so prevent a pile-up on your desk which is both stress-inducing and counter-productive.

Fear of delegation

Most owner-managers are proud of the fact that they have built up their own companies from nothing. In the beginning, entrepreneurs often perform all the tasks of running the business. Reasonable enough, but as the operation grows they may have to hang on to too many jobs. They may believe that nobody else can do the job, and conversely it is just possible they may fear being shown up. It is also possible that through pressure of work or else the gradual nature of the expansion they simply have not reviewed the day-to-day management of their time.

Another reason for small business owners not delegating is that sometimes the routine is preferable to the difficult. Writing invoices is easier than preparing the new cash flow for the bank!

What has to be recognized is that when you delegate, both you and your employees grow. The work gets done and your employees get a chance to broaden their skills. Through delegation you can ease your job of managing and thereby increase the effectiveness of both yourself and your workers – and thus your organization.

Benefits for you

1 *Allows time to achieve more.* An owner-manager who can delegate effectively is likely to achieve greater output. Through the proper selection, assignment and co-ordination of tasks, a manager can mobilize resources to achieve more results than would have been possible without skilful delegation.
2 *Allows time for managerial activities.* Delegation allows the owner-manager an opportunity to handle aspects of the job that no one else can do – project planning, plans for developing the business, monitoring how the business is doing, monitoring staff performance and dealing with any problems arising.
3 *Provides you with back-up.* By delegating responsibility in different areas you will create a back-up workforce who can take over in times of emergency.

Benefits for employees

1 *Develops employees' skills.* Owner-managers who fail to delegate effectively deprive employees of opportunities to improve their skills and assume greater responsibility. Since employees are likely to realize that they are not learning and gaining experience, they may well leave your firm in order to find a more challenging and supportive environment. This happens most frequently with those employees who are most talented – precisely the people that you least want to lose. What is a routine job for you is often a growth opportunity for an employee.
2 *Increases employee involvement.* Proper delegation encourages employees to participate more in understanding and influencing their work. By increasing their involvement in the workplace you will also increase their enthusiasm and initiative for their work.

Benefits for your organization

1 *Maximizes efficient output* – by making the best use of available human resource so as to achieve the highest possible rate of productivity. It also provides the right environment for employees to offer new ideas that can improve the flow and operation of the workplace.
2 *Produces faster and more effective decisions* – since an organization is most responsive to changes in the environment when individuals closest to the problems are making the decisions about resolving those problems.
3 *Increases flexibility of operations* – effective delegation trains several people to perform the same tasks. As a result, when someone is absent or when a crisis requires others to assist with functions not regularly a

part of their job, several individuals will already be familiar with the assignment.

Delegation prepares more people for promotion or rotation of responsibilities. It also eases your job of finding someone to supervise when you are absent.

Your five-point plan

1 *Decide what and what not to delegate.* The general guidelines for deciding what should be delegated are:
- the work can be handled adequately by your workers;
- all necessary information for decision making is available to the worker being delegated the task;
- the task involves operational detail rather than planning or organization;
- the task does not require skills unique to the owner's position;
- an individual other than you has, or can have, direct control over the task.

Therefore any routine jobs, or information collection or assignment involving extensive details such as making calculations, etc., are things that can be delegated.

Tasks that should not be delegated include the delegation process itself, employee evaluation and discipline, planning and forecasting, confidential tasks, complex situations and sensitive situations.

2 *Decide to whom to delegate.* Obviously your ability to delegate will be governed by the size and quality of your workforce at any given time. However, three factors are of primary importance when selecting the right person for an assignment: (a) an employee's skills; (b) an employee's interest; (c) an employee's workload.

3 *Communicate your decision.* Describe what it is you are delegating and give the other person enough information to carry out the task. Presenting the directive in writing will prevent the 'I didn't know' syndrome. If a gap exists between the assignment and an employee's skills you must be very clear and concise in describing the steps of the task. Bear in mind that a new assignment, particularly one involving several stages, is unlikely to be completely understood on the first explanation. Make yourself available for further clarification as the employee works through the assignment. Closely monitoring the employee will save time in the long run.

4 *Manage and evaluate.* From the beginning clearly establish set times when you will meet with the person to review their performance. The secret of delegation is to follow up.

5 *Reward.* Results that are recognized get repeated. You must monitor and respond to the person's performance. Otherwise it's like playing a game without score, which in the end is not motivating.

Part of the essence of delegation is thoughtfully judging when a new employee is ready to handle a more stimulating assignment. If necessary delegate in stages, starting with small tasks and working up to more challenging projects.

Of course, the one thing you can never delegate is accountability. No matter which employee handles the task, as the business owner it is your reputation that is on the line.

Delegation is a form of risk-taking. If you can't deal with a few mistakes you will never be able to delegate. Nevertheless, effective delegation which is carefully planned and well executed will result in a freeing-up of your time and a more efficient and more profitable business.

MOTIVATION

Professor Frederick Hertzberg, an American professor of psychology, discovered that distinctly separate factors were the cause of job satisfaction and job dissatisfaction. His study of 200 engineers and accountants showed that five factors stood out as strong determinants of job satisfaction: achievement, recognition, responsibility, advancement and of course the attractiveness of the work itself.

When the reasons for dissatisfaction were analysed they were found to be concerned with a different range of factors: company policy, supervision, administration, salary, working conditions and interpersonal relations. Hertzberg called these causes of dissatisfaction 'hygiene factors', reasoning that the lack of hygiene will cause disease, but the presence of hygienic conditions will not, of itself, produce health.[1]

So lack of adequate 'job hygiene' will cause dissatisfaction, but its presence will not itself cause satisfaction. It is the 'motivators', such as recognition, responsibility, achievement, etc., which cause satisfaction. Both hygiene and motivator factors must be considered if you are to be successful at the art of effective management.

Having got the right people to implement your strategy, the problem is to keep them. If morale and levels of job satisfaction are low, then performance will suffer, the team will be affected and often people (usually those you want to keep!) will leave. Holcot Press is a service business, Richard Meredith, its managing director, says 'Keeping people and good morale is crucial to our business'.

One of the biggest mistakes you can make is the assumption that money alone is the only way to motivate staff. See Figure 10.3 which gives a graphic example of how minor is the motivating effect of a salary increase by itself.

In fact, it is not so much the amount of money awarded that is important – expectation is all. The 'S'-shaped curve shows that the effect of a salary increase on job satisfaction and, therefore, performance, depends on what you expected. Thus, if you expected a salary increase of £2,000 and this is

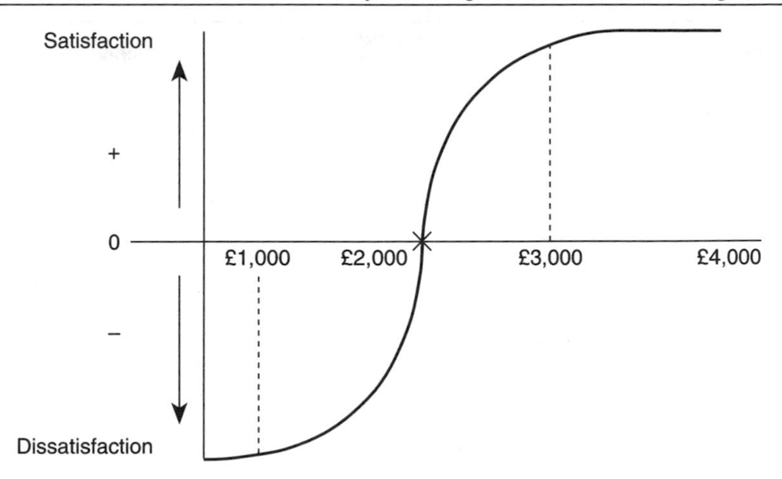

Figure 10.3 The effect of a salary increase on job satisfaction

what you got, then the effect is zero. If you expected an increase of £2,000 and were given £3,000, then your job satisfaction will increase. You will have a warm glow but the feeling soon tails off! Similarly, if you expect £2,000 and are given £1,000, you'll actively be demotivated!

Maslow's famous hierarchy of needs shows just how many other factors are involved in job satisfaction, from physiological, through security and social needs to the needs for self-esteem and self-actualization. In fact, the problem is not so much that of motivating people, but of avoiding demotivating them! If managers can keep off the back of employees, it is quite possible that they will motivate themselves. After all, as Hertzberg established years ago in his interviews at Pittsburg Iron and Steel, most of us want the same things: a sense of achievement or challenges, recognition of our efforts, an interesting and varied job, opportunities for responsibility, advancement and job growth.

You can gain a lot of mileage by arranging the context so that people can find more motivators in the jobs they do. You will also keep them longer and they will be more likely to empower the business change you are seeking.

There are some key measures which you can use to benchmark the morale of your people. They are:

- monitor labour turnover regularly
- carry out exit interviews
- survey levels of job satisfaction.

When ICL was trying to stay alive in 1983/84 the annual labour turnover of the Reading Division was 25%. This was against a Thames Valley 'norm' of around 12%. A clear signal of low morale! When anyone leaves, it is a

Question	Rating* 0...5...10	Comment
1 How would you assess your morale right now? Please explain why.		
2 What action would help to move your score up and increase your job satisfaction?	Comment only	
3 How well does the management team manage?		
4 How effective are our internal communications up, down and across? What improvements would you suggest?		
5 How clear are you about what is expected of you (targets, etc.)?		
6 How adequately are you rewarded and recognized for good performance?		
7 How well does the appraisal process work? Any recommendations?		
8 How fully are we using all your talents? How could we do better?		
9 What do you most like about working for this business? (What's special about us?)	Comment only	
10 To what extent do you feel part of the total team? How could we involve you more?		

*Rating: 0 = very poor; 5 = average; 10 = excellent

Figure 10.4 Some ideas on a simple attitude survey (to use as an annual benchmark)

good idea to get a reliable and trusted member of staff to carry out an 'exit' interview. In this way you can discover the real reasons people are leaving and identify sources of internal dissatisfaction. If, every year or every two years, you carry out a simple internal survey of staff attitudes you will be able to pinpoint problem areas in the parts of your business which you

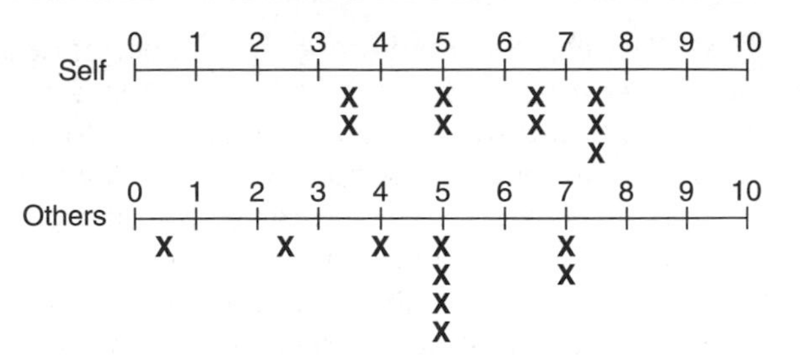

Figure 10.5 The morale of Holcot Press Management Team and their subordinates in 1990

can't reach. (See Figure 10.4 for a sample survey questionnaire.) Even a simple 0–10 scale will give valuable information.

For example, Holcot Press management team defined the morale of those under them on a simple scale, reproduced in Figure 10.5. The difference in rating indicates the work they had to do in 1990 to bring the motivation of all employees up to the level of the management team.

APPRAISAL

Appraisal lies at the heart of assessing, improving and developing people's performance for the future of the business. However, to be an effective tool, appraisal needs to be approached seriously and professionally by all involved.

> EXAMPLE: Two years ago, Innovex, which provides marketing services to the pharmaceutical industry, had a fairly half-hearted appraisal system. Not all managers carried out appraisals, some interviews only took half an hour or so, assessment of areas for improvement was distinctly lacking, there were no clear objectives, people were assessed against personality characteristics (such as 'common sense') rather than results. Yet the great issue for Innovex is the lack of depth of management resource. This could easily become a limitation on its phenomenal growth rate. There are no obvious successors and managers are already 100% stretched in their current jobs. The requirement is 'to grow people to run businesses in the UK and Europe'. There are some significant gaps between the management 'animal' of today and the one Innovex will need for the future. As Barrie Haigh Chairman of Innovex plc says 'The key is to look hard at our people, look hard and develop'. The mechanism for doing this is appraisal.

Innovex has put all its managers and secretaries through appraisal interview training (video) and has taken a good look at its appraisal system and re-vamped it along the following lines:

- Appraisal as a 'talk between people who work together'.
- Open two-way discussion, both appraiser and the person being appraised prepare for the interview in advance.
- Results orientated rather than personality orientated. The appraisal interview starts with a review against objectives and finishes by setting objectives for the year to come.
- The appraisal 'format' is a narrative rather than tick boxes and ratings. It covers a discussion of achievements, areas for improvement, overall performance, training and development and career expectations.
- Plenty of time is allowed for each appraisal interview (one and a half hours on average).
- Appraisals are once a year with more regular quarterly reviews.
- Training needs are identified and acted upon by those concerned.

Recognition and rewards

As businesses grow it is common to find that rewards are encouraging the performance you need now. Different stages of growth demand different reward packages, from the hands-on commission-based sales linked rewards of an infant business, through the cost and budget management of an adolescent into the challenges of giving the whole management team a share of the future which comes as a business matures.

As the business climbs the Greiner (1972) curve it is likely that the recognition and reward package will need to be slanted to:

a) encourage genuine 'ownership' of and commitment to the business (share options?);
b) provide some element of reward for team performance as well as individual success;
c) demonstrate a direct relationship to performance.

EXAMPLE: Richer Sounds, a small specialist hi-fi chain, gets most of its best ideas from its own staff. A discount scheme which boosted sales of cassette tapes tenfold; a bell at waist height to allow disabled customers to ring for attention; a policy of telephoning customers to check that they were satisfied with its repair service. All were proposals made by Richer's 70-plus employees through the company suggestion scheme.

To encourage staff to come up with the ideas Julian Richer, founder of the £12 million a year turnover company, funds a monthly brain-storming session in local pubs for the teams of employees from each of his 12 stores. As an additional incentive the number of suggestions also counts towards a monthly competition for most highly rated score.

Richer, who devotes considerable time to his company's Business Planning for Growth programme, spends one week in two at his Yorkshire mansion headquarters. On his regular train journey north, Richer scrutinizes the 80 or so suggestion cards that come in each fortnight and scribbles a comment on each one. 'The suggestions have to be seen by someone that staff will want to impress, not by a committee. You have to reply to them quickly – I do it within 14 days – and the good suggestions have to be used. I hit the department involved with the suggestion and make it happen.'

Richer also takes the view that all suggestions must be rewarded, although many companies only pay for suggestions which are adopted. The simpler suggestions made by Richer's staff win between £5 and £25 while the people who make the best two suggestions each quarter win a gold badge (another part of the company's incentive scheme) and a trip on the Orient Express.

Once regarded as only being appropriate in large manufacturing companies, suggestion schemes have increasingly found favour in white-collar organizations like banks and building societies, and in small firms such as Richer Sound. And while large organizations such as British Airways and the Inland Revenue run successful schemes, some privately owned businesses and small divisions of large companies have also found them to be of value.

Jean Balcombe, co-ordinator of the Industrial Society's suggestion scheme campaign, estimates that between 400 and 500 schemes are in operation in Britain. The UK Association of Suggestion Schemes (UKASS), founded in 1987, has just over 100 members, although Andrew Wood, chairman, expects more companies to join.

The most recent survey of suggestion schemes, carried out by the Industrial Society showed that the 103 schemes identified had received more than 73,400 suggestions or five for every 100 employees. Just over 16,000 suggestions were adopted, a success rate of 22%. Savings worth £18 million were achieved in 1991 by the Rover Group alone. Employees' proposals during 1991 cut production costs by £7 million. Another £11 million was saved by suggestions implemented in previous years, said Rover. The £18 million is considered one of the best totals in industry, although the United Kingdom

Association of Suggestion Schemes estimates more than £1 billion could be achieved if every firm matched the Japanese and secured an average of 32 staff contributions a year.

The suggestion schemes currently in operation save UK firms an average of £265,000 per scheme.

Six rules for success

1 New suggestion schemes must be carefully planned and provided with the resources and management backing to sustain them over the long term. There are a lot of dead schemes around, they die very quickly if they are not properly run.

Several schemes running when the Industrial Society carried out its 1988 survey have since folded. Angus Modelmakers, a Glasgow company employing 27 people, said it dropped its scheme a year ago because of 'patchy response'. Interox Chemicals, part of the Laporte group, said its suggestion scheme was 'in abeyance' after the flow of suggestions dried up two years ago.

2 They require constant promotion. 'We have a virtually continuous publicity campaign', says Dunlop. 'As soon as you stop putting articles in the company magazine people forget about it.' The Dunlop scheme, which dates back to 1929, fell into disuse in the mid-1980s and drew just four suggestions in 1986 but has since been revived and now attracts more than 150 a year.

3 They should be fun. Dunlop gives away pens with the company logo to all suggestors and a mug bearing the legend 'I am a Dunlop Bright Spark' to people submitting ideas which are adopted.

Schemes can be enlivened with short-term campaigns aimed at encouraging suggestions in areas such as energy-saving, the environment or customer care. League tables, a lucky dip from a tub of accumulated suggestions or a chairman's prize for the best of the year, can all sustain interest.

4 Suggestions must be handled quickly and efficiently. 'If the guys on the shop floor have an idea and get excited they should not be kept waiting more than 24 hours for an acknowledgement', advises Jim Byers of Ingersoll Engineers, a manufacturing consultancy. 'The company should come up with a response to the suggestion within a week.' If the suggestion is turned down, employees should be encouraged to submit new ones. Dunlop describes ideas it turns down as 'not adopted' rather than 'rejected'.

5 Suggestions should be rewarded – though opinions differ on the scale of payment. One school of thought believes the rewards should be significant. Businessmen like Richer, however, believe in giving 'a little and

often'. On average, schemes surveyed by the Industrial Society paid out 18% of savings made.

6 The move to more broad-based quality programmes need not signal the end of suggestion schemes. Dunlop is introducing BS5750, the main UK quality standard, and intends to keep its suggestion scheme, although Dunlop wonders what would happen if the BS5750 procedure and the suggestion scheme both throw up the same ideas for improvements.

Modern quality methods encourage people to work as teams, says Andrew Wood of UKASS. There is still a place for a system which encourages the individual to come up with good ideas. UKASS is at St Nicholas, Hoe Court, Lancing, West Sussex BN15 0QX (Tel: 01903 755188).[2]

The Industrial Society also runs regular one-day seminars and training courses, one dealing with setting up and revitalizing a scheme, the other with new ideas and initiatives, including the contribution of suggestion schemes to a total quality environment. The Industrial Society also makes available a suggestion scheme training pack of two BBC videos, a book and notes.

ESOPs

Employee Stock Ownership Plans or ESOPs have been used in the UK since the late 1950s to spread ownership of companies by helping to finance buy-outs of companies by their employees and to upgrade benefit packages.

Around 10,000 companies have adopted ESOPs for one reason or another since Louis Kelso, a San Francisco lawyer, their inventor, helped the employees of Peninsula Newspapers of Palo Alto, California, buy out their owner in 1957. According to Gianna Durso of the National Center for Employee Ownership in Oakland, California, companies continue to adopt ESOP at a steady rate of perhaps 800 a year, including roughly one million more employees. There are now estimated to be around 10,000 companies which have adopted plans covering 10 million workers.

Figures from the centre suggest that companies which had adopted ESOPs in a five-year period up to 1986 have grown by as much as 11% faster than companies without plans. The evidence from individual companies which sold out to their employees is highly positive. At Avis, the leading car rental company which has been 100% owned by its employees since 1987, service has improved and profit growth is extremely healthy.

Even Weirton Steel, a once troubled steel company, has consistently outstripped its competitors since it was bought by its employees through an ESOP in 1984.

The ESOP has a rather shorter history in Britain, and in the past two decades government support for it has fluctuated. The Heath Government established tax concession for all-employee savings-related share option schemes in the 1973 Finance Act. These were promptly abolished by the incoming Labour Government in 1974.

In 1978, however, during the term of the Lib–Lab pact, Approved Deferred Share Trust (ADST) schemes were launched, which carried with them income tax concessions. Following the Conservative victory in the 1979 election, the development of profit sharing went on apace. Save-As-You-Earn (SAYE) share option schemes were introduced in 1980, followed in 1984 by tax relief for executive share option schemes and in 1987 by tax concessions for profit-related pay schemes.

The benefits to the firm

Share option schemes can be attractive for a number of reasons. They can help to:

- create a closer identity of interest between employees, shareholders and the company, reducing the 'them and us' attitude which traditionally exists in workplaces
- foster a greater understanding by employees of how their performance affects company profitability, encouraging them to become more cost-aware and profit-conscious and more likely to hold down excessive wage claims which could damage company profits
- provide an incentive to employees to work harder and more productively
- maintain company competitiveness in the labour market and reduce labour turnover rates
- cushion the impact of a downturn in the firm's market by reducing the profit-sharing element of pay, rather than causing lay-offs or redundancies
- provide companies with a flexible and tax-efficient method of rewarding staff for their commitment and loyalty
- they provide a way for companies to pass on share benefits to their employees without diluting the holdings of existing shareholders through the issue of new shares. That is important for any company coming up against the 10% ceiling imposed by the Association of British Insurers. This has been one of the strongest motivations for the creation of ESOPs so far
- create a market in a company's shares – potentially attractive to a company that does not want to go public
- create a defensive barrier against hostile takeovers.

Benefits to employees

Share option schemes provide employees with a tax-free addition to their incomes and give them a stake in their own company.

In addition to benefiting from the company's prosperity in good times, as shareholders the employees also have a voice – albeit small on an individual basis, but potentially significant collectively – which has a right to be heard at shareholders' meetings.

A further advantage is that the schemes cause employees very little inconvenience. ADST schemes require them only to exercise patience to reap a 'something-for-nothing' bonus, while the rewards to employees from investing monthly savings in SAYE share option schemes carry no risk. If the share price hits rock bottom, employees can simply take the cash they saved plus statutory bonuses. SAYE schemes have thus been described as a 'heads you win, tails you can't lose' deal.

The drawbacks

- *Schemes can be complex.* Profit sharing and share option schemes can, however, have a number of drawbacks. Some schemes can be complex and difficult for employees to understand, although most companies produce explanatory booklets to help to simplify them.
- *You may have to wait for rewards.* Both ADST and SAYE schemes only provide the rewards in the long term. In an ADST scheme employees have to wait for at least two years before being able to cash in their shares, and to be able to do so with full tax-exemption they must wait for five years. Employees taking out SAYE contracts have to wait either five or seven years, depending on the contract.
- *Irregular payouts may damage morale.* While regular profit-sharing payments may be good for morale, commitment and loyalty, schemes which pay out rarely (because of low company profitability, for example) may have a detrimental effect on employees' morale.

Model ESOPs

A 'model' employee share ownership plan (ESOP) has been drawn up in detail, with the blessing of the Inland Revenue, offering smaller and medium-sized businesses, in particular, a budget path to securing ESOP tax benefits.

It could precipitate a surge of ESOPs because it should short-circuit the many complexities associated with setting up an ESOP, according to David Pett, of Pensent & Co., the Birmingham law firm, which has prepared the model for the ESOP Centre.

Most ESOPs in the United Kingdom have been created on a 'case law' basis, but the model opens the way to establishing new ESOPs on a statutory basis. The model should make it possible for a company's legal adviser to draw up an agreement in weeks instead of months. A statutory ESOP confers corporation tax benefits while shareholders selling a sizeable stake can roll over capital gains tax.

Copies of the model trust deed cost £500 for ESOP Centre members and £750 for non-members. Details from: Sheila O'Connor, The ESOP Centre, 2 Ridgmount Street, London WC1E 7AA.[3]

MANAGING YOURSELF

It is hard to see how anyone can seriously expect to become an effective business manager until they can first manage themselves.

There are three aspects to managing yourself that need to be kept under regular review and these have a major impact on the ability of the rest of your staff to be able to perform.

The first is managing your own time – vital if you are to win back the opportunity to think and plan; the second is Managing Meetings – or other people's time – vital if your team is going to have a chance to do their job effectively; the third is communication.

Managing time

Most owner-managers have a false impression of how they use their time and how it affects their performance. There is a strong body of research that suggests that a typical MD could improve his or her output by at least 10% and save time by as much as 20–30% in a typical working day.

A prize such as having an eight- or nine-day week at your disposal, is surely worth a modest investment of time and energy.

There are many time management systems in the market, but you can realize many of the benefits yourself immediately without any expertise.

Step 1

Have a daily and weekly 'to-do' list. Most senior people in business have diary scheduling meetings and the like, but do not have a list of key tasks to be completed each day and each week. It follows that without set of daily objectives key priorities cannot be established, nor can you commit to driving hard to achieve those objectives.

Step 2

Establish the key priorities. A manager's day is made up of different types of priorities:

- 'A' priorities are highly essential activities which must be completed or progressed substantially.
- 'B' priorities are less essential activities which can be deferred because the time element is less critical and the impact on job performance is lower.
- 'C' priorities are non-essential activities which can be scrapped, screened out, handled by other people or handled at low priority times.

- 'X' priorities are activities which require immediate attention. There may be queries, requests for information, crises and emergencies, boss demands or interruption. You can have 'AX', 'BX' or 'CX' priorities.

One of the golden rules of time management is based on the Pareto or 80/20 rule. This suggests that 80% of your performance will come from 20% of your activities and 20% of your performance will come from 80% of your activities.

When you assess your own time usage and your own performance in the day you will find that the majority of your time has been spent on lower priority work. Log the following:

- For each activity calculate the time you spent on it.
- For each activity assign a ABCX priority.
- Work out the total time spent on ABCX priorities as a percentage of the total day.
- Ask a very frank question about your 'A' priority activities 'Did I achieve what I intended to achieve?'
- Estimate the time you could have saved, by better discipline and control, on each low priority activity.
- Make a judgement about your achievement on the day, how much 'continuous' time you spent on your top priority work and how much 'total' time you could have devoted to high priority work if you had exercised better control and discipline.

When you go through this assessment you will find that you are not spending enough time on your top priority work in order to achieve, and that the majority of time (which could be as high as 60% or 70%) will be spent on low priority work of which you could have saved at least 20% by better control and discipline.

Step 3

Review how you spend your time. This is a simple technique whereby you sum the total amount of time (in percentages) you spend in certain categories of activities. Typical categories are: meetings; telephone; secretary; correspondence; project work; report writing; reading, etc. Each manager will have different categories and different times; however, managers usually find they spend at least 40–50% of a typical day in some sort of meeting.

If you made an assessment of the amount of time you saved by 'crisper' management of these activities you would find that your time saving could be between 20% and 30%. The four priority areas for time saving and better self-management are: delegation, meetings, planning and personal organization.

Making a start

You can make a start on improving your time management by keeping a daily time log for three or four days, reviewing how you spent your time – and then look for ways to save time, improve performance or delegate tasks (see Figure 10.6).

Time	Start and finish time	Activity	Time taken (minutes)	% of the total day	ABCX priority (%)	Was this a main goal activity?	Estimate of time saving on this activity. How?	Could this activity be delegated? Why not?
Totals				A B C X		%	%	%

Figure 10.6 Daytime log

MANAGING MEETINGS

Meetings consume between one and three days of a business week. It follows that anything that can be done to make them more effective must be good news. Meetings are vital. They are a forum for exchanging business ideas and gaining fresh thinking – a way to communicate complex information – a way to gain consensus and commitment to key decisions. Unfortunately, most people see most meetings as a complete waste of time – including the person who called the meeting!

Here are some points to help make your meetings more effective:

Define the purpose

Knowing exactly what you expect to achieve. Meetings without set objectives demotivate people. The purpose might be to inform staff of new initiatives/ procedures (in many instances a memo would be a quicker, cheaper and just as efficient a way of doing this); it might be to identify and resolve a particular problem, to review progress and give people and opportunity to express their views.

Asking yourself what would happen if the meeting was not held is a great help in defining its objectives.

Decide who should attend

The fewer the better if the meeting is going to achieve its objectives in a reasonable length of time. However, research has shown that larger groups often come up with sounder decisions than individuals or a small number of people – but take much longer to do so.

Ensure everyone prepares properly

A meeting is going to be much more successful if all the participants have prepared in advance, yourself included. If possible, circulate beforehand a note giving notice of the meeting with the agenda items. The note should state the purpose of the meeting and its probable duration (to give people a chance to organize the rest of their day).

An agenda is vital for any meeting – it acts as the control device, establishing order and sequence, assigning tasks and providing guidelines for the timing of each item. If a meeting is called on the spur of the moment, it should still have an agenda, even if it is just jotted down on the back of an envelope. An agenda sent in advance, though, gives people a chance to do their homework.

If participants need to have absorbed specific information before they can discuss it, e.g., budgets, plans, proposals, it is much better to send these out well in advance since nothing wastes time more than people sitting reading during a meeting.

Be a good listener

People who chair meetings need to listen more carefully than anyone else in the group since it is their job to make sure the real point of someone's contribution is not being missed. They need to pick the right moment to move on; clarify points when people are getting in a muddle and summarize all the views when it is time to push for a decision.

Involve all the participants

People are likely to feel far more committed to the meeting and the decisions reached if they have had a chance to say their piece. And, indeed, people should not be at the meeting unless they have something to contribute. It is your task to ensure that everyone has a chance to participate.

Use open-ended questions to get people to talk (questions that start with words such as how, what, why, when – these are impossible to answer with a yes or a no). Making positive noises throughout the session – 'Anybody add to that?' 'Any more?' – also encourage the shy, and checking round the group – 'Let's see where we all stand on that, Tim you first' – not only forces people to speak but generally mobilizes and motivates the meeting.

Closed questions (those that begin with do, can, are, which are usually only answerable with a yes or a no) can be used to bring the talkative to a halt – 'So do you think we should proceed on that basis?'

Keep the meeting on course

Red herrings and ramblings are the chief dangers when you are trying to stay on course and keep to time limits. There are polite ways to stem the speaker's flow – cough, lean forward, raise your eyebrows – or the more positive: 'We're getting off the point aren't we?', 'That's your two minutes up, we have to move on.' Don't be too tolerant with people who regularly take the meeting off at a tangent or you'll lose the respect of the others who want to see your hand firmly on the wheel.

Control aggression

Conflict can be healthy in that it encourages new ideas and new ways of solving problems and it is the chairperson's job to ensure that everyone has a fair say and a fair hearing even if they are disagreeing. However, some control may need to be exercised if things are getting particularly ugly or someone with strong views is being very vocal.

You must avoid taking sides or apportioning blame. This almost always provokes an argument and the chairperson who loses his/her temper loses credibility in the process.

Check that everyone understands

You need to know both that the rest of the group is not at cross-purposes with the speaker, and that they understand what he or she is trying to convey, so check assumptions by asking follow-up questions: 'So you mean that if we improve x we'll get better results from y?' Make a habit of providing a summary of what has been said.

Decide on action

The purpose of meetings is not to impose decisions but to achieve decisions by consensus. Once decisions have been made, define clearly how they are to be acted upon, by whom and by when.

Memories being short, it is essential to produce minutes (or at least some notes) of every meeting, if for no other reason that to prevent subsequent arguments over who was responsible for what. Another of the chairperson's tasks is to ensure that this is done, although he/she may well prefer to delegate minute-taking to someone else in the group or a secretary.

The minutes should be brief and strictly factual, describing what happened without distortion or comment, sticking to suggestions and proposals with the names of the people who made them, actions agreed and the name of the person responsible for each action.

Make sure decisions are implemented

If the meeting was worth having, the decisions are worth implementing so your job doesn't stop when the meeting finishes. You need to monitor progress which may involve holding a follow-up meeting, asking for interim reports or carrying out day-to-day checks.

EXAMPLE: John Harris is MD of Carpaints, a 10-year-old company supplying car refinishing paints which employs 20 people and has an annual turnover of around £2 million.

John knew where he wanted to go, and how he wanted to get there, but he realized when considering the company's future while on holiday last year that he needed to acquire the skills to ensure success. He applied to go on the BPG and, in his own words:

'I enjoyed the course right across the board, it covered so

many things which were all thought-provoking, and made you study all aspects of business marketing.

'Ours is a business which has undergone constant expansion, but with the recession really starting to bite we realized we had to control our development with the help of a good business plan. Carpaints needed a kickstart to budge it from a position of complacency and to do that I needed to stand back, take a good look and get ready to really develop.

'Basically the effect of the BPG has meant changes in practically everything, including the way we answer the telephone! Even the sales team, in what I thought was the 'organized' side of the business have made changes, they now all have clearly defined roles, so there aren't black holes in responsibilities – and we're on the scent of a new £500k account at the moment. With six-weekly sales meetings, and working towards formal bi-weekly joint meetings for sales and technical staff as well as office meetings on a weekly basis I'm looking forward to everyone setting their own targets, being sales driven, so that should I disappear tomorrow the company could pretty much run itself.'

COMMUNICATION

The principal ways to communicate are by the spoken word and in writing. Good verbal communication is a two-way process. The speaker gives the listeners the opportunity to ask questions and make comments about what has been said in order to clarify. The objective of verbal communication is to give a message in such a way as to be readily understood by the listeners – and to be sure that they understand it.

There are, however, a number of barriers that get in the way, distorting or even shutting out, the messages we try to send.

Such barriers include physical distractions such as noise, temperature, lighting; emotional distractions such as personal prejudice, experience, assumptions or values and beliefs. Finally, certain words can cause us to stop listening altogether. This can happen when people are moralizing, threatening, criticizing or just using jargon. So a good starting point in improving communication is to think about these barriers and prepare your communications with them in mind. Talk to people in an atmosphere free of interruptions and use words that don't rub people up the wrong way. While you can't do much about other people's emotions, you can do something about your own. Stay calm and neutral. If you sense emotional barriers in others either keep your conversation brief and to the point, or postpone it.

Speaking effectively

Research has shown that each of the following elements has a specific value in transmitting the 'true' message:

- words 7%
- tone 35%
- non-verbal or body language 58%.

You may disagree with these percentages, but think about it for a moment.

You have complete control over the words that you use. You have less control over the tone as your emotion begins to take over. Try saying the phrase 'Where did you go last night?' without emphasizing any of the words. Repeat it, putting an emphasis on the first word, then again, this time emphasizing the word 'you'. Three different 'True' messages will be conveyed to the listener and they will respond accordingly. You have virtually no control over the non-verbal, your body language. Subconsciously your body will reveal what you really mean and think.

If you sit with your arms and legs crossed, this is a defensive posture and indicates a hostile attitude towards the other person and/or the message. Sitting with your arms folded with your thumbs up, shows a superior attitude. Leaning forward indicates either interest or intimidation. People who rest their chin on one hand and have a finger in or near their mouth, need reassurance. Those who rub their chins are thinking or making a decision and will not be listening to you, so stop talking.

Gestures are intentional movements and should not be confused with body language.

You may be able to control your body language at the beginning of a conversation, but the more you become involved, the more your subconscious will take over.

To back up the importance of body language at the beginning of a conversation, it should be noted that of information relayed, 87% is via the eyes, 9% is via the ears, and 4% is via the other senses (taste, touch, etc.).

A vital part of speaking effectively is being sure people understand what you mean. This is best done by asking questions. Never say 'do you understand?', as this puts the onus on the listener and rather than appear stupid they will probably say 'yes'. If you say 'Have I explained that satisfactorily?' then the responsibility rests with you. The listener does not feel threatened and can answer honestly.

Written communication

Much of our written communication is made unnecessarily hard to follow. Research into the subject has shown that two things make life hard for readers: long sentences and long words. Back in 1952 Robert Gunning, a business language expert, devised a formula to measure just how tough a letter, report or article is to read. Called the Fog Index, these are the four steps:

1 *Find the average number of words per sentence.* Use a sample at least 100 words long. Divide total number of words by number of sentences to give you the average sentence length.
2 *Count the number of words of three syllables or more per 100 words.* Don't count (a) words that are capitalized; (b) combinations of short easy words like 'bookkeeper'; (c) Verbs that are made up of three syllables by adding 'ed' or 'es' – like 'created' or 'trespasses'.
3 *Add the two factors above and multiply by 0.4.* This will give you the Fog Index. It corresponds roughly with the number of years of schooling a person would require to read a passage with ease and understanding.
4 Check the results against this scale:
   - 4 and below very easy, perhaps childish
   - 5 fairly easy: tabloid press, hard selling letters
   - 7 or 8 standard: *Daily Mail*, most business letters
   - 9–11 fairly difficult: *The Times*, good product literature
   - 12–15 difficult: *The Economist*, technical literature
   - 17 or above very difficult: *New Scientist*, no business use, except to bamboozle.

MANAGEMENT IN THE FAMILY BUSINESS

Management issues in family-owned businesses include all of those covered in this chapter – plus a few unique problems. Factors which have helped British family-owned businesses outperform the stockmarket by 80% over the last two decades include less risk-taking and consistent objectives, according to research.

Family-owned companies claimed reduced vulnerability to takeover bids and the ability to take a long-term view also contributed. The Family Business Index, run by accountants Stoy Hayward, has tracked the share price of 71 family companies and shows that nearly half achieved a tenfold growth during the period. They beat the market even during the boom years of the late 1980s, and unlike other quoted companies were unaffected by the stockmarket crash of 1987.

The conclusion is that family businesses are the best placed to lead Britain out of recession. The research shows their ability to weather the ups and downs of the economy, and they benefit from goals which are less concerned with short-term gain and more focused to longer term wealth. (Contact: Moira Lewis, Stoy Centre for Family Business, 8 Baker Street, London W1M 1QA, Tel: 0171 486 5888. Annual subscription £120, plus VAT.)

Keeping your business in the family

If your inspiration is to build up an enduring family business then beware the old adage 'clogs to clogs in three generations'. In fact the average life-cycle of a family business is 24 years, which coincides with the average tenure of the founder. Only 33% of family businesses reach the second generation, less than two-thirds of these survive through the second generation while only 13% survive through the third generation!

Although these statistics illustrate the fragility of the continuing family business you should not despair: more than 98% of US corporations including some of the largest multinationals (Heinz and Campbells soup, for example) are family owned. In fact about 42% of the largest companies are controlled by one family.

Family businesses have both strengths and weaknesses. By being aware of them you can exploit the former to do your best to overcome the latter to give your business a better chance of survival.

The overwhelming strength of the family business is the different atmosphere and feel that a family concern has. A sense of belonging and common purpose which more often that not can lead to improved performance.

Another advantage is that the family firm has greater flexibility, since the unity of management and shareholders provides the opportunity to make quick decisions and to implement rapid change if necessary.

EXERCISES

1 What kind of a leader do you think you are, hero, meddler, artisan or strategist? What consequences do you think this has for your firm±s growth prospects?
2 Prepare a five-point plan for delegation along the lines shown in this chapter.
3 Carry out an attitude survey in your firm to get some feel for how your employees are feeling.
4 How do you appraise performance and reward achievement? Will these methods help you achieve your future goals?
5 Calculate the Fog Index for the next six important letters or reports that you write. Are you happy with the result and if not what can you do about it?

NOTES

1 Herzberg, Frederik *et. al.* (1993) *The motivation to Work*, Reprint, USA.
2 Useful reading: *Ideas Unlimited: How to Run Suggestion Schemes Successfully.* This is published by the Industrial Society, Quadrant Court, 49 Calthorpe Road, Edgbaston, Birmingham B15 1TH (Tel: 0121 454 6769).

3 More information about ESOPs is available from the Industrial Participation Associates, 85 Tooley Street, London, SE1 2QZ (Tel: 0171 403 6018) and from these publications: *ESOPs: Employee Share Ownership Plans*, available from Unity Trust Bank, 130 Minories, London EC3N 1NP (Tel: 0171 481 3110); *ESOPs in the UK – A commercial guide*, can be obtained from NBS Publications, Tallis House, 2 Tallis Street, London EC4Y 0BJ. For explanatory notes from the Inland Revenue, get a copy of Income Tax Explanatory Note: SAYE Share Option Schemes (IR 98), from Inland Revenue, Enquiry Office, West Wing, Somerset House, London, WC2R 1LB (Tel: 0171 438 6420/6425).

SUGGESTED FURTHER READING

Arthur, Michael B and Jones, Alan (1995) *Strategy Through People*, International Thomson Business Press, London.

Fisher, Martin (1996) *Performance Appraisals*, Kogan Page, London.

Greiner, L.E. (1972) Evolution and Revolution as Organizations Grow, *Harvard Business Review*, July–Aug, 37–46.

Taffinder, Paul (1995) *The New Leaders: Styles and Strategies for Success*, Kogan Page, London.

McGregor, D. (1960) *The Human Side of Enterprise*, McGraw Hill, New York.

Chapter 11

Can marketing strategy be optimized?

From start up, through early growth, we have argued that successful companies should have been able to demonstrate product or service differentiation and clear customer focus.

> EXAMPLE: Michael Gregson's innovative first aid pack, containing 'easy to read' medical instructions alongside the equipment necessary to apply to specific injuries, sold well in his early targeted mountain climbers and canoeist market sectors. One pack, taken on an early Chris Bonnington Everest expedition, was actually instrumental in saving the life of one member of the expedition. The resultant PR helped sales of the Gregson pack throughout specialist climbing shops in the UK and export opportunities began to develop. Michael Gregson, at the outset, had fortunately patented several of the innovative mechanical features of the pack, which was to stand him in good stead five years later as he contemplated the ever rising promotional expenditures necessary for him to penetrate his biggest target market sector, the private motorist market. Unable to secure a major motoring organization's endorsement, he realized penetration of this tempting vast market required resources beyond his capacity; when approached by a major competitor, with assured distribution power, Michael had no difficulty in agreeing a sales price for his company combined with a royalty payment on each future patented pack sale!

Michael Gregson had realized that he simply did not have the amount of time and resources necessary to upgrade his product from what the Boston Consulting Group (BCG) would have termed a 'Question Mark' product, i.e. a product generating profits but not significant cash flow, into a 'Star' and ultimately a 'Cash cow', i.e. leading edge products able to provide future profits and considerable cash flow. A starting point for optimizing marketing

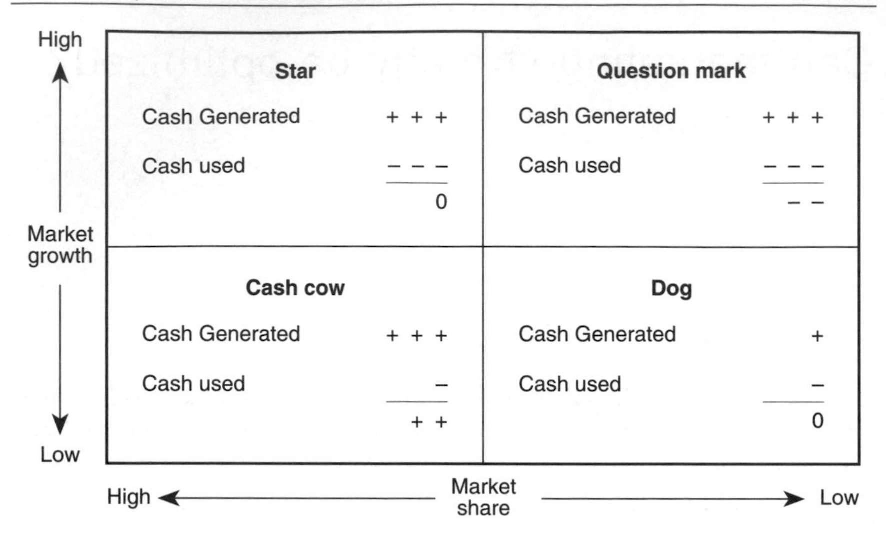

Figure 11.1 Boston matrix

strategy might be to clarify your products and services in terms of the 'Boston Matrix' as developed by BCG in the 1970s and 1980s.

PRODUCT PORTFOLIO ANALYSES

Your company's products should be classified according to their ability to generate or consume cash, against two dimensions of market growth rate and market share. This process is summarized in Figure 11.1.

The concept behind this 'product portfolio' approach is, of course, to seek to use cash generated by 'Cash cows' to invest in 'Stars' and a selected number of 'Question Marks', while considering dis-investment for 'Dogs'. Cash flow is used, rather than profits, as it is the real determinant of a company's ability to develop its products/services. Investment is directed in favour of achieving market share or growth while maximizing cash flow, as shown in Figure 11.2.

A software writing company might have several prototype products in research and development in the 'Question Mark' box, which if tailored to a specific client could become profitable 'Stars' for the company. Ultimately, they could be 'Cash cows' if applicable to a broader range of companies, before becoming obsolescent and 'Dogs' requiring disposal, when new products and technology replaces them. Classifying your products and services in this way should give some insight into the type of marketing strategy now appropriate for the products and services in your company portfolio. It would not be sensible, for example, to invest heavily in

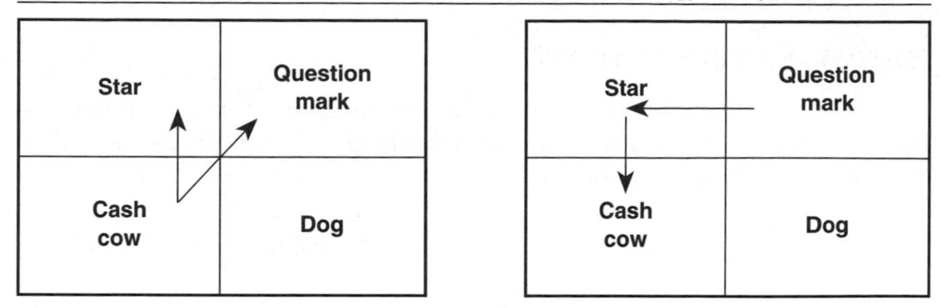

Figure 11.2 Matrix suggesting investment direction

products nearing the end of their life-cycle, unless, like Betty Crocker and BISTO, some evidence exists that marketing expenditure can enhance the life of the product for a new generation of customers.

OPTIMIZING PRODUCT/SERVICE RETURNS

Having classified your products and services, it is now important to determine how the return on each can be optimized; this can be done by answering the two major marketing questions:

1 Can we improve productivity for the business unit?
2 Can we increase volume sales for the activity?

These questions are not mutually exclusive, but each has a different focus and elements as the chart in Figure 11.3 shows.

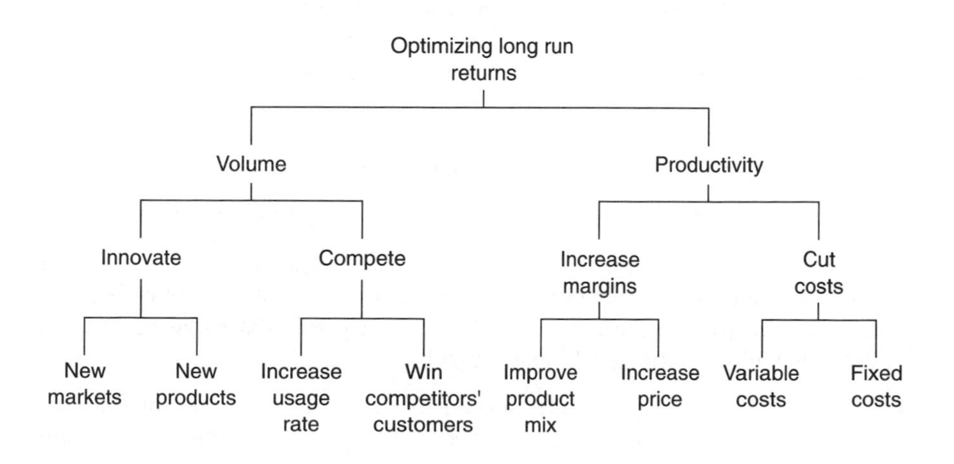

Figure 11.3 Optimizing product source returns

IMPROVING PRODUCTIVITY

Improving productivity is a constant requirement for growth-minded business, not simply an activity during periods of economic recession (when it is still, nevertheless, important – one way to 'delight' customers as many mission statements demand, is to maintain rather than increase prices or to 'share' productivity improvements as many major retailer customers demand).

Cutting costs

Costs need to be constantly controlled and balanced against the needs for good quality and good service. In particular you need to separate and act on your variable and your fixed costs:

- Variable cost cutting is always in evidence in recession, witness the automotive and banking staff cuts in the early 1990s. Some employers aim to keep flexibility.

EXAMPLES:
Bagel Express in 'rolling out' its formula bagel bars in Central London in the mid 1990s, employed primarily visiting American students, whose maximum stay was known to be six months. More permanent staff were only employed once the location was deemed to be successful.

Similarly, Richard Branson's Virgin Airlines in the early 1990s found that its growth had been halted by the system of allocating airport slots, leaving the company over-manned. In Richard Branson's own words, 'short-term interests of the shareholders would have been best served by declaring 200 redundancies but we have put people first, by using a whole range of flexible arrangements to keep them employed. Now that we are growing again, the positive response is already repaying short-term costs.'

Other companies sought actual pay cuts rather than redundancies, which would have led to a new competition, together with tight control on expensive overtime. Focusing attention on the 20% of items that make up 80% of your costs will probably yield biggest results.

- Fixed cost reduction, similarly, should not include scrapping investments in technology that could bring economies and extra nimbleness in the future (like flexible-manufacturing facilities, where, for example, Peugeot has invested in product lines that can turn out two models at once). Many firms, following Japanese practice, increase their use of sub-contractors to help offset increased risk.

Marks and Spencer have grown dramatically in recent years by doing just this, but equally share some of the risk with suppliers, ensuring loyalty to the firm when better conditions prevail.

Equally, alliances between firms, aimed to reduce fixed cost investments, can be advantageous.

EXAMPLE: Andy Ingleston of Dockspeed, rather than invest in a new fleet computerized control system, agreed to an unusual equity swap with an indirect competitor, Inter City Trucks. While both retained their independence Andy traded 25% of his own company's private stock for 20% of Inter City Trucks; this provided Dockspeed with access to Inter City's computer system, as well as permitting better buying by the combined companies, saving Dockspeed £70,000–£80,000 pa on diesel, tyres and ferry spaces.

Increasing margins

Increasing margins may be the result of the variable cost control actions noted above or through better buying (quantity discounts, payment term discounts), or by increased investment. It can also result from external market appraisal leading to changes in your product mix sales or even from increased prices.

- Product mix analysis requires that your accounts give you accurate costs and gross margins for each of your product/service lines.

EXAMPLE: Autoglass, at a time of depressed sales, recognized the extra margin from fitting laminated compared with toughened windscreens. An incentive scheme for fitters, combined with display aids for customers emphasizing the extra benefits of laminated vs toughened, saw an increased proportion of laminated sales in a static market, and a marked improvement in gross margins.

- Increasing price is always difficult; you know what to do when cutting prices to stimulate demand: you make a lot of noise and publicity! Some people think that increasing price should be the opposite, being silently

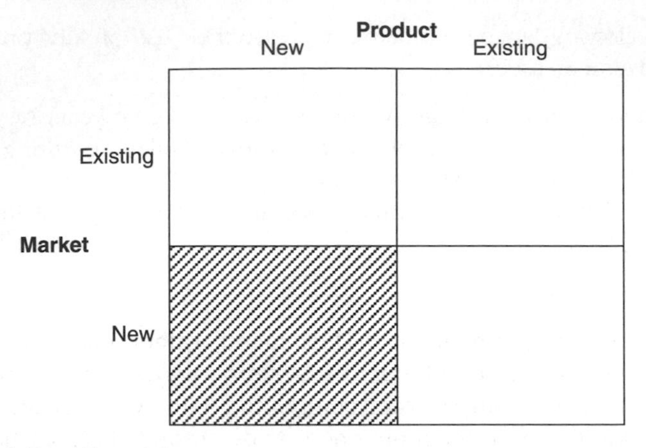

Figure 11.4 Growth matrix

passed through to suppliers and customers alike. This is rarely the way to generate long-term loyalty! Better companies seek to combine increases with improvements in service or product offerings.

> EXAMPLE: The Post Office in the early 1990s, was able to coincide a postage price increase with the re-introduction of Sunday collections, which went some way to improve its public service image.

Equally, warning retailers of planned increases may enable you to reduce slow moving stock and build longer term customer/supplier loyalty.

INCREASING VOLUME

A systematic approach to building sales volume was early devised in the form of a matrix by Igor Ansoff as shown in Figure 11.4.[1]

In terms of risk, developing new products for new markets is clearly the most difficult strategy; by keeping one of the variables constant, either an existing product or an existing market, you are clearly ensuring, in military terms, that 'you are keeping one foot on the ground' and reducing risk. The lowest risk is in competing more strongly with existing products and existing markets, the two strands of strategy in terms of priority are therefore:

- to compete more strongly
- to innovate, with new products and new markets.

Compete

Competing more strongly with existing products within existing markets may be less glamorous than launching new products into exotic markets, but usually ensures better returns. What is required is to sell more to existing customers – to increase their usage rate – then to capture customers from competitors.

- Increased usage rate is possible because customers have a life-cycle curve just like products, winning their early business (courtship) does not mean that you are their only supplier. Winning more of their business (wedding) is clearly a priority.

> EXAMPLE: Equinox Furniture Design, being a UK producer, supplied UK retailers with small 'top-up' orders, as overseas suppliers insisted on minimum orders of at least a dozen items. Equinox decided to offer customers an incentive to place a minimum order of five of each product. This virtually doubled their 'sell-in' to many customers, while still leaving them competitive with overseas suppliers, in terms of size of minimum order.

Equally, deadlock and divorce can loom with existing customers if you do not actively seek to maintain the marriage relationship; setting up computer links to facilitate direct customer ordering, carrying out joint promotions, or simply sharing information may be the way to build customer loyalty and sales. Building databases of customers, devising bonuses to reward loyal customers and detecting more easily those who have not ordered recently and therefore need visiting, can also be important. None of these actions require the expensive promotional costs of attracting new customers, which is why increasing usage rate has to be the most attractive method to build sales volume.

- Winning competitors' customers again means following a low risk strategy of working with existing products in existing markets. Gaining entry to a competitor's customer is never easy, unless they are in the wedlock-divorce stage. To know this requires constant market intelligence, to reveal when a competitor's quality is down, deliveries are late or a trusted salesperson has left. Your attention should always be to focus on added value rather than price: there is no point in growing unprofitably.

> EXAMPLE: Equinox Furniture, emphasized their production and small order delivery flexibility to gain entry to customers with

foreign suppliers. Prices were not discounted. Only when they were accepted as a trusted supplier did the company seek to improve orders by offering minimum order incentives.

As you seek to win competitors' customers you may also be seeking to convert the sizeable army of non-users of whatever you and your competitors sell. This usually involves seeking referrals from existing customers, sometimes by offering incentives, and can also involve buying mailing lists of customers with a similar socio-economic grouping as your present customers.

Innovate

Innovation, involving new products and new markets is clearly higher risk. But there are exceptions:

- New markets may mean simply taking existing proven products/services into a new geographical area, as Amberly Plc successfully achieved by taking British rising damp cures and selling methods on to the Continent. The challenges involved coping with languages (recruitment), adapting promotional methods (using multinational advertising agencies) and expanding under control (good accounting systems).

EXAMPLE: It may mean simply expanding the range of your existing products as Goldsmiths Ltd did in adding soft drinks to its portioned snacks business and, doubling sales to snack bars as a result, together with geographical expansion. In this situation businesses are basically expanding their 'core' businesses, the ones they know best. (Sir Graham Day, Chairman of Rover and Cadbury's once described a core business as 'one you can bet on'. Peters and Waterman describe it as 'sticking to your knitting'.)

- New products may equally mean simple line extensions of our existing core businesses:

EXAMPLE: Autoglass realized early that success in establishing a windscreen replacement business would still leave seasonal troughs in their fitting business. By expanding into side windows (vandal area) and glass run-roofs (peaking in season of lowest windscreen replacement activity) the company was able to build a balanced product line, with good labour utilization, concentrated none the less on 'automotive glass'. Even glass polishes and cleaning items provided a useful added contribution.

You should clearly be seeking to extend your existing product lines and seeking new market segments for your existing business. Yet major successful companies, like Marks and Spencer with food now providing 40% of their turnover or Sainsbury's with Homebase, are clearly able to launch new products and enter new markets, the most risky combination of all. How is this done? By hastening slowly and sometimes by acquisition, i.e. careful market testing in one's own premises, listening to one's own customers and employees (such as Stue Leonard's Dairy in Peters and Waterman's classic example) and careful acquisition of proven earnings. Beware synergy, which should really be spelt sinergy, unless you can actually quantify the extra discounts, reduced price competition through acquiring significant market share – both of which Autoglass finally achieved in buying its major competitor, Windshield Enterprises. Careful test marketing has to be the key, as in new products/ new markets. Murphy's law prevails: if a thing can go wrong it will.

EXAMPLE: Lucius Cary, the successful owner of Venture Capital Report, invested £5,000 seed capital to help David Vint develop a prototype of his new wax-filled hot water bottle. The 'Huggie' as it was labelled, was designed to provide a safer alternative to the traditional hot water bottle. A good working prototype resulted in a further £100,000 investment in manufacturing facilities and although the Christmas launch went well, a large number of Huggies were returned as faulty. Many of the thermostats did not work properly, while the wax oil filling started to penetrate the skin of the bottle when stored for a time. With hindsight, Lucius admitted 'we are trying to break too much new ground'. The inventor, David, remains unabashed: 'If we had £200,000–£300,000 more, I think the product would be a world-wide best seller.' The assets of the business were bought from the liquidator by an industry competitor.

The careful process of screening new ideas, developing the product, thoroughly testing prior to launch, is time-consuming and expensive. But much less expensive than jumping all those hurdles and rushing into the market. Hastening slowly but surely must be the key.

None of the above marketing strategic options may sound very exotic, particularly when compared with the predatory activities of a Hanson Trust!

EXAMPLE: Perhaps the most daring strategic change in Europe since the war by a single man was the way in which Antoine Ribaud transformed BSN from being one of Europe's leading flat glass manufacturers into a leading European branded food company! This extraordinary achievement, by an extraordinary man, came after his failure to take over the leading European flat glass manufacturer St Gobain. Thwarted in this attempt, Antoine sold his low-yielding glass business to his major competitors and invested the enormous proceeds into the higher yielding branded food business.

Less dramatic, but nevertheless equally daring was Richard Branson's diversification from music retailing into airlines!

EXAMPLE: 'It was the experience of watching Freddie Laker and admiring him that drew me into the airline business. David versus Goliath is a clear pattern running through my life,' Richard Branson has explained. 'The reason that drives us to start something new is when we feel that something hasn't been done very well by other people, so we can do it better. The importance of having a name like Virgin cannot be over-emphasized. Over the next 20 years, we can use that brand name to break into a number of different areas and hopefully create a number of other quite successful companies.' Even Branson had some caution: 'We do not want to be a pioneer. Follow the leader is all right and we will always fight the "not invented here" syndrome in Virgin.'

Virgin Atlantic may not have been the brainchild of Richard Branson (the idea came from Randolph Fields, a 31 year-old California lawyer, who had founded British Atlantic in 1984 and appealed to Branson for financing). Seeing David (Freddie Laker) cut down by Goliaths and recognizing the value of his own brand name, gave Branson the drive and value added potential in diversifying so radically.

At the simplest level, it might even come down to lateral thinking.

EXAMPLE: Mrs Eugene Barter tried unsuccessfully to sell her luxury country home in S W France to a variety of buyers in Europe and the Far East. When she finally re-advertised it as a guest house, with a source of income and database of 500 happy holidaymakers, it was sold within 3 weeks!

Redefining your products and markets may sometimes prove useful!

Extraordinary strategies and strategists do exist; for the growing business incremental options, such as we have outlined above, come first. When totally frustrated, however, as Antoine Ribaud was, or when all incremental options have been exhausted, you may need to completely re-think! If you divested all your businesses, or your major business, as Branson did with music retailing, what new diversification would you seek? Are the green pastures next door really greener? Antoine Ribaud and Richard Branson proved it could be done!

SUMMARY

Optimizing your marketing strategy, as either a prelude for further growth (e.g. Autoglass) or seeking an exit from your sector (e.g. Connectair or Gregson's Pack) is clearly important for maximizing the return on your activity. Possible outcomes of this process include deciding whether the winning marketing formula that you have developed, which, after organization, can be 'rolled out' to other outlets (e.g. Bagel Express) or needs such substantial funding/development that the alternatives such as franchising, trade sale, or new 'business angel' equity backing needs to be sought. Different ways of raising this funding for your proposed marketing strategy is what we will examine finally in the next chapter.

EXERCISES

1 What are the directional implications from your products/services of the Boston Matrix analysis?
2 What opportunities are there for you to improve productivity in your business?
   (a) Cutting costs
   (b) Increasing margins
3 How can you increase volume in your business?
   (a) Compete
   (b) Innovate
4 What are your diversification or divestment possibilities?
   (a) Diversification
   (b) Divestment
5 What are the funding requirements for your marketing differentiation strategy?

NOTE

1 Ansoff, Igor (1965) *Corporate Strategy*, Penguin, London, p. 109.

SUGGESTED FURTHER READING

Dick, R. and Kretz de Vries, M. (1995) *Richard Branson: The Coming of Age of a Counter Culture Entrepreneur*, INSEAD, Fontainebleu. (European Case Clearing House, Cranfield University, Cranfield.)

McDonald, Malcolm (1989) *Marketing Plans*, 2nd edn, Heinemann, Oxford.

Chapter 12

Can you withstand the financial pressures?

WHY SELL UP?

Every year, tens of thousands of entrepreneurs sell up all or part of their business. The reasons for doing so are legion. Some want to retire, others want to get out of a business they are bored with and need the resources to get into something new. Some feel their business has reached the point where association with a larger business is either desirable or even essential.

Many firms who have taken venture capital on board will find their erstwhile partners become restive after a few years and seek to influence both the choice and the timing of an exit-route for their investee firms.

These examples give a flavour of some of the main reasons for selling up.

EXAMPLES

Scientific instruments

From its origins in a garage in the early 1970s one small British manufacturer of scientific instruments managed to finance expansion from retained profits. Despite all the efforts of its management, however, the company faced three seemingly insuperable barriers to growth.

It lacked the resources to develop its own computer systems; it was unduly dependent on an overseas supplier; and it was unable to break into the UK market because its products were not sufficiently competitive. These problems were compounded by a new product which suffered from technical and design failings.

By 1978, the company, which then employed 20 people, appeared to have reached a limit to its growth. It was helped out of this impasse when it was acquired by a larger company. This allowed the smaller firm to finance a new research and development programme and invest in production capacity.

With the help of its larger parent the smaller company has since grown to turnover of £11 million (in 1987) and a workforce of 245. Seventy per cent of its production is exported and it spends 12% of turnover on R & D.

Thomas Goode
In January 1991, Thomas Goode's 60 family shareholders decided that the business, which has been financially weakened in recent years by failed diversifications and the tough retailing market, could best be taken forward as part of a larger organization. They also wanted to realize some of the capital tied up in the business, which they hoped would fetch about £10 million.

Hambros Bank was asked to look for suitable buyers and very quickly received several preliminary offers from potential purchasers in the UK as well as from North America, Japan and continental Europe.

The business started in 1827, when Thomas Goode opened a china store in Hanover Square. The shop moved in 1845 to its present site in South Audley Street and consists of an enticing maze of small showrooms displaying ornate glassware, porcelain and fine china.

Mrs Robinson, a former executive editor of *Vogue* Magazine who also worked as a main board director at Debenhams, gradually transformed the business after her appointment as managing director in 1988, and also brought in outside professional managers.

They modernized the shop, speeded up service, introduced computer technology, achieved faster stock turn-round and improved the availability of goods. They also introduced a range of branded goods, ranging from pottery to playing cards, and are looking at further licensing and franchising opportunities. Thomas Goode has retained three royal warrants, which are proudly on display near the entrance. Other precious objects are also on show and two seven foot high Minton china elephants stand guard in the window.

However, by 1991 the company had reached an impasse and was finding it hard to expand without further injections of cash. The company was hit badly by the collapse of a pottery manufacturer it ran in Stoke-on-Trent and an unfortunate – and expensive – attempt to stage an exhibition in the US on the day the Wall Street market crashed in October 1987.

Like many other UK retailers, Thomas Goode suffered from the harsh trading climate in the early 1990s and was further hampered when some large orders from Kuwait and Iraq were cancelled because of the Gulf War. Sales in the 12 months to 31 January 1991 rose from £3.4 million to £3.6 million but the company still made a small loss at the pre-tax level.

Technophone

Finland's largest private company, Nokia, became the world's second biggest manufacturer of cellular telephones after Motorola of America, after paying £34 million for Technophone, a British company set up seven years ago with a share capital of just £3.3 million. The agreement made Hans Wagner, Technophone's chairman, and Nils Martensson, managing director, millionaires many times over. Together, they held 60% of the share capital. Mr Martensson remained in charge of Technophone and joined the board of Nokia-Mobira, the cellular telephone arm of Nokia.

The 1991 deal was the fruit of more than 12 months of talks between the companies. It put Nokia in a position to take advantage of the rapid expansion in demand for cellular telephones expected in the wake of agreement on a common European technical standard and fast-rising usage of the equipment worldwide. Mr Martensson claimed at the time that both companies would benefit from economies of scale as production volumes increased, and from shared research and development.

Technophone was set up in Camberley, Surrey, in 1984 and established a reputation for innovative lightweight telephone designs. It has manufacturing plants at Camberley and in Hong Kong, which together employ 500 people, as well as a research and development staff of 150 at Camberley.

A study at Cranfield published by Sue Birley and Paul Westhead, with support from Price Waterhouse and Lloyds Bank, came up with the following statistics on why entrepreneurs sell up (see Table 12.1). For the 2,000 owners who responded to this part of the research study, 17% indicated specific strategic reasons, 23% either wished to retire or were selling due to ill health. By far the largest majority, however, were either in receivership (28.7%) or administration (23.9%).

WHERE ARE THE EXITS?

The Cranfield study mentioned earlier revealed for the first time the overall pattern in business sales for a five-year period (see Table 12.2). By far the most common method used by owners to realize their investment in their business is sale through advertisement. The option of a listing on the Stock Exchange, whether it be a full listing, or a partial listing on the Unlisted Securities Market (USM) or the then Third Market, was a route used by just over 1,000 businesses during the period studied. The USM and Third Market were replaced in 1995 by the Alternative Investment Market. *The BBC Small*

Table 12.1 Reasons why private company owners sell up

Reason for sale	*Number*	*Percentage*
(a) Strategic		
1 For development	41	2.1
2 Cash for incorporation of business	4	0.2
3 Lack of funds	5	0.3
4 Exchange shares for PLC shares	11	0.6
5 Wishing to diversify	3	0.2
6 Seeks acquisition	14	0.7
7 Strategy/policy misfit	190	9.5
8 Explore other interests	59	3.0
(b) Personal		
9 Retirement	397	19.9
10 Ill health	53	2.7
(c) Ceased to trade		
11 Receivership	574	28.7
12 Liquidation	82	4.1
13 Insolvency	1	0.1
14 Administeration/joint administration	478	23.9
15 minimize capital gains	1	0.1
16 Tax losses/ceased trading	87	4.4

Business Guide, published bi-annually, gives a directory of all sources of capital for the growing business.

There are two possible stock markets on which to gain a public listing. A full Stock Exchange listing calls for profits of at least £1 million. In practice, unless there are exceptional circumstances, most advisers will insist on profits of between £2 million and £3 million. A full listing also calls for at least 25% of the company's shares being put up for sale at the outset. In addition, you would be expected to have 100 shareholders now and be able to demonstrate that 100 more will come on board as a result of the listing. This is rarely an appealing idea to entrepreneurs, who expect to see their share price rise in later years, and are loath to sell off so much of the business at what they believe to be a bargain basement price. There is also the threat of a takeover with so many of the shares in so many people's hands.

The Alternative Investment Market (AIM) is a much more attractive proposition for entrepreneurs seeking equity capital. Formed in 1995 specifically to provide risk capital for new rather than established ventures, it has an altogether more relaxed atmosphere.

After the failure of the Third Market and the imminent demise of the unlisted securities market, some may ask why the Stock Exchange is bothering to start another secondary share exchange. AIM was conceived

Table 12.2 Exit routes for each year, 1983–87

Year	*Private advertised sales*	*Public listing*	*USM listing*	*Third Market listing*	*Mergers listed on the Stock Exchange*	*Independent acquisitions on the Stock Exchange*	*Management buy-outs*	*Receiver independent company management buy-outs*	*Private/ family/ retirement/ company management buy-outs*
1983	868	79	88	0	68	43	189	6	13
1984	1,168	87	101	0	90	69	209	8	19
1985	1,393	80	98	0	104	94	255	0	53
1986	1,338	136	94	0	132	115	312	2	56
1987	1,522	155	75	35	161	125	335	1	49
Total	6,289	537	456	35	555	446	1,300	17	190

after pressure mainly from venture capitalists who want a way of investing in companies and realizing their profits more quickly.

The authorities accept that small companies suffer generally from a scarcity of investment capital in relatively small amounts. This is an attempt to bridge the gap. The Stock Exchange decided it was easier to start again rather than amend existing rules. AIM will replace two existing secondary markets. The Unlisted Securities Market, which enjoyed success in the 1980s but will close at the end of 1996, has ceased to be distinct from the official list – the main part of the stock market – partly because European securities laws enforce similar entry requirements.

Frequently there is no match, leaving the would-be seller with highly illiquid shares. The Stock Exchange hopes AIM will mean lower costs, greater liquidity and a higher profile for small companies.

AIM will be a separate, less regulated market, run by an independent management team with its own marketing arm, although it still will be part of the Stock Exchange. The shares are not alternatives to mainstream shares. Small, young and growing companies are likely to be attracted. They may be management buy-outs or buy-ins, family-owned companies, former Business Expansion Scheme companies or even start-up businesses. Around 75 are expected to join the market this year. A young company which may be typical is the Old English Pub Company, which recently raised £2 million to refurbish rundown pubs and hopes to be one of the first to trade on AIM. 'Whatever we do we have always been very aggressive,' says managing director Barry Warwick.

Pan Andean Resources, an exploration company, will also join AIM but is not alone in voicing disquiet about the cost. Some companies claim to have been asked to pay up to £100,000 to advisers, but Pan Andean is paying only £25,000. Moreover, a listing on the Stock Exchange does not automatically imply that the owner(s) or investor(s) have realized the whole of their equity stake in the business, but that they have merely diluted their ownership. Thus, for example, only 22% of businesses admitted to a full listing sold shares through an offer for sale. This caveat also applies to the 446 independent acquisitions listed on the Stock Exchange.

Over the five years, the results show a clear growth in exit route activity in all markets except for the USM which has remained fairly stable at around 90 businesses per year. The smaller number in 1987 reflect the October stock market crash of that year. The Third Market was initiated in 1987 as a response to the perceived need for a market in the shares of the smaller, newer business, but in the first year only 35 businesses were traded. These positive trends in exit route activity are also reflected in the growth of management buy-outs, which continue to be an attractive option for entrepreneurs and managers alike. (The USM and Third Market have now been replaced by AIM.)

Table 12.3 The leading agencies advertising private sales in 1983–87

Agency sales	*Number of business sales*	*of total business*
Peat Marwick McLintock	284	4.5
Grant Thornton	204	3.2
Cork Gully	155	2.5
Price Waterhouse	117	1.9
Arthur Andersen	111	1.8
Touche Ross	108	1.7
Arthur Young	94	1.5
Ernst & Whinney	93	1.5
Deloitte, Haskins & Sells	83	1.3
Spicer, Pegler & Partners	67	1.1
Robson Rhodes	59	0.9
Stoy Hayward	55	0.9
Edward Symmons & Partners[a]	46	0.7
Henry Butcher Business Brokerage[a]	46	0.7
Binder Hamlyn	37	0.6
Coopers & Lybrand	37	0.6
Humberts Chartered Surveyers[a]	37	0.6
Christie & Co[a]	35	0.6
A.P. Locke & D.R.F. Sapte	32	0.5
Levy Gee & Partners[a]	26	0.4

[a]Essentially dealing in real estate.

TRADE SALES

Table 12.3 covers the principal organizations involved in selling private companies in the UK. Over the five-year period covered in the Cranfield study, 624 agencies were involved in advertising 3,322 private business sales. A significant minority of companies advertised their own firms themselves. Not surprisingly, the majority of agencies represented the leading firms of chartered accountants, most of which have significant geographic coverage, although five leading agencies (Edward Symmons and Partners, Henry Butcher Business Brokerage, Humberts Chartered Surveyors, Christie and Co and Levy Gee & Partners) were dealing with real estate based retail businesses. However, even the 20 most active agencies listed in the table accounted for only 27.4% of the advertised sales. Indeed, 537 firms (86.1%) appeared to have very little experience on which to draw, since they were only involved with one or two sales during the five-year period. On the basis of this evidence, it was decided in the Cranfield study to classify active agencies as being those agencies which had dealt with more than 10 private sales each over the five-year period.

Table 12.4 Industrial category of private business sales by different data sources, June and November 1987

Standard industrial category	*ata Source*									
	Financial Times		*aily Telegraph*		*The Times*		*usiness Assets*		*Western Mail*	
	No.		*No.*		*No.*		*No.*		*No.*	
Primary	12	3.9	1	0.4	1	1.5	2	3.4	24	8.7
Manufacturing	112	36.0	7	2.5	13	19.7	26	44.8	7	2.5
Construction	13	4.2	5	1.8	1	1.5	0	0.0	3	1.1
Services	168	54.0	270	95.4	49	74.2	30	51.7	241	87.6
Not known	6	1.9	0	0.0	2	3.0	0	0.0	0	0.0

Table 12.5 Selling price (£s) of private business sales by different data sources, June and November 1987

	Selling price					
ata	*Mean*	*Standard deviation*	*Minimum*	*Maximum*	*Number valid cases*	*of valid cases*
Financial Times	455.027	526,780	3,500	3,000,000	55	17.7
aily Telegraph	288,988	284,692	20,000	2,000,000	225	79.5
The Times	174,513	208,048	10,500	1,100,000	36	54.5
usiness Assets	230,667	164,020	50,000	450,000	6	10.3
Western Mail	68,253	70,957	1,875	600,000	172	62.5

The media used by these organizations to sell private companies were studied in a two-month sample out of the whole period. To do anything else would have involved an enormous volume of data and perhaps little greater accuracy. Alongside the heavyweight nationals, the specialist periodical *Business Assets* and a representative local newspaper, the *Western Mail*, were included.

Table 12.4 shows that the *Financial Times*, *Daily Telegraph* and the *Western Mail* were all important media for the sale of private companies. The *Financial Times* was particularly strong with regard to manufacturing companies, while the *Daily Telegraph* heads the lists for service companies.

When it comes to the size of businesses being sold, the *Financial Times* is the clear leader (see Table 12.5). The average business on offer was priced at £455,027 compared with the *Western Mail* where the asking price was only £68,253.

DRESSING TO KILL

If you are thinking of selling it certainly pays to plan ahead and prepare your business to look its best. Your buyer will be looking, at least, at your last three years' performance, and it is important that your figures for these periods are as good and clean as possible.

Taking the latter point first, private businesses do tend to run expenses through the business that might be frowned upon under different ownership. One firm, for example, had its sale delayed for three years while the chairman's yacht was worked out of 'work in progress'. There can also be problems when personal assets are tucked away in the company, or where staff have been paid rather informally, free of tax. The liability rests with the company, and if the practice has continued for many years the financial picture can look quite messy.

The years before you sell up can be used to good effect by improving the performance of your business relative to others in your industry. Going down the Profit and Loss Account and Balance Sheet will point out areas for improvement. Once the business is firmly planted on an upward trend, your future projections will look that much more plausible to a potential buyer. You should certainly have a business plan and strategic projections for at least five years. This will underpin the strength of your negotiations by demonstrating your management skills in putting together the plan, and show that you believe the company has a healthy future.

Some entrepreneurs may wonder if such an effort is worthwhile. Perhaps the following example will show how financial planning can lead to capital appreciation for the founder.

EXAMPLE: A 34-year old owner-manager built up a regional service business in the United States that had a 40% compounded annual growth rate for the five most recent years. He employed an experienced CPA (chartered accountant) as his chief financial officer. This person developed budgets for one- and three-year periods and a detailed business plan charting the company's growth over the next five years. The owner's objective stated to his directors was to be ready to sell his business when the right offer came along.

A UK company interested in acquiring a leading service company in the region and finding a manager with the potential for national leadership carefully analysed the company and came away impressed with management's dedication to running its business in a highly professional manner. Because the previous year's after-tax profits had been 500,000 on sales of 10 million, the UK company offered 4 .5 million on purchase, and 4.5

million on attainment of certain profit objectives (well within the growth trend). The transaction closed on these terms.

The 9 million offering price, representing 18 times net earnings, was 50% higher than the industry norm and clearly justified the owner's careful job of packaging his business for sale.

VALUING THE BUSINESS

There are no mathematical-based or accountancy-based formulae that will produce the correct value for your business. There are some principles that can help, but the figure you end up with will in all probability have more to do with your negotiating skills, than with audited accounts.

EXAMPLE: Robert Wright, a Cranfield MBA who started up his venture, Connectair, immediately after completing his MBA in 1985, is a suitable cautionary tale. He sold out to Harry Goodman late of International Leisure fame in 1989 for around £7 million. Not bad for just under five years' work. However, negotiations with Goodman took up nearly a year, and his opening offer was under £1 million.

The starting point has to be how much you want to make from the sale. If you are planning to retire you will be unpleasantly surprised to discover exactly how much cash you need now to produce anything resembling a decent real salary for the next 20 years. If inflation runs its historic course you can expect the value of your nest-egg to halve every seven years.

The next task is to revalue your assets for sale rather than their continued use in the business. It seems incredible, but companies still leave assets at book value when planning to sell up. Quite recently there was widespread publicity about the sale of a major advertising agency where the buyer found he was able to recoup a large chunk of the sale price by selling off an under-valued office building in Tokyo. Good news for the buyer, galling for the seller.

It will always be helpful to develop some logic for setting the selling price. The most common valuation method is to use a Price–Earnings Ratio. So if your profits are £100,000 dependent on the sector and the economic climate a business could be worth anything from four to 16 times profit. Interest in this area is such, a new society was formed in 1996 to advise on this subject. (They can be contacted at Bruce Sutherland & Co, Stoneleigh House, Moreton in Marsh, Glos GL56 0AT, Tel: 01608 651091.)

SCRUTINY, RARITY AND UNIQUENESS

There is much anecdotal evidence to demonstrate that purchasers are prepared to pay more than a financial valuation alone would support, when suitable companies are rare in a given sector.

For example, Laura Ashley paid rather more for Penhaligans, the up-market toiletries business, than they eventually got when they sold the business on a couple of years later. But Penhaligans was unique, and in the toiletries sector small retail chains are rare. It also seemed a perfect fit to Ashley's style of business. But when their profits slid in the early 1990s, as did many UK retailers, they had to concentrate on their core business and sell off everything else.

The example given earlier of Thomas Goode's is one where prospective buyers were acquiring a name and a collection of royal warrants as much as an income stream. A private company not under the same compulsion as public companies to achieve immediate earnings growth may be prepared to pay more for these intangible benefits.

AFTERWARDS

What happens afterwards rather depends on your goals in selling up. If you are retiring then your plans should be well laid beforehand. If you are staying on as a member of a larger group, as Technophone's Nils Martensson did, then you need to be prepared for corporate rather than entrepreneurial life. This can be hard, and few people make the transition successfully.

If you are walking away with a large cheque, as Robert Wright did, then your experiences may bear a close resemblance to a bereavement. He, and many others who have sold up, have taken years to find the right opportunity to get back into business. What they have found helpful is to set themselves up as a sort of one-man venture capital and management consultancy business. By putting the word out that they are interested in buying or backing ventures in the field they understand best, they receive a steady stream of proposals and presentations, from which they hope to fund their next venture.

GOING PUBLIC

A public flotation is a major project and proprietors would be well advised to plan some three years ahead to ensure that the company is in the best possible shape when it comes to market. The objective must be to present a sound profit record and balance sheet, along with prospects of further growth, which will make the company attractive to investors.

As you draw up your flotation plan and timetable you should have the following matters in mind according to accountants Touche Ross:

- *Advisers*: You will need to be supported by a team which will include a sponsor, stockbroker, reporting accountant and solicitor. These should be respected firms, active in flotation work and familiar with the company's type of business. You and your company may be judged by the company you keep, so choose advisers of good repute and make sure that the personalities work effectively together. It is very unlikely that a small local firm of accountants, however satisfactory, will be up to this task.
- *Sponsor:* You will need to appoint a financial institution, usually a merchant banker to fill this important role. If you do not already have a merchant bank in mind your accountant will offer guidance. The job of the sponsor is to co-ordinate and drive the project forward.
- *Timetable:* It is essential to have a timetable for the final months during the run up to a float – and to adhere to it. The company's directors and senior staff will be fully occupied in providing information and attending meetings. They will have to delegate and there must be sufficient back-up support to ensure that the business does not suffer.
- *Management team:* A potential investor will want to be satisfied that your company is well managed, at board level and below. It is important to ensure succession, perhaps by offering key directors and managers service agreements and share options. It is wise to draw on the experience of well-qualified non-executive directors.
- *Accounts:* The objective is to have a profit record which is rising but, in achieving this, you will need to take into account directors' remuneration, pension contributions and the elimination of any expenditure which might be acceptable in a public company, namely excessive perks such as yachts, luxury cars, lavish expense accounts and holiday homes. Accounts must be consolidated and audited to appropriate accounting standards and the audit reports must not contain any major qualifications. The auditors will need to be satisfied that there are proper stock records and a consistent basis of valuing stock during the years prior to flotation. Accounts for the last three years (two years in respect of the USM) will need to be disclosed and the date of the last accounts much be within six months (nine months for the USM) of the issue.

The rewards

In the first nine years of the USM's existence over 500 entrepreneurs were made millionaires. The top USM millionaires are John Aspinall, the Kent zoo-keeper, and Sir James Goldsmith. They shared £48 million in equal halves when the Aspinall Casino Group was floated. In fact, going public is about the only way you can become seriously rich in business and stay in control of your company. With venture capital you are always susceptible to the pressures of the capital providers. They want an exit route so they can plough their clients' funds into new and 'even more exciting ventures', so if the opportunity for a trade sale comes along the chances are they'll sell you to the highest bidder. This may make you rich, but it's unlikely to make you seriously rich and it will certainly leave you in the passenger seat rather than the driver's.

Banks, as we have already discussed, are largely fair weather friends, and you certainly will not get rich borrowing from them.

Going public also puts the stamp of respectability on you and your company. It will enhance the status and credibility of your business, and it will enable you to borrow more against the 'security' provided by your new shareholders, should you so wish. Your shares will also provide an attractive way to retain and motivate key staff. By giving, or rather allowing them to earn, share options at discounted prices, they too can participate in the capital gains you are making.

With a public share listing you can now join in the takeover and asset stripping game. When your share price is high and things and going well you can look out for weaker firms to gobble up – and all you have to do is to offer them more of your shares in return for theirs. You don't even have to find real money. But of course this is a two-sided game and you yourself may now become the target of a hostile bid.

The penalties

So much for the rewards. The penalties are equally awesome, and they can happen before you even get a listing.

EXAMPLE

Before

Kevin McNeany, founder and managing director of Nord Anglia Education, spent four months and £300,000 preparing his company for a flotation on the USM. On the day before the price of the issue was due to be announced, McNeany decided that his company, which runs 16 private schools and five language schools, was being valued too cheaply and cancelled the flotation.

'I wasn't willing to accept the price because it was 20% less than what had been suggested before', says McNeany, a former teacher who, over the past 18 years, has built up a company with turnover of £8.2 million and pre-tax profits of £610,000.

'My financial advisers said: "You can't do this", I said: "I am",' recalls McNeany, Disappointed, despondent and £300,000 poorer, McNeany took the train back to Manchester from London to re-negotiate credit lines with his bankers which he had thought the flotation would render unnecessary.

After
Debbie Moore's Pineapple dance studios was introduced to the USM in 1982 by its venture capital providers. Its shares quickly went to an 85% premium. Profits rose by 50% in 1983, as forecast, and the company raised a further £1.5 million via a rights issue. Ms Moore was even given the coveted Businesswoman of the Year award.

But this time the moneymen were not so fortunate. In 1985 aerobics began to lose its popular appeal as health experts cast doubts on its efficacy. By May the company was in a nose-dive, showing half-year losses of £197,000. In the latter half of 1985 Peter Bain, a new boardroom recruit, evolved a strategy to turn the company into a marketing services group. After several acquisitions and total change of direction, Pineapple reported profits of £1.25 million in 1986.

But the dance studios clearly couldn't be made to work. 'It soon became obvious', to quote Moore, 'that it was difficult to deliver the kind of money the City wanted out of dance.' Ms Moore resigned from the Pineapple Group in December 1987, taking the loss-making dance studios with her for a nominal sum, leaving the rest of the Group to pursue its new strategy.

The next penalty is that public companies come under the greater scrutiny of a larger and more perceptive investment community. For example, Spice, the motor parts distributor which has gone into receivership, was scuppered in its first attempt to join the USM when the Stock Exchange found that the financial controller had been convicted of fraud. Another company that came unstuck after its flotation was Sharp and Law, a shopfitter, which joined the Unlisted Securities Market in 1987. Two years later, it discovered errors in its 1987 figures where payments for some large contracts had been double-counted.

Arthur Young, the accountants, who were called in to investigate, produced a report calling for improvements to the company's senior financial management, the appointment of a managing director and organizational systems and computer department reviews. The company never recovered and went into receivership.

You may also find that being in the public eye not only cramps your style but fills up your engagement diary too. Most entrepreneurs find they have to spend up to a quarter of their time 'in the City' explaining their strategies, in the months preceding and the first years following going public. It's not unusual for so much management time to be devoted to answering accountants and stockbrokers questions, that there is not enough time to run the day-to-day business, and profits drop as a direct consequence.

The City also creates its own 'pressure' both to seduce companies onto the market and then expects them to perform beyond any reasonable expectation.

For example, Michael Aukett, Chief Executive of Aukett, the architectural practice, is less sure that he would not reconsider his options if he had his time again. Aukett went public in February 1988 and maintained its steady promise in June by turning in highly respectable interims. Profits shot up 24% to £947,000.

Yet Michael Aukett says: 'The City is responsible for creating the hype that any size of business should go on the market, but architectural firms are basically too small. We don't begin to command any position under a market capitalization of £50 million.'

With the benefit of hindsight, Michael Aukett believes now that he should have waited another three years to grow to a bigger size before tangling with the institutions: 'They seduce you to go in and when the market goes on its knees, they don't support you. How do our shareholding staff feel when they see the market dip?'

One final penalty is the apparent lack of a direct relationship between the business's profit performance and its share price. Confidence, rumour and the sentiment for certain business sectors which fall in and out of favour, all play a part in moving share prices up and down – and at the end of the day that's all public shareholders and City institutions care about. Polly Peck is a vivid example of this problem. The auditors report, dated 17 April 1990, showed the company had made £161 million profit and the share price stood at 417p making the company worth £2 billion, on paper. By 20 September the company's shares were suspended at 108p on the back of rumours about alleged share dealing irregularities. A month later the company went into administrative receivership and the shares were declared 'worthless'.

Whatever the downside risk on going public it is as well to remember that several thousand private companies go bust for every public company that goes under. In the long run the only realistic way to get big, very rich, and to survive is to go public.

PROFESSIONAL ADVICE

Nothing said in this chapter should be construed as a substitute for taking professional advice. Most people only sell a business once in their lives. The best professional advisers in the field sell a dozen or so each year. A good tax and pension strategy can double the end value you receive and legal advice on warranties can make sure you get to keep the money.

EXERCISES

1 Prepare two lists in balance sheet style setting out the pros and cons of selling up now and in say five years time.
2 If you had to get out of your business for any reason, which exit route would you favour?
3 What value would you put on your business now and in say five years time?
4 What will you do when you exit?

SUGGESTED FURTHER READING

Nash, Tom (ed.) (1994) *Buying and Selling Private Companies*, Director Publications, London.
Walker, Ian (1992) *Buying a Company in Trouble*, Gower, Aldershot.

Index

NOTE: Page numbers in italic refer to information found only in a table. Page numbers in bold refer to information found only in a figure.

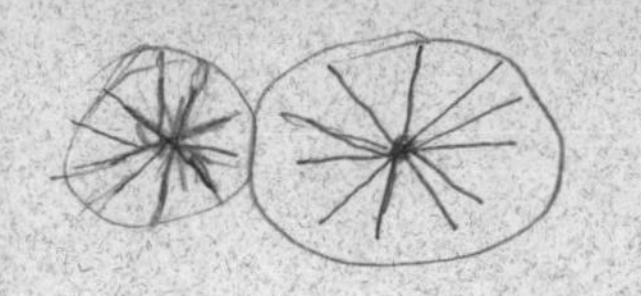